Wakefield Press

RED SILK: THE LIFE OF ELLIOTT JOHNSTON QC

Penelope Debelle is an award-winning journalist who began her career at *The News* in Adelaide. In 1983 she moved to Melbourne and worked as a political reporter at *The Herald*, then as Melbourne writer for *Good Weekend* magazine. In 1995, after the birth of her daughter, Honey, she and Robert returned to Adelaide where she worked as Adelaide correspondent for *The Age* for a decade. In 2008 she joined *SA Weekend* magazine at *The Advertiser* as a senior writer, winning the SA Press Club 2009 Gold Award for a feature on former South Australian Premier, John Bannon. In 2010 she won the National Press Club Engineer's Australia award for an article on maths. She has a Bachelor of Economics degree from Flinders University (Hons arts).

Watercolour by Paul Heywood-Smith, painted in 1983 from a photograph in *The Advertiser* on the appointment of Elliott Johnston to the Supreme Court Bench.

RED SILK

The Life of Elliott Johnston QC

Penelope Debelle

Wakefield Press
1 The Parade West
Kent Town
South Australia 5067
www.wakefieldpress.com.au

First published 2011

Edited by Penelope Curtin
Digital photography by Bryan Charlton
Cover design by Stacey Zass, Page 12
Typeset by Wakefield Press
Printed and bound by Hyde Park Press, Adelaide

National Library of Australia
Cataloguing-in-Publication entry

Author:	Debelle, Penelope.
Title:	Red silk: the life of Elliott Johnston QC / Penelope Debelle.
ISBN	978 1 86254 956 2 (pbk.).
Notes:	Includes index.
Subjects:	Johnston, Elliott.
	Judges – Australia – Biography.
	Lawyers – South Australia – Biography.
	Political activists – Australia – Biography.
Dewey Number:	340.9423092

Publication of this book was assisted by the Commonwealth Government through the Australia Council, its arts funding and advisory body.

Contents

Foreword

A biographer should be so lucky: a subject who lived in interesting times, who participated in many of the major events of the twentieth century and was an observer of others and who, above all, remains interesting in his own right.

I met Elliott Johnston on only a few formal, legal occasions. I regret that I did not know him well – a regret that is magnified by this account of his life and times. On any view, Elliot was and is a complex character: a lifetime Communist, but not an ideologue; a critical thinker who, at times, was naively optimistic about the political cause he espoused, a person who believed that there could and should be a better political system, but who was prepared to work within the current system and, even, accept some of its privileges and honours. Above all, however, he believed in equal justice. That belief sustained his professional life and, perhaps, goes some way to explaining his political beliefs.

This book is not simply an account of Elliott Johnston, the lawyer. It is also an account of a student radical who, even then, would put his belief in freedom of thought and speech above his personal interests, a Communist warrior whose ideas and principles were not well understood even by his comrades. It is the story of a husband separated from his young wife, Elizabeth, during the Second World War and later while he was a student in China, a wife whose beliefs, integrity and industry matched his own and with whom he had a long and loving relationship. The backdrop to all of this is a fascinating picture of Adelaide life and society, particularly student life in the late 1930s when Elliott's fellow students included Max Harris and others associated with the Angry Penguins, as well as Fin Crisp who, with Elliott's help, founded the National Union of Australian University Students. Equally fascinating is the account of the privileged circumstances of Elizabeth's family, the Teesdale Smiths.

What comes through this account of Elliott Johnston's life is his complete and unswerving commitment to improving the lives of others, both by political means and practical assistance. This practical assistance was not confined to his work as a lawyer. For example, when stationed in New Guinea during the Second World War, Elliott ran literacy classes to help other soldiers write letters home. However, it was as a practising lawyer that this aspect of his character came to the fore, fighting workplace injury cases and representing ordinary men and women whose ability to pay his legal fees was never an issue. He also appeared in complex criminal cases, both for the defence and the prosecution. Elliott was a skilled advocate and his courtesy and charm won him many friends and admirers within the legal profession. One such admirer was Chief Justice Bray, who provoked considerable controversy when he nominated Elliott for silk in 1969.

The controversy surrounding the appointment of a member of the Communist Party as Queen's Counsel delayed Elliott's appointment until 1970, when he became Australia's first Communist silk – the 'Red Silk'. He remained an active member of the Communist Party until his appointment to the Supreme Court of South Australia in 1983 – the first openly avowed Communist to be appointed to a superior Court in Australia.

Being 'a first' of anything nearly always involves difficulties, especially in the Law, which remains an essentially conservative profession, and was even more so in the 1970s and 1980s. At the very least, being 'a first' usually involves a higher level of scrutiny than would otherwise be the case. Elliott seems not to have been confronted with many difficulties, either as the first Communist Queen's Counsel or as the first avowed Communist appointed to the Supreme Court of South Australia. Perhaps, in part, that was because of his social connections through Prince Alfred College and the Teesdale Smiths. Certainly, it was partly due to his courtesy, charm, integrity and professionalism. It was also due in part to the South Australian legal profession, which boasted a progressive, independent and outstanding Chief Justice in the person of Sir John Bray and which produced Australia's first female Queen's Counsel in the person of Roma Mitchell, who later became the first woman to be appointed to an Australian Supreme Court. Certainly, I have always found the South Australian legal profession to be open-minded, progressive and tolerant. I suspect Elliott's professional life might have been more difficult and more controversial in any other state.

Elliott's commitment to equal justice has been and continues to be an inspiration to many, including those who had the privilege of working with him before his appointment to the Bench. That commitment underscores his work on the Royal Commission into Aboriginal Deaths in Custody following his retirement from the Supreme Court. His commitment to equal justice for Indigenous Australians has a long history, including as first Chairperson of the Aboriginal Legal Rights Movement. Despite Elliott's work on the Royal Commission, equal justice remains elusive for many Indigenous Australians. It is to be hoped that, sooner rather than later, the recommendations of the Royal Commission become established both in law and in fact. That would be a fitting tribute to the work of Elliott Johnston, a good man and a great Australian.

Mary Gaudron
7 December 2010

Preface

This biography of Elliott Johnston is not an authorised work in the accepted sense. It was commissioned by lawyers who had worked with Elliott and wanted his extraordinary life to be remembered. Elliott cooperated with generosity, efficiency and a good deal of grace, but he had no direct hand in what appears on these pages. He has not read it (although his son, Stewart, has) and the analysis is mine and not his. It is a book about Elliott, not by him.

Red Silk places on record Elliott's personal involvement in international events that took place more than half a century ago. The Depression shaped his Communism but he was equally committed to the great cause of peace. His presence at the 1950 Peace Congress in Sheffield, which moved to Warsaw after the Attlee Government prevented some delegates from entering the country, place him in an incredible moment in world history. Pablo Picasso was there, and Elliott sat a few feet from him. He returned from Warsaw through Stalinist Russia at the invitation of the Communist Party of the Soviet Union. Five years later he went to the People's Republic of China for 18 months to study Communism as a guest of Chairman Mao Tse-tung, returning again through Russia. Elliott's personal recollections, combined with the historical record, memoirs and reports from the time, provided the basis for writing about these events. (I am indebted, with a healthy dose of irony, to ASIO for their diligence in bringing to my attention articles from sources as diverse as *On Dit* and *Truth*.)

Elliott's commitment to Communism ran parallel to his practice of the law. For many people their co-existence in one man was at best perplexing, at worst something to be feared. Even those close to Elliott were not entirely sure how a man of such intelligence could remain a follower of Communism after the horrors committed in its name. I was unsure how the two could be reconciled. Part of the book's purpose, then, was to make sense of a life that seemed riven by fundamental contradictions.

Elliott is that gift to a biographer, a good record-keeper. In his personal papers he held letters, press clippings, notes from speeches, and seminal Communist Party of Australia documents going back to the late 1940s. They are a treasure trove for any future Communist historian and provided me with a firm foundation from which to understand our conversations.

The initiative taken by the commissioning panel turned a good idea around a dinner table into a reality: they are Andrew Collett, Mick Doyle, Paul Heywood-Smith QC, Carmel Kerin, Robyn Layton QC, Peter McCusker, Ann McLean and Lindy Powell QC.

The degree of goodwill towards Elliott, and as a consequence this project, was striking. He had his enemies, but he was also widely venerated, admired and loved. In that spirit, I was given generous help. Many of Elliott's colleagues and friends contributed ideas, stories, guidance and support. All direct quotes included in this book, including from Elliott, were from my interviews unless footnotes indicate otherwise. I particularly thank Chris Sumner, John Bannon, Greg Crafter, Ted Mullighan QC, Justice Kevin Duggan, Sam Jacobs QC, Max Basheer and Professor Carol Johnson from the Politics department of the University of Adelaide for her early guidance. I was greatly assisted by my brother-in-law, Bruce Debelle AO QC, who helped me to move an early draft into a more finished manuscript, particularly in relation to Elliott's practice of the law. His thoroughness allowed me to proceed with a great deal more confidence. Others who assisted with proofreading were Jean Lamensdorf Debelle and Rachael White.

On a number of occasions Elliott asked me – always with the greatest respect – to make sure that Elizabeth's contribution was properly acknowledged. He would have preferred a biography in which husband and wife received equal billing. The reality is that Elliott was more at the forefront of public life and that Elizabeth preferred it that way. Her life was interwoven with his and she appears throughout the book, including a chapter dedicated to who she was and what she achieved. In life they were equal partners.

I am extremely grateful to Stewart Johnston for his help, advice, photographs and information. He very graciously allowed the book to take shape beyond the reach of family control and I hope his faith has been rewarded.

Wakefield Press has proven again its invaluable role as a supporter of histories and biographies that might fall short of the commercial bar set by the larger publishing houses. The sage guidance of Michael Bollen has been greatly appreciated. I was also privileged to have as an editor the talented Penelope Curtin.

My final thanks go to Elliott. His unfailing good humour made our regular meetings around his kitchen bench table unexpectedly pleasurable. More importantly, he is the real thing. It was gratifying to delve deeply into his life and to discover that up close he is a man of integrity.

Penelope Debelle
February 2011

Chronology

1918	Born 26 February at Gover Nursing Home, Adelaide
1932	Elder Scholarship to Prince Alfred College
1935	Tops South Australia Leaving Honours in Economics
1936	Commences Law at University of Adelaide
	Articled clerk with Povey Waterhouse
1937	Secretary of University of Adelaide Peace Group
1938	Business editor of *Phoenix*
1939	Joint founding editor of *Obiter Dicta*
	Meets Elizabeth Teesdale Smith
1940	Stood down from University of Adelaide
	Enlists with Australian Military Forces
	Graduates and begins private practice
1941	Student dunking in River Torrens
	Elliott and Elizabeth join Communist Party of Australia (CPA)
	Called up December 15
1942	Marries Elizabeth April 17
1943	Stationed in New Guinea
	Joins Army Education Services
1944	Promoted to Lieutenant
1945	Demobbed. Returns to Povey Waterhouse
1946	Starts own practice
1948	Wins Clerks Award
	First South Australian Supreme Court appearance
1949	Birth of only child, Ian (Stewart) Johnston
1950	Sheffield Peace Congress (transferred to Warsaw)
	Visits Russia
1951	Returns to Adelaide on *Orcades*
	Full-time organiser with SA branch of CPA
1953	CPA candidate for seat of Stuart in state election
1954	Elected to state committee of SA branch of CPA

1955 Study trip to People's Republic of China

1957 Returns from China

Resumes legal practice

1959 Joined by Elizabeth at Johnston & Johnston

1964 First High Court appearance (workers compensation)

First murder trial

1969 Rejected as Queen's Counsel by Hall Government

1970 Appointed Queen's Counsel by Dunstan Government

Purchased 345 Carrington Street

1971 Elizabeth joins Crown Law office

Chairman of Aboriginal Legal Rights Movement

1975 Privy Council appeal in London in Van Beelen case

Laverton Royal Commission

1976 Elizabeth first female assistant Crown Solicitor

Elizabeth chairs first SA Sex Discrimination Board

1980 Communist candidate for Port Adelaide at federal election

1983 Appointed South Australian Supreme Court judge

Resigns from CPA

Visits China

1984 Elizabeth on board of SA Housing Trust

1988 Retires from Bench

Royal Commission into Aboriginal Deaths in Custody

1989 Appointed lead Commissioner after Jim Muirhead resigns

1991 Royal Commission hands down report

1992 Associate Professor, Flinders University Law School

1994 Order of Australia

1996 Honorary doctorate Flinders University

2002 Elizabeth Johnston dies

2006 Honorary doctorate from University of Adelaide

CHAPTER 1

A revolutionary in China

On a bridge above the Pearl River in Guangzhou, Elliott Johnston looked out at a new Communist nation that was coming to life. It was January 1957 and the young lawyer from Adelaide was dressed in the blue uniform of a Chinese cadre. After 18 months in Chairman Mao's China, Elliott believed that he was seeing his dream of a workers' paradise come true. Around him he saw signs of a nation that was embracing the Communist ideal of men and women working side by side, in harmony, for the good of all. This vision of a more enlightened way of living, in which the state protected the weak and distributed wealth according to need had made him a Communist 16 years earlier. First Russia, now China ... Elliott burned with hope that Australia, too, would be a Communist nation one day. At the end of a long immersion in Red China, Elliott was convinced that a new world order had been born. It was the single greatest moment of his life.

This was his second time on the bridge. Elliott, 39, had arrived 18 months earlier as one of a group of Australian Communists handpicked to study Chairman Mao Tse-tung's revolution. The new People's Republic of China had established a school in the capital, Beijing, and had invited comrades from around the world to study the second great Communist movement of the twentieth century.

Soon after arriving in August 1955, Elliott had found his way to the Pearl River. There he saw farmers on their way into Guangzhou (then Canton), hurrying over a bridge spanning a river that teemed with sampans. Travelling either on foot or bicycles, and balancing long poles on their shoulders that supported bamboo baskets overflowing with rice, eggs, vegetables and chickens, the peasants poured in from the countryside to the busy port, much as they had done for a thousand years.

Eighteen months later, the scene had changed. Peasants still crossed the bridge carrying produce, but travelling in the convoy were two of the very earliest trucks manufactured in China. They were white utility vehicles that had been dispatched by the Communist government to communes in the country and the cities. Elliott had seen the first of them a few months earlier lined up outside a factory in Changchun, close to Inner Mongolia, and at the time he had wondered how they would be used. Now Chinese people were seeing tangible rewards for their efforts. It was a sign to Elliott that China was being transformed into a vibrant Communist economy. He could not know then that he had been exposed to only the best of what Chairman Mao wanted the 12 Australians to see.

It was the second visit to China by an invited group of Australians who were being groomed for Party leadership. What they learnt was meant to strengthen the ideology and practice of the Communist movement at home. During the first China trip, from 1951 to 1954, Chairman Mao had personally welcomed the Australians; they were comrades from a nation destined to join an emerging Asian Communist bloc.

Elliott, married with a young son, was a prominent member of the South Australian Party branch and on the Party's orders had ceased practising law in Adelaide in 1951 to become a full-time Communist organiser. He was being schooled for leadership and had attended two Party seminars in Sydney before being taken quietly aside and told to prepare for China. He should not alert anyone to where he was going or how long he would be away.

In Australia in 1955, as the Cold War took hold, Communism was feared. A referendum to ban the Communist Party of Australia (CPA) four years earlier had failed, but national sentiment against Communists was strong. Anti-Red hysteria worsened as Right-wing Industrial Groupers, backed by the charismatic Catholic anti-Communist, Bob Santamaria, formed cells inside trade unions to fight Communist control. The first trip to China had been illegal under Australian law. Three years later travelling to Red China to study was permitted but hardly smiled upon.

Very little was known in the outside world about China, its people, culture and conditions. In 1927 the dominant Kuomintang (Chinese National People's Party) led by Chiang Kai-shek had turned on the fledgling Chinese Communists and killed many of its leaders. Twenty-two years later, on 1 October 1949, the Communist leader Mao Tse-tung stood in triumph in Tiananmen Square and proclaimed the People's Republic of China. But the Australian Government had no contact with the Chinese Communists nor was the Communist government recognised by Australia or the United States of America, and, with the exception of notable correspondents like Mao Tse-tung's American biographer Edgar Snow, there were few first-hand reports describing the vast country or the people and their politics.[1] Deep-set patterns of suspicion and mistrust were taking hold. One of Elliott's travel companions, Bernie Taft, had to be taken outside the Melbourne Party office to be informed of his trip because officials believed the rooms were bugged. Spies from the newly formed Australian Security Intelligence Organisation (ASIO) were listening, and Elliott was already under surveillance.

He had discreetly made his arrangements. It meant leaving his wife Elizabeth and young son Ian, but Elizabeth was a loyal Communist too, and the couple did what the Party wanted. During the 18 months Elliott was away, Elizabeth had no clear idea where her husband was and she had expected him home four months before he returned.

Elliott's application for a passport to attend the Communist school had set off alarm bells in Canberra. His stated intention of travelling to 'China, the USSR, Czechoslovakia and Poland' caused a flurry of departmental exchanges and was considered at the most senior levels. Elliott had to explain why he wanted to visit China and possibly countries behind the Iron Curtain. He notified the Department of Immigration by letter that his reasons were tourism and to study 'legal-constitutional arrangements'.[2]

He was the only South Australian in the group, which had flown to Hong Kong and entered the People's Republic of China by

---

1 Snow's book, *Red Star Over China,* published in 1937, introduced the Communist Party of China to the outside world.

2 Department of Immigration, 'Elliott Johnston', National Archives of Australia, Canberra, 1950–55.

train. Those with him included Bernie Taft, Ted Bacon, who later headed the Queensland branch, Laurie Aarons, Harry Stanistreet and Harry Bocquet from Melbourne, and from Sydney, Joyce Stevens, the only woman.

Hong Kong was, as it still is, glittering and exotic. The group was met by representatives of the Chinese Communist Party (CCP) and booked into the Miramar hotel. After a banquet, they took an evening stroll, stepping over a Chinese woman and her baby who lay prostrate on the ground. There was nothing they could do to help her, but they were filled with hope that life would soon be different.[3]

Two days later, they boarded a train for Red China and arrived in Guangzhou, a trading port from the second century and accustomed to dealing with the outside world. It was a noisy introduction to the Chinese mainland, which contained more than a fifth of mankind. After two days on a train, they arrived at the Communist school on the outskirts of Beijing (then Peking). The small Australian group was part of an Asian contingent that included Communists from New Zealand, India, the Philippines, Burma, Indonesia, Vietnam and Pakistan. There was also a group of guerrilla fighters taking a break from the jungles of Malaya, where they were fighting British colonial rule.

The school was in a large complex with a high brick wall enclosing a series of two-storey buildings, and it was Elliott's home for the next 18 months. They were made welcome with gifts of blue Maoist workers' uniforms and poetic Chinese names, but they were also heavily supervised.[4] They were cared for by a large Chinese staff of lecturers, translators, administrators, cooks, security and medical personnel, and had access to sporting facilities and laundries, even a modern theatre equipped with earphones for the translation of films. About 200 comrades from different countries ate together three times a day, sometimes unable to communicate but united by Communist ideology. In sparse lecture rooms with concrete floors the group studied the history and achievements of the CCP. Elliott, who had read the original doctrines of Marx and

3 Bernie Taft, *Memoirs of Bernie Taft*, Scribe, Melbourne, 1994, pp. 77–8.

4 Bernie Taft was named Bo Ming, meaning 'bright and clear'. Elliott did not record his Chinese name.

Engels, had nothing but admiration for the way Communism in China was taught and practised. He attended lectures six days a week on the foundations of Marxism–Leninism, political economy and dialectical and historical materialism. He learnt how, by organising along Soviet Communist lines, the Communists had brought order to a war-weary and depleted country, and how Chairman Mao had heroically led his Red Army on the Long March to Yan'an, in the north-western province of Shaanxi.[5] He had an English translator, a delightful young man who had lived in Australia and who spoke English with an Australian accent. Lessons were in Chinese or Russian and each group sat in its own language area with an interpreter, who translated according to the language of the specific group, painstakingly word for word.

From behind the walls the comrades saw little of the real China, and when they ventured outside they were presented with a stage-managed view of Communist life. They were invited guests but were not free to wander. They could not explore on their own nor become too friendly with the local Chinese. None of them, including Elliott, thought this was odd or suspicious and they felt honoured to be part of China's political rebirth. Organised exercise was an integral part of the learning regime and every morning saw some form of activity – volleyball, running or walking. On the long train journey to Beijing, Elliott had woken in alarm when the train stopped suddenly and brisk military music blared out from the speakers. The Chinese jumped from their seats and threw themselves vigorously into an exercise routine, touching their toes and leaping into the air. This went on twice a day, and one of the few things Elliott brought back from China was a recording of the military music that accompanied the Communist callisthenics.

The Australian contingent elected a committee, headed by Laurie Aarons, and including Elliott, Ted Bacon and Bernie Taft, to maintain morale and liaise with the Chinese. They celebrated birthdays, drank beer, and saw parts of the ancient Great Wall, rebuilt under the Ming Dynasty to keep out marauding nomadic tribesmen. The pale-faced comrades in their blue uniforms were

---

5 Chairman Mao's mythologised leadership of the Long March is challenged in Jung Chang and Jon Halliday's bitter revision of history (*Mao: The Unknown Story,* Jonathan Cape, London, 2005).

objects of blatant curiosity to ordinary Chinese people and when they visited landmarks like the Forbidden City in central Beijing and the lakes and bridges of the Summer Palace, they were surrounded by locals who stared and laughed at the hairy foreigners, calling out 'monkeys, monkeys'.[6]

Everything in China, from agriculture to theatre, seemed to revolve around the revolution and the common good. All cultural activities, including operas and plays, commemorated Maoist heroes and no aspect of daily life was too insignificant to be regulated. Beijing was in the grip of a plague of flies and Elliott was allocated a quota of ten flies a day to kill in the name of the revolution. Ideological remodelling was an essential part of the armoury of Chinese Communism and Elliott learnt how to be a dutiful Communist. Good cadres scrutinised their personal lives for evidence of the bourgeois traits of selfishness, ego or desire for the limelight. These were to be renounced. Revolutionaries had to be motivated by the most honourable of reasons. Modesty was a virtue, and individuals, they were told, should be heroes. Self-examination and self-criticism were milestones on the rough road to self-improvement, and in Elliott's classes these sometimes took the form of public confessions before fellow students. 'You've told us the good reason; now tell us the *real* reason', the Chinese would say when a student sought to rationalise his actions.[7] But the psychological pressure imposed on the students was relatively mild, and the brutal personal censure used in the Cultural Revolution to turn student against teacher and son against father was still a decade away. Elliott did not find the public self-examination intrusive or irksome and he saw nothing to cause alarm.

Although he appreciated it only later, Elliott was in China at the best possible time. In the mid-1950s, the country enjoyed, at least superficially, an interlude of intellectual freedom unlike anything before or after. It was a lull between the period of revolutionary establishment, known as 'Liberation', and the beginning of the next of Mao's dramatic set pieces, the 1958 'Great Leap Forward', whose policies of forced collectivisation caused mass starvation and devas-

---

6 Taft, p. 89.

7 Eric Aarons, *What's Left*, Scribe, Melbourne, 1993, p. 97.

tating suffering. Forty million people died as a result. While Elliott was there, Mao Tse-tung invited gentle criticism of his regime in the episode known to the rest of the world as the time of 'a hundred flowers', a phrase from a work by a Taoist sage, 'Let a hundred flowers blossom, let a hundred schools [of thought] contend'.[8] In this spirit of openness, Mao urged Chinese intellectuals to speak from their hearts and to offer criticism in the manner of a breeze of mild rain.

Elliott believed that Mao was on a genuinely inclusive path. The spectacle of brainwashed Chinese Communists standing before the National People's Congress to make excoriating public confessions to kill off their old reactionary selves was not part of his experience. Later the period of 'a hundred flowers' was seen for what it was, a veneer of openness that gave the illusion of intellectual vigour. Worse, Mao was deliberately flushing out the dissenters before embarking upon a brutal cycle of recrimination and purges. 'Let a hundred flowers bloom and a hundred thoughts prevail became, let one thought prevail', Elliott said later, with some bitterness.[9]

Everything he saw at the time convinced him that the Communist experiment was a success. When he quizzed a sweeper on a train, the worker told him pay and conditions had never been better. He said he worked harder now because he had a share in the railways and he took pride in keeping the train clean in order to keep down disease.[10]

It was true that China was making great economic strides. Two years earlier, the first of the Five Year Plans had been announced and vast armies of workers had been mobilised to build massive infrastructure projects, like the 300-kilometre railway line in the south-west province of Szechuan, completed at great speed and then used for domestic propaganda to show what Communism had achieved. Elliott heard how a thousand grateful delegates gave Chairman Mao a three-minute standing ovation at the 1956 National Congress of the Communist Party of China in Beijing's

8 Roderick MacFarquhar, *The Hundred Flowers*, Stevens, London, 1960, p. 8.

9 Unless otherwise stated, all comments attributed to Elliott Johnston were made in interviews with the author between 2005 and 2009.

10 Australian Security Intelligence Organisation (ASIO), 'Elliott Frank Johnston', National Archives, Canberra, 1957.

Great Hall of the People. Extravagance and waste were criticised, and the finance minister warned that China must not sacrifice quality and safety in production by being impatient and taking risks.

Most pleasing of all, China seemed to be following a consensual pace of change that made allowance for human adaptation. The transition to Communism seemed to be progressing at just the right rate. Land redistribution and the collectivisation of agriculture were underway, and it appeared to be happening voluntarily, with some land still in private hands. Elliott visited a show farm north of Beijing, where he marvelled at the small weirs and dams ingeniously carved out of the countryside's hills and valleys. Man-made canals were dug and fish had been introduced, and Elliott thought it a great example of how cooperation helped everyone. On the same farm he saw a giant hothouse made entirely from soil strengthened with grass and peat, its roof and three sides enclosed. The fourth side was a wall of glass designed to trap the sun and heat the interior. Inside, a fire raised the temperature just enough to enable vegetables to grow during the winter when the land was under snow. Elliott talked to some of the farmers who were wearing boots for the first time and who told him their lives had never been better.

In late 1956 the group travelled to the vast expanse of northern China which, with Russia's help, was being opened up to economic growth. State quotas were driving the iron and steel, coal, cotton and cloth industries, and production targets had been established for factories, workshops, teams and individuals. New plants, like the factory where Elliott had seen the first vehicles coming off the production line, were huge in scale and in ambition. They were shown a factory manufacturing the tools and equipment needed to set up a power industry. A peasant society, which for centuries had laboured from dawn and gone to bed at dark, was being transformed by electricity. In Shanghai he visited the home of a man who owned a profitable metal factory. The man spoke with enthusiasm about his arrangements for a staged handover; he would remain the manager and receive a declining percentage of the profits over time. After 15 years, his equity in the factory would be extinguished, the factory would be state-owned and he would be paid a salary. ASIO reported later that Elliott was struck by 'the happy look worn by people of all classes, both workers and intelligentsia'.[11]

Six months after Elliott had arrived in China, the news of Soviet Russia's terrifying experiences under Joseph Stalin leaked out. The practice of mass extermination and terror had been Russia's dirty secret, but in 1956 President Nikita Khrushchev made his 'secret speech'. Speaking in a private session at the Twentieth Party Congress in Moscow, Khrushchev denounced Stalin, his predecessor, as a cruel despot and madman who for 30 years murdered his countrymen on a whim. Court cases had been fabricated and false confessions of guilt extracted under torture; innocent people were exiled to the gulags or shot. Western intelligence translated the speech and circulated it. Elliott heard whispers, which were confirmed when the Victorian Communist, Ted Hill, who had been at the Congress, returned through China and showed the group the speech reproduced in full in the *New York Times* newspaper. No one could doubt that it was genuine. Elliott read with silent horror what a new leader was saying about the giant who had led post-revolutionary Russia for three decades.

There was still a huge stock of goodwill on which to draw and enough excuses to go around. Here was Russia admitting its mistakes and making a commitment to a more transparent future. Best of all, Elliott believed that here was China presenting a smiling socialist alternative to the mistakes of Stalin.[12] As if to emphasise that China had nothing to hide, Elliott's group was later supplied with reports from the European press, in which Stalin's crimes were analysed and discussed.[13]

Russia and China were close and remained so while Elliott was in China. Russia supplied teachers to the Communist school and helped China's industrial program by providing advice and expertise. But China's ambitions were being unleashed and while Elliott was there Mao would say, 'The Soviet Union's today is China's

---

11 ASIO, 'South Australia: Elliott Frank Johnston', National Archives of Australia, Canberra, 7 June 1957, p. 100.

12 Bob Walshe, '1956: The secret speech and reverberations in Sydney', *The Hummer*, publication of the Sydney Branch, Australian Society for the Study of Labour History, vol. 3, no. 10, 2003.

13 Taft, p. 93.

tomorrow'.[14] China took an enigmatic position on the Khrushchev speech, announcing that Stalin's contribution to Communism had been 'seventy per cent positive and 30 per cent negative'. China had clearly determined its own trajectory free of Russia; the message was that Australia should do the same. Elliott believed China was adapting Communism to fit the circumstances of its history and people and he took this as a lesson that Australia, too, should find its own way.

After 18 months, the group was tired and rundown. The poor-quality food had stripped them of weight and they were isolated in a country not diplomatically recognised by Australia. Elliott did not want to draw attention to Elizabeth by sending letters post-marked 'China' and they had corresponded irregularly and briefly. In late 1956, they were instructed to burn all papers and documents, including, regrettably, all photographs. It was time for Elliott to start making his way home. Most of the group were to return by rail across China and to the British Crown Colony of Hong Kong, but Party headquarters in Australia intervened. Elliott and three others were diverted to the Soviet Union for a short study visit. He went without question.

Although the timing was opportune for learning first-hand about Russia after Stalin, it proved a desultory experience. Elliott had already visited Moscow in 1951 and was impressed then by the industry and purpose of the Soviet experiment. He resolved on this visit to discover the reaction of ordinary people to the Khrushchev revelations. Illness intervened. He arrived in Russia in December 1956 and was taken almost immediately to Moscow General Hospital for minor surgery. The operation went badly and he needed a lengthy convalescence which isolated him from the rest of his group. (On his return to Australia he defended the failed operation, claiming, according to his ASIO file, that he had 'the best surgeon there', but he had reached the hospital too late.)

When he emerged from hospital four weeks later, he asked to visit a factory where he could question the workers. He was taken to the outskirts of Moscow where tools for the power industry, similar to those he had seen in China, were manufactured. The factory,

---

14 Ross Terrill, *China in Our Time,* Hale & Ironmonger, Sydney, 1992, p. 14.

which had been built in the late 1920s by workers and students, was in a compound that included blocks of flats and a giant hothouse. It was on the eastern periphery of the city and had been on the frontline of the attack in 1941 when Hitler's 4th Panzer Division came within 30 kilometres of the Kremlin. As the Nazi army approached, the factory had been packed up and relocated to the other side of the Ural Mountains. 'Before the war we only had one factory,' the manager shrugged, 'now we have two'.

Elliott's visit was on a Saturday and although the factory closed at lunchtime, some of the workers had stayed behind. Elliott's Russian translator was an older man who had witnessed the Bolshevik Revolution and had fled to the United States of America, returning home after the war. Through him, Elliott asked the workers what they knew about Stalin's reign of terror and how their lives had been affected. Yes, they knew the details, they said; a meeting had been called at the factory to explain what Stalin had done. But instead of crying out for anger and justice, they were dull and resigned. We all make mistakes, they told Elliott; you can tell us now what we are doing wrong. Elliott persisted: 'What will stop it happening again?' he asked them. They seemed not to know or care.

Dispirited, Elliott saw that their vision did not extend past the factory floor. Their docility, in particular, troubled him. Back at his hotel, Elliott made one more attempt at digging beneath the surface. The woman who looked after his room spoke faltering English and had told him that her daughter danced with the Bolshoi Ballet. But she shrugged him off saying she knew nothing about politics. He gave up and presented her with the fragrant flowers given to him by the chair of the factory's hothouse committee.

Elliott returned to China and made his way by train to Hong Kong. On 20 February 1957 he was back in Adelaide, reunited with Elizabeth and Ian, and looking somewhat older, according to ASIO's spies, with patches of grey above his ears. The next day an official from the South Australian branch of the Communist Party of Australia (CPA) rang and asked Elliott to deliver a report on his trip. He spoke glowingly, at length and from the heart, about what he had seen and learnt about the practice of Communism in China, how it was poised on the brink of great economic progress, and how state control was being erected on a structure of thoughtful, consensual transition. He told them he had witnessed an enlightened form of Communism, driven by intellectuals who were shaping the principles of Marxism to China's history and circumstances. One of the members, Jim Mitchell, had a question: 'What I want to know is why have we never received a report like this about the Soviet Union?' It was some time later Elliott before learnt the truth: that the Chinese people were being as cruelly repressed by their leaders as had the Russians.

In Adelaide silence fell as the Party members who toiled away at factories at General Motors-Holden's and Simpson Pope pictured a Marxist-Leninist Utopia blossoming in a faraway land. They believed that through Communism the lives of ordinary working people would be transformed; the poor would have dignity; wealth would be shared communally; the sick would be cared for; children would be educated; and the weak would have protection. This was Elliott's vision for Australia. It sustained him for the whole of his life.

CHAPTER 2

A better world

Elliott became a Communist because he wanted to improve the lives of working people and make the world a better place. Communism frightened many Australians but Elliott embraced it in the manner of a religious conversion. He was sustained by it and guided by it. He joined the Communist Party of Australia in 1941 and despite all the terror that was inflicted and the evil that was done in the name of Communism, he never wavered in thinking he had done the right thing. He was one of hundreds of young 'Depression Communists' who signed up in the 1940s, men and women who made an idealistic commitment to create a political economy that was kinder and fairer than capitalism. The 1929 Great Depression had crushed Australia's spirit, destroying the old certainties of work, stability and progress. The economic structures on which the developed world had been built were shown to be flawed and when they failed, human misery seemed boundless. Elliott thought that Communism had the capacity to prevent a repetition of this kind of mass suffering. As though further argument was needed, the CPA was a marshalling point for opposition to war. As Fascism began to take a hold on Europe, Elliott signed up to its campaign for peace.

In 1918, the year Elliott was born, Adelaide was on the brink of catastrophe. Drought and depression had led up to the First World War when 28,000 young men had left South Australia to fight. One in 20 died on the battlefield and almost half returned wounded. Although the city staggered to its feet, barely a decade later drought again stalled the economy. The Wall Street crash on the New York Stock Exchange in 1929 accelerated a decline that was already underway. By 1933 the unemployment level in Adelaide was the highest of any Australian city and more than one in three men was out of work.

Born on 26 February 1918, at Gover Nursing Home in North Adelaide, Elliott was only 11 years old when the Depression overshadowed a childhood that had been secure and carefree. As the crisis deepened, his father, William Stewart Johnston, worried that he would lose his job as an accountant in the cashier's department at Harris Scarfe, a department store in the city. Elliott, his older brother Ross and younger sister Marjorie would lie in bed at night listening as their parents talked in hushed tones. William Johnston, one of ten surviving children, and his wife, Elsie Vivian Elliott, one of nine, understood what a struggle life could be. Elliott's paternal grandfather, a Presbyterian Scot, had fallen in love in Liverpool with a young woman from an Irish Catholic family. You can marry him, her family said, but never darken our doors again. The young lovers fled to Australia. His mother's parents were Cornish and had met at Kapunda, north-east of Adelaide, where Joseph Elliott at different times ran the Kapunda Arms, the Railway Hotel and later the Ramshead Hotel at Evanston, a small north-eastern town closer to the city.

Named after Elsie's brother, Frank Elliott, who had died fighting in the Somme, Elliott grew up at 39 Balham Avenue in leafy Kingswood, a suburb south of the inner city. His childhood was happy, with weekends spent playing in the nearby paddocks on the Waites' family property, Urrbrae.[1] Elliott began his education at Highgate Primary School, but his time there was brief, a victory for the territorial magpies that swooped on him on his way to school. Elliott had been born blind in his left eye and his parents, concerned for his sight, moved him to Unley Primary School. There he spent much of each day wearing a patch over his working eye in a misguided attempt to prompt his left eye into sight. He walked into people and crashed into walls and eventually the treatment was abandoned. The cause of his blindness was never diagnosed or understood and Elliott never regarded it as a handicap.

At school, young Elliott played cricket and football, sang badly, learnt Tennyson's 'Charge of the Light Brigade' and played in a large yard divided by a fence that separated the girls from the boys.

---

1 This large tract of land in the south-eastern suburb of Urrbrae became the Waite Institute after it was given to the University of Adelaide in 1922. It remains a major agricultural and animal research hub.

His father had topped his final year at school and won the right to borrow from the local library and so the Johnston home was filled with the works of Shakespeare, Wordsworth, Browning and Keats.

Elliott progressed to Unley High School, and at the end of his second year applied for a scholarship to Prince Alfred College (PAC), a Methodist private boys school on the eastern edge of Adelaide's inner city. He had been encouraged to do so by the example of his older brother Ross, a good footballer who had won a sporting scholarship to PAC. In 1932 Elliott won the Elder entrance scholarship, arriving at PAC when the Depression was at its most severe. By the beginning of Elliott's second year, enrolments had fallen from 400 to 315, and staff were being retrenched, while at home, his father's job seemed to hang by a thread. The school had an egalitarian Methodist background and was conservative in its policies on education. Elliott's first headmaster was John Ward, who pledged to provide a sound liberal education and a varied curriculum. In a setting reminiscent of a grand English boarding school, tradition was emphasised and discussion was encouraged.

Families during the Depression were not merely worse off; many of them lost everything and were struggling to survive. Another college boy who lived just a few streets away from Elliott, the master painter Jeffrey Smart, asked his father what life had been like before the Depression. As an old man, he remembered his father's answer: 'Life [was] heaven'.[2] In later life Smart still has the excruciating memory of a schoolboy incident that illustrated the desperation of the Depression. He and other students from Pulteney Grammar School on the southern parklands encountered a woman at lunchtime selling home-made chip potatoes from a cheap suitcase for a penny a bag. The boys ran over to the woman, inspected her chips and pronounced them the wrong sort because they were flaked ovals instead of chips. Later, Smart was appalled at how callously they had treated this poor woman. 'It was my first intimation that there was absolutely no justice in the world – it made me physically ill and I got the squitters.'[3]

---

2 Jeffrey Smart, *Not Quite Straight: A memoir*, William Heinemann, Sydney, 1996, p. 31.

3 ibid. p. 32.

Once a man lost a job, it was not regained for years. Possessions were sold, houses were repossessed and banks raised signs, 'House deserted, whereabouts of owner unknown'.[4] Desperate families rented accommodation, dodged the bailiffs, then moved out in the dead of night in what became known as the 'midnight flit'. By June 1931, almost 40 per cent of Adelaide's workforce was receiving unemployment relief and six thousand homes had been deserted. Families slept rough – in the sand dunes at Semaphore or in the terrible shanty towns along the banks of the River Torrens, in makeshift humpies with walls made from flattened kerosene tins, bits of old wood or iron, or chicken wire.[5] Men went on the swag or knocked on doors begging for work. They offered for sale pitiful items, pieces of wire bent into coat hangers or handmade pegs. It was a heart-wrenching time.

Around Elliott's middle-class neighbourhood, people knocked on the door selling fish from the Onkaparinga River or rabbits trapped in Carey Gully in the Adelaide Hills. Families shared fruit from backyard orchards, although raiders often stripped the trees during the night. His mother Elsie, a kind and gentle woman who devoted herself to family, gave eggs to neighbours and offered anyone who came to the door a piece of iced cake. Her natural compassion guided Elliott. One day when he was young, Elsie paused while scrubbing his back in the woodchip-heated bath. 'I hope you'll be like Uncle Jim and look after the poor', she said to him. Jim Johnston, William's eldest brother, sold men's clothing in Adelaide's East End, but Elliott understood what she meant. Uncle Jim led a humble life but he was a kind, decent man.

Although Elsie remained fearful that disaster would strike her family, the Johnstons weathered the tough years better than most. Some of the staff at Harris Scarfe lost their jobs, but Elliott's father was promoted to cashier, replacing an older man who retired early. William Johnston held the same job for more than 50 years, earning a gold watch, which he wore with pride.

Elliott loved sport and at PAC he began a lifelong passion

---

4 Ray Broomhill, *Unemployed Workers: A social history of the Great Depression in Adelaide,* University of Queensland Press, St Lucia, 1978, p. 115.

5 Valerie Howe, *And the Lions Roared at Night*, Flinders Press, Adelaide, 1998, p. 5.

for Australian Rules football, most of it spent as an enthusiastic spectator. His allegiance was always to the Sturt Football Club, formed in 1901 with players from the Unley area, which adjoined Kingswood. At school, despite his blind eye, he made the 'A' team and his sense of fair play was evident. 'A fast and dashing player who leads and passes perfectly', his captain wrote in September 1935, after a win against St Peter's College. 'His clean play has saved the side in the matter of unnecessary frees. He must endeavour to check his man when defending.'

But Elliott's strength was English and the exchange of ideas. He joined the debating team and in his Leaving year his English teacher encouraged him to study for the Shakespeare prize. He missed out on his first attempt, but the following year he won the George Thorburn Melrose Prize for Shakespeare. The idea of studying law was slowly taking shape, although where this ambition came from was unclear. There were lawyers in the family, notably his cousins Don, Keith and Jack, who were the sons of Elsie's brother Ronald (known in the family as Darby). Don, the first of the Elliotts to graduate as a solicitor, was older than Elliott, and the next in line, Keith, suffered ill health and had an uncertain career before dying in 1950 from a cerebral haemorrhage. In 1933 Jack Elliott was articled to Don's firm, R.D. Elliott & Co. Don became a Magistrate in the Juvenile Court and Jack became a prominent criminal barrister, best known for his defence in the Privy Council of a South Australian Government appeal against the conviction of a farmhand accused of murdering a local grazier. The Elliotts lived not far from the Johnstons and on Sundays Jack came by to chat in the garden with William, Elliott and Ross. Elliott and Jack were closest in age and Jack's love of language and his willingness to challenge authority may have left their mark.

At PAC the great themes of war and peace, politics and the economy were widely discussed and students were encouraged to question events taking place in the world around them. In his four years at the college, Elliott increasingly contributed to a profound schoolboy debate about the kind of society in which he wanted to live. In his Leaving year he led an intercollegiate debate against arch-rival St Peter's College, whose team boasted the great Fin

Crisp.[6] In the view of the school magazine, Elliott trounced Crisp on the topic 'that democracy is doomed'. According to this account, Crisp opened the debate with 'a slashing attack on everyday life and modern institutions generally but seemed to have very little to substitute for them'. Elliott, in what was judged to be the best speech of the night, explained that democracy for all its flaws was the most practical system yet formulated. On this occasion PAC defeated the St Peter's debating team for the first time.[7]

He loved ideas and debating came naturally to him. He became a member of the Christian Union and wrote a paper that traced the history of the missions from Christ's disciples to the twelfth century. In his final year he gave a speech on the life and work of David Lloyd George, and at Methodist Ladies' College he participated in a lofty mid-winter discussion about whether it was in the best interests of all nations that armaments be abolished. Not all student debates were about international politics; the school magazine recorded such topics as 'the advantages of semi-deafness' and 'the virtues of the abdominal muscles' and Elliott once gave an impromptu speech on the question, 'can a baby think?' Nor were his political writings entirely serious. He penned a piece of absurdist schoolboy wit for the magazine about the League of Nations and its impotence in the face of Mussolini's invasion of Abyssinia.

STOP PRESS

Geneva, December 23rd, 1935

We have it on good authority that the committee of 18, acting at the instigation of the committee of five, has intimated to the committee of 13 that it intends to warn the committee of nine to advise the committee of 12 that steps be taken to put an end to the present unfortunate conflict between Italy and Abyssinia.

E.F.J[8]

---

6 Leslie Finlay Crisp became a Rhodes Scholar, academic, influential public servant, biographer of Ben Chifley and author of *The Australian Federal Labor Party 1901–1951.*

7 *Prince Alfred College Chronicle*, December 1934, Prince Alfred College, Adelaide, p. 171.

8 *Prince Alfred College Chronicle*, December 1935, Prince Alfred College, Adelaide, p. 174.

There was much to talk about and consider. This was an era defined by the Great War, followed a decade later by widespread financial ruin, where economies simply crumbled. In Europe, another war was brewing. Spain was on the brink of a civil war, with the Loyalists in a stand-off with the Fascist-supported armies of General Francisco Franco. Elsewhere in Europe, Fascism and Nazism were on the march. All sense of an ordered universe had vanished and this was felt even by schoolboys; immediately after Elliott left for university the boys of PAC and St Peter's College raised funds for victims of the Spanish Civil War.[9]

Elliott began to engage seriously with international political thought. In his final year at school he was head of the library committee, which meant examining every new acquisition and assigning it a classification number. One particular book – Emil Ludwig's *July 1914* – moved him so profoundly that he never forgot it. The book gives an account of last-minute efforts by the European Socialists, particularly the Socialist parties of Germany and France, to prevent the outbreak of the First World War. Ludwig, a lawyer who worked as a foreign correspondent, wrote about 'the stupidity' of the men who took Europe to war while others made no attempt to stop them. Elliott, by now a young pacifist, was impressed by the ideas expressed in the book and wrote about it glowingly in the school magazine. 'In this very fine book, which should be read by every statesman in the world, the author points out the causes which led up to the final outburst, the ways in which it might have been avoided, and the lessons we can learn from the mistakes of that fatal month.'[10] In his final term, Elliott led a debate in which he argued, with conviction and without notes, that nationalism threatened civilisation because it made peace impossible.

At the end of 1935 he won a bursary scholarship to the University of Adelaide to study law, leaving behind an outstanding school record. In the 1935 South Australian Leaving Honours exam he topped the state in Economics, came fifth in English and was seventeenth on the Honours List. At school, he won the Alan Johnson

9 Amirah Inglis, *Australians in the Spanish Civil War,* Allen and Unwin, Sydney, 1987, p. 69.

10 *Prince Alfred College Chronicle*, September 1935, Prince Alfred College, Adelaide, 1955, p. 281.

Memorial prize for coming top in Intermediate, the inaugural J.C. Sunter Memorial prize for languages, the Harold Fisher prize for English literature and the Shakespeare prize.

At Adelaide University law school he was in a class of about 15 students, among them Gwenneth Woodger with whom he later edited the student newspaper, *On Dit.* They were a colourful bunch: one student was jailed for extortion in his first year, another was killed in a motor-cycle accident, and two became Rhodes Scholars. One of the Rhodes Scholars, Richard Arthur (Dick) Blackburn, became the first Chief Justice of the Supreme Court of the Australian Capital Territory, and the other, Duncan Campbell Menzies, a good friend of Elliott, studied at Oxford but died a harrowing death at the hands of the Japanese in Burma in April 1943.

At university, the constant intellectual searching that propelled Elliott through his final years at school was channelled more closely. Apart from his studies – Elements of Law, Contracts, Latin and English – he threw himself into student life and began a lifelong habit of joining clubs and organisations, mostly on the Left. He was a great participator; in his last year of school he had been a prefect, a member of the school magazine committee, head of the library committee, patrol leader of a Scout troop, and a member of the Christian Union, the concert committee and the debating society. At university he joined the Law Students' Society, which still took only men, and the Student Christian Movement, which he left a year later, but not before he had made his mark as a potential Christian leader. 'He has a true interest in the welfare of humanity which will enable him to make good use of his training so as to do good work in the future', wrote Reverend Leslie Parkin from the Memorial Congregational Church in Tasmania in a reference for Elliott.

Just as these were extraordinary times, so the students at Adelaide University in the late 1930s were a truly brilliant crowd. The English faculty was brimming over with personalities who left their mark on literature and who were building a new tradition of cultural modernism. 'The decade 1935 to 1945 was a seminal period in South Australia's (and Australia's) cultural history, falling roughly between Rex Ingamell's first book of verse, *Gumtops,* 1935, and the last issue of *Angry Penguins* in 1949', wrote a fellow university student, author Colin Thiele, in a foreword to *Lost Angry Penguins.*[11]

Thiele, who became a Fulbright Scholar and wrote more than one hundred books including *Storm Boy,* was two years ahead of Elliott and studied English with the flamboyant prodigy, Max Harris, who strode around the campus with great élan, usually in the company of his firm friend Mary Martin. Rex Ingamell was the founder of the Jindyworobaks literary movement, which eschewed the culture of Europe, instead looking to Australian and Aboriginal culture for inspiration. In its early stages the movement attracted Max Harris and another poet, Wilf (Flexmore) Hudson. Harris, along with the modernist poets Sam (Donald Bevis) Kerr, a dashing, romantic figure on campus, and Paul Pfeiffer, co-founded the famous Adelaide University literary magazine, *Angry Penguins.* Another founder was Geoffrey Dutton, who studied English at Oxford under C.S. Lewis and who later established Penguin Australia.

Elliott and Sam Kerr were the best of friends, although Kerr was a year behind at university. They had met in the refectory over lunch in January 1938, and Elliott, who was then joint editor of *On Dit,* invited Sam to contribute. Kerr, handsome with thick, dark curly hair, agreed to write a regular page three column that would be provocative and questioning. Kerr wrote under the homonym 'Cur', Latin for why. Elliott and Kerr were on the university debating team together and travelled to Brisbane and Mount Gambier for intervarsity and competition debates. Over the Christmas of 1939, just three months after Britain and Australia had declared war on Germany, they went swagging together for a week and slept out under the stars in the Adelaide Hills, talking, walking and reading.[12] Kerr would give Elliott his sonnets to read. 'Lady, Amen', written about a woman Elliott knew, was his favourite, particularly the final lines: 'At the last I find I still/ Regret your hard irreverent laughter'.[13]

Elliott was also a friend, but not a disciple of Max Harris. Harris and his literary crowd enjoyed jazz, listened to Bach, and under

---

11 John Miles, *Lost Angry Penguins: D.B. Kerr and P.G. Pfeiffer: A path to the wind*, Crawford House, Adelaide, 2000, p. vii.

12 ibid., p. 74.

13 ibid., p. 206.

the mentorship of English Professor Charles Jury, published avant-garde poetry and literature that defied the classical constraints. Elliott was friendly with them on campus, went to the same parties and shared their passion for words and ideas. The precursor to the *Angry Penguins* literary journal was the Adelaide University Union publication, *Phoenix*. Sam Kerr edited it with Max Harris, and in 1938 Elliott became its business editor, a role that required him to round up a handful of advertisers for each edition. The job was a consolation prize after an article he submitted on peace had been knocked back. From 1935 until 1939, *Phoenix* published original art work, poetry, prose and political discussion, but it fell out of favour on campus and in 1939 the money ran out. The following year *Angry Penguins* began, named by its patron Charles Jury who borrowed the marvellously enigmatic phrase from a Max Harris poem, 'Mithridatum of Despair':

> We know no mithridatum of despair
> as drunks, the angry penguins of the night,
> straddling the cobbles of the square,
> tying a shoelace by fogged lamplight.[14]

The new journal attracted attention from around the country and by 1941 it had become a national publication of genuine literary value.[15] But Elliott's main interest was in the world of political ideas, not literature.

He was already very serious about the law. In 1939 he became a joint founding editor, along with Duncan Menzies and Howard Zelling, of the Law Students' Society publication, *Obiter Dicta*.[16] Promoting itself ambitiously as 'a journal of persuasive authority', the first issue was introduced in March 1939 by the Professor of Law, A.L. Campbell, with an invitation to students to look beyond the mechanics of their training and consider the world around them. Dick Blackburn wrote a colourful piece, 'The historical aspect of conspiracy as a tort', which described case law based on an inci-

14 Samela Harris, 'Ern Malley: Angry Penguins', <http:www.panda.nla.gov.au>.

15 Miles, pp. 93–4.

16 *Obiter dicta* is a Latin legal term for an incidental remark or passing comment.

dent at Covent Garden, where the audience booed the actors off the stage at the behest of the Duke of Brunswick. Duncan Menzies contributed a piece regretting the implications for Australia of the Shropshire Union case, in which a British union disguised its interest in a company through a trust in the name of one of the members who then sold it, legitimately as it turned out. Elliott made a stolid contribution, 'The divisibility of the Crown' and its implications for the debts of a Queensland company. *Obiter Dicta's* second issue a year later was more modest and Elliott, still a co-editor, examined what the abdication by King Edward (later the Duke of Windsor) meant for the divisibility of the Crown. By the third and final issue in 1941 Elliott was no longer involved and many potential contributors were away at war, including Dick Blackburn, Sam Jacobs, Brian Magarey and E.B. (Eb) Scarfe, each of whom later became noted practitioners. Sam Jacobs, a Queen's Counsel, became a Judge of the Supreme Court of South Australia; Brian Magarey was a founding partner of a successful legal firm; and Eb Scarfe QC became Crown Prosecutor.

In the late 1930s Elliott was one of the best debaters on campus. He was on the committee that ran university debates and was part of the victorious 1939 intervarsity debating team with Sam Kerr and Victor Matison, who later became a magistrate. He was a leader of Left-wing intellectual and political student discussion and by 1941 was at the forefront of every debate on student democracy and Left-wing politics. 'It is largely by the vigour of his rhetoric he has ridden to power and popularity. In the last two years most debates in the union have been his debates, remembered at once for his eloquence and the superb assurance with which he put across the most aged of wisecracks', an anonymous profiler wrote in *On Dit*.[17]

While Elliott was popular, not everyone appreciated his wit or liked his extremist views, particularly in the emotional climate of a nation at war. He had supporters on the university staff, but one famous academic, Sir Douglas Mawson, was not among them. Knighted in 1914 after leading the Australasian Antarctic Expedition, an extraordinary voyage of scientific exploration and discovery, which he barely survived, Sir Douglas returned to the

17 *On Dit*, July 1941, University of Adelaide, Adelaide.

University of Adelaide in 1919 as professor of geology and mineralogy. He was a conservative thinker with an irascible personality and he had no time at all for Elliott. They disagreed openly at meetings and Elliott accepted that Sir Douglas, a great man in almost every sense, disliked him. They clashed late in 1940 at a meeting held to elect the new president of the University Union, a body comprised of student representatives and staff members that included Sir Douglas. After Elliott had been nominated, Sir Douglas suggested the union consider a female president and nominated a friend of Elliott's, Sam Jacobs's sister Doreen. Elliott took it as a clear signal that Sir Douglas did not want him. But Doreen, who was for a time president of the Women's Union, declined the nomination. She had already been sounded out as a possible challenger and refused to stand. They were friends and if there was to be an election, her vote was with 'Johnny'. Elliott was duly elected and for a short time in 1941, he was president of the union, with Doreen as his deputy.

A year or so ahead of Elliott was another exceptional student who left his mark on history, Elliott's schoolboy debating opponent Fin Crisp. Crisp was appointed in 1974 to the Board of Directors of the Commonwealth Banking Corporation after a distinguished career as an author, academic and public servant. He graduated from the University of Adelaide with First Class Honours in Political Science and History, won a Rhodes Scholarship in 1938 and the following year began studying at Balliol College, Oxford. Tall and brilliant, he was active in student politics and in 1938 he and Helen Wighton, the feminist student he later married, founded with Elliott's help the National Union of Australian University Students (NUAUS), the first student-only representative body. Elliott was passionate about student democracy and was appointed as one of three Adelaide representatives on the first council of NUAUS, representing the university at one of its annual conferences. 'No undergraduate has stimulated so much activity in local affairs and no undergraduate in Australia has, with more tenderness and zeal than he, nursed the NUAUS', *On Dit* said of Elliott.[18]

But Elliott's path was weightier than student democracy. In the late 1930s the Civil War in Spain preoccupied Left-wing thinkers,

18 ibid.

on and off campus. The war became an international rallying point for the fight between Fascism and democracy, with Elliott supporting the Communist-backed Republican Loyalists against General Franco. Internationally, the sides were lining up: the Soviet Union supplied the Republicans with weapons and volunteers, while Franco's Nationalists were backed by the Fascist governments of Italy and Germany. Although Spain later played no part in the Second World War, it was seen at the end of the 1930s as the battlefield where the rise of German militarism and the next war might be stopped.

In 1937, motivated by rising international tensions, Fin Crisp formed the University of Adelaide Peace Group, and Elliott became the secretary. Among its members was Maurice Finniss, a tutor at St Mark's University College; on occasions the group met at the home of his father, Canon Finniss, in North Adelaide.[19] The Peace Group opposed all wars rather than any particular battle, but it viewed the way events in Europe were unfolding as ominous. There were around 60 members, male and female, including Archibald Grenfell Price, the Master of St Mark's College.

Elliott's fight on the side of the Australian worker began taking on a more solid form. In late 1938 the federal Attorney-General, Robert Menzies, was embroiled in an ugly dispute on the docks at Port Kembla in New South Wales. The waterside workers refused to load pig iron from BHP on to a ship bound for Japan, arguing that it could be used by Japan for bombs and weapons to attack China, and that Japan could turn on Australia. Menzies, soon to be nicknamed 'Pig Iron Bob', threatened to bring in strike-breakers. The Port Kembla dispute was for a time a focus for the peace movement, but by January 1939 seven thousand waterside workers were out of work and they capitulated. It was a partial success; the two ships waiting on the dock were loaded but it was agreed there would be no more exports of pig iron to Japan. Elliott was impressed by the use of industrial power to further the cause of non-aggression.

In 1940, wishing to explore the larger themes of peace, politics and the economy, Elliott established his own university forum, the

---

19 Miles, p. 71.

Radical Club, of which he became president. Its 25 members, who included Max Harris, drew up a constitution that set out radical objectives. They included modifying or replacing the present system of production and distribution and seeking a permanent peace based on a just distribution of economic resources. Elliott's lifelong commitment to a better world for the working man and woman was taking shape. He was not yet a Communist, but he was beginning to think like one. The club elected officials and prepared a white paper on free speech. A draft was circulated and agreed changes were made. The paper attacked wartime censorship which suppressed criticism of government policy, although it recognised the need to protect military secrets. Censorship during war sprang from fear, Elliott argued, and was a return to the uncivilised instincts to kill and destroy that which did not conform. 'The argument is always the same and it is always wrong. It is used by those who fear what they do not understand, who fear the truth which may emerge from free discussion and who seek to support their own uncertain power by attacking the liberties of those who oppose them.' This, he wrote, was the very argument Hitler used.[20]

Free speech on campus was a delicate issue and *On Dit*, in a decision by its editorial committee a month earlier, had endorsed the need for wartime censorship. Elliott had objected and wrote that the issue was far more vital than the usual student concerns about refectory lawns and union crockery. The argument for transparency that he put then, and believed throughout his life, was that there was no situation so desperate and no government so perfect that its policies could not be bettered by open examination and debate.

His cry for free speech in the white paper was put dramatically to the test. As it was being typed, the head of the University Union walked by. Elliott was summoned to the office of the Vice-Chancellor, Professor Sir William Mitchell, who told Elliott the Radical Club would be banned from the university for the duration of the war. Any student who criticised the government would also be banned. Elliott considered that Mitchell was being unreasonable and autocratic and attempted to argue his case. Unmoved, the

20 University of Adelaide Radical Club, 'White Paper on Free Speech', p. 4. Elliott Johnston private papers.

Vice-Chancellor stood Elliott down for a fortnight, advising him that he would report the matter to the University Council. It was agreed that Elliott would be permitted to write to the council to present his point of view.

Elliott consulted the Radical Club committee and on 30 May 1940 typed a two-page letter in which he defended the right of the Radical Club to exist. He argued that suppression was an extreme reaction to a club which had been active for little over a month and had done nothing subversive. It was also foolish to expect students not to argue about politics at a time of war. Better to have orderly discussion in guided study circles than secret talks between individuals who were embittered by suppression, he argued. On the threat of punishment, Elliott asked only to be treated in the same way as someone outside the University. 'We do not seek for any distinction to be drawn between the University and the rest of the community; we do not seek a greater freedom but we do wish to maintain an equal freedom'. Finally, he raised the issue of his growing reputation as a Left-wing radical, referring to Communism for the first time. 'I am informed by the Vice-Chancellor that it was mentioned at the last meeting of the Council that I was personally an "avowed Communist". I think it right to say, not in self-protection, but because the statement as it stands may prejudice the Radical Club, that this is incorrect.'[21] The unspoken fear was that the Radical Club was a Communist front and Elliott addressed this in a separate letter to the Vice-Chancellor after their meeting. 'I understand that it is feared by some that the Club consists of a number of students connected to some particular political faith who will run the organisation for the spreading of propaganda in support of that faith. This is far from being the true position as the constitution, I think, readily demonstrates.'[22] It was a fine distinction nevertheless, given the Club's commitment to changing, or replacing, the present economic system.

Elliott received a formal reply dated 1 June 1940 that read: 'The Council at its meeting yesterday decided that the Radical Club be excluded from the University for the duration of the war. It took

---

21 Letter in Elliott Johnston's private papers.

22 Private papers.

this decision unanimously notwithstanding its appreciation of the quality of your letter.'[23]

There was a minor flurry of protests on campus, including objections from two members of staff, the Professor of History and Political Science Gerry Portus, and the Elder Professor of Anatomy Frank Goldby, who spoke in Elliott's defence. But discussion of the event was banned from *On Dit*, and a letter written to it by Elliott defending the Radical Club was never published. Sam Jacobs, who now was jointly editing *On Dit* with a fellow student, Primrose Viner-Smith, ran into Elliott on his way to the Law School and told Elliott that his letter had been withdrawn. Jacobs, who much later sat on the Supreme Court Bench with Elliott, was prepared to resign in protest but he was called away to war. By early June, Jacobs was at officer training at Liverpool in New South Wales.

There was some support for Elliott's position from interstate. The University of Melbourne Students Representative Council sent a mild letter of protest, couched in terms of inquiry into what had taken place. 'I think you will appreciate that the actions alleged in Adelaide University are of great interest to students in all universities and that they are of particular interest to the Melbourne SRC as a constituent member of the National Union', wrote the president, George Shaw, who became a good friend of Elliott.[24] In response, the Registrar of the University of Adelaide confirmed the Radical Club's exclusion during the war but praised Elliott's defence of it. 'The president's letter was read and highly appreciated ... I suggest that you get a copy', the Registrar wrote. He denied that *On Dit* had been formally censored, claiming that the editors had voluntarily withdrawn Elliott's letter after learning that the Vice-Chancellor would recommend the suspension of any student who criticised the government's prosecution of the war.[25] The University of Sydney Labour Club presented a tougher protest, noting that if the Council of the University of Adelaide considered that the discussion of social change and civil liberties impeded the war effort, they were out of touch with the wishes of the public. 'If it cared to listen, it would

23 ibid.

24 Letter in Elliott Johnston's private papers.

25 ibid.

find that the opinion more widely voiced than any other is that things must change, that they cannot go on after the war in the same way as they went before.' The letter was signed by the secretary of the Sydney University Labour Club, Eric Aarons.[26]

Being stood down was not the harsh punishment that it seemed. Elliott was suspended on the final day of the autumn term for the duration of the two-week May break. Friends rallied, including Max Harris, who went to the Vice-Chancellor and argued that he, too, should be stood down. His request was denied.[27]

The argument over the Radical Club subsided, but divisions on the campus were deepening. The war was intruding into everyday life and students disappeared from the refectory and lecture rooms to battlefields in Europe, North Africa and the Pacific. Political arguments were riven with emotion and personalities clashed. Aligned with, but not part of Elliott's Left-wing political thinkers, was the literary crowd of Angry Penguins, minus Sam Kerr and Paul Pfeiffer, who had left at the end of 1940 and who by mid-1941 were on active war service. Harris – Max Hashish as *On Dit* playfully called him – headed the Angry Penguins and his presence on campus was for some a provocation in itself.

In mid-1941, a spiralling exchange of angry views between students and some staff fuelled this tension and forced to the surface antagonism between the groups, which were broadly split into Right and Left. The stand-off culminated in a mass dunking in the River Torrens, an episode which has over the years been widely misrepresented and misunderstood. Often regarded as aimed at the literary renegades, particularly Harris, the catalyst for the dunking was Elliott, who, by an accident of timing on the day, avoided getting wet.

In the lead-up to the dunking, Elliott had got wind of a decision by the Sports Association to invite students to register to help the government in an emergency 'such as a strike that hindered the war effort', effectively putting their names down to act as strikebreakers. Elliott, who had finished his degree but was still president of the University Union, immediately wrote a letter to *On Dit* to

26 ibid.

27 Based on Elliott Johnston's recollections.

defend workers' rights. He opened courteously; if he was wrong in believing the Sports Association had resolved to form a squad of students willing to be strike-breakers, then he apologised. But if he was right, he opposed it on every ground. 'The Sports Association resolution means, if supported, that the students as a body declare their support for those who stand opposed to the workers, it declares that the student body lays the blame for strikes on the workers, that the students believe that the strikers have not been prompted by serious grievances which could not have been settled by other means.'[28]

The letter provoked a fierce battle over Elliott's radicalism and his right to speak for the union, and his loyalty as an Australian citizen was called into question. Following its publication on the cover of *On Dit,* he was gagged by the union committee. Elliott felt aggrieved and misunderstood. He was not advocating strikes during wartime, he was opposing the formation of a strike-breaking student group. Undercurrents of anger, suspicion and hostility surfaced and the union committee accused Elliott of acting against the war effort. Those who lined up against him included his old foe, Sir Douglas Mawson. 'We believe in democracy. How then could we support strikes? Mr Johnston's views were not such as should be held by a President', Sir Douglas thundered.

An angry third-year medical student, Nigel Abbott, whose father Charles Lempriere Abbott was soon to become the state's Attorney-General, considered Mr Johnston little better than a political agitator. His feelings were shared by others, including Cairns Villeneuve Smith, later a Queen's Counsel and Victorian County Court judge, who questioned Elliott's loyalty to his country. 'Neither the loud-mouthed bellowing of Mr Elliott Johnston, nor the shrill rantings of Mr Max Harris and his lickspittle associates will deter those whose loyalty is to Australia first and anything else second. The political rabble have held sway too long at this University and they must either declare themselves in full support for the war, or else take the consequences', Villeneuve-Smith wrote in *On Dit.* Their collective anger was not aimed solely at Elliott but also at those on the publishing committee of *On Dit*, like Harris, who took his side.

---

28 *On Dit*, July 1941, University of Adelaide, Adelaide.

This torrent of bad feeling overflowed dramatically at an outdoor lunchtime meeting on the university campus on 11 August. The meeting was called in an attempt to rescind the motion preventing Elliott from speaking publicly, but the numbers were against him. Elliott tried to calm the mood, but had to return to work in his law office before the meeting ended.

The anger that had been simmering on campus for weeks erupted into violence that was partly personal and partly ideological. In a potentially dangerous turn of events, students were thrown into the River Torrens. The fracas began when unidentified students threw three members of the *On Dit* publishing committee – editor Max Harris, business manager Bob Schulze and sub-editor Robert Hamilton – into the freezing river from the Footbridge behind the university. In the ensuing free-for-all, seven students from both factions were hurled into the water. No one was hurt, but the violence was serious enough to be written up in local and interstate media. Melbourne's *Truth* newspaper, always one to relish a drama, described the Torrens as so filled with bodies as to resemble the sacred River Ganges.[29]

Although Harris was in the thick of it, the dunking did not in fact represent a cultural condemnation of the Angry Penguins; rather, it was an expression of student anger towards the radical *On Dit* set, who had supported Elliott, their political ally. Harris was in the Torrens because he backed Elliott against the strike-breakers, as had the two other members of the *On Dit* publishing committee. It was a hostile act, planned in advance, and was supported by most of the two hundred students who were at the meeting. A report of the meeting in *On Dit* a few days earlier had warned that a 'surprise' was being organised by those who opposed restoring Elliott's right to speak, and students from the conservative engineering faculty had turned up armed with ropes, as if preparing to tie someone up. *Truth* suggested it might also have taken place with the tacit knowledge of the University Council. Elliott heard later from a senior figure in the law that it was remarked over drinks at the conservative Adelaide Club that he and his clique 'had it coming'.

---

29 'Students ducked: Heated rumpus over strike-breaking plan', *Truth* August 1941, Melbourne.

The dunking took much of the heat out of a campus divide, with Elliott left on the losing side. A spokesman for the students against Elliott and the *On Dit* group told the Adelaide afternoon newspaper *The News*: 'It will all die down now. We have achieved our object.' Max Harris declared himself too emotional to describe the events in the next issue of *On Dit*, but it was reported that the meeting censured Elliott and a vote of confidence in his presidency was lost.

Elliott was oblivious to the violence until later that day. He escaped the river but he had lost the confidence of the students and declared that he would stand down, without saying when. Two months later his hand was forced after his political affiliations became so extreme they were unacceptable to the student body and, on 17 October 1941, *On Dit* reported that Elliott had resigned. His departure was initially resisted, but only until the committee learnt that Elliott was secretary of the newly formed South Australian division of the Australian Soviet Friendship League.

Notwithstanding his increasingly extreme political beliefs, Elliott had a year earlier applied for a Rhodes Scholarship. He had the credentials for studying at Oxford, a glittering array of awards and prizes, an obvious gift for literature and debating and a vigorous engagement with political thought and ideas through student activism and *On Dit*. In his application he warmly supported liberal concepts of free speech and individual rights. He also wrote that capitalism had shown itself unable to deal with the manifest injustices of society as they existed, namely poverty, malnutrition, poor housing and the fear of unemployment. He believed capitalism could be replaced with socialist reforms that placed capital and political power in the hands of the state. 'It would be my desire after leaving Oxford to return to South Australia and join some existing group or help to found some new group advocating such a policy', he wrote. At the interview for the Rhodes Scholarship, the panel asked for his opinion of the Soviet Union, his reputation having preceded him. He answered frankly, saying he thought their economy was very good and that, although they were not yet democratic, he believed they would become so. On his way in to meet the Rhodes interviewing panel at Government House, the door was opened by a friendly young man in military uniform who was an old scholar of St Peter's College. 'Old blue, no doubt?' he asked Elliott. 'No,' replied Elliott, 'as a matter of fact an Old Red'. (PAC's maroon colours only partially explained the reference.)

CHAPTER 3

Comrade Johnston

In 1936, at the end of his first year of law, Elliott had been employed as an articled clerk by the small city firm of Povey Waterhouse. Following the practice of the time, his father had borrowed one hundred pounds, which he placed in trust to be paid back to Elliott as wages over the next four years. Ted Povey and David Waterhouse ran their general practice from a first-floor office at 24 Waymouth Street and Elliott was trusted with minor legal matters, house sales, infringements, wills, divorces and accident compensation claims. He occasionally interviewed clients, but he mostly searched land titles and prepared documents for property transfers or deceased estates.

Elliott spent four years learning the fundamentals of law at the University of Adelaide, attending lectures six times a week. He took three subjects a year, including International Law and Legal Ethics and, despite the distractions, he was a student of merit. A sketch in *On Dit,* unsigned but probably by Max Harris, described him in glowing terms:

> He is reported to have said once that if he spent a third of the time that he passed on talking on working, he could give a fair imitation of genius. This story may have grown, but it gives an idea to the uninitiated. But he was not missed out when Fate portioned out the brains of the world. He gained a bursary from Prince's in the Leaving Honours and without dying of overwork, has managed to keep his name out of the dust since then.[1]

In his final year of law, he won the David Murray Scholarship for outstanding results.

1 'E.F. Johnston', *On Dit*, June 1939.

He only rarely attended court. The young clerk, who had taken to wearing fashionable owl-rimmed glasses, never argued a case but would sometimes sit behind one of the partners, eager to do their bidding. Very occasionally, he was invited to check an actual point of law.

On a 1939 intervarsity debating trip to Brisbane with his friend Sam Kerr, he met Elizabeth Teesdale Smith, a handsome girl with wavy hair who was studying first-year law and who was representing the university hockey team. She was smart and athletic and she came from a well-off family with substantial holdings of land in the city and the Adelaide Hills. She was already fiercely Left-wing. It was family legend that when she was 15 years old, her father gave her George Bernard Shaw's *The Intelligent Woman's Guide to Socialism and Capitalism*. Shaw's vision of a peaceful transition to socialism permanently changed her thinking.

Back in Adelaide, Elliott set upon inviting Elizabeth for lunch. He wrote an invitation and left it in her university pigeon hole. A week later he retrieved it, untouched, and found Elizabeth in the reading room of the Barr Smith library, her head buried in books. He strolled past and dropped the invitation on her desk. They had fish and chips that day in the Italian section of the Botanic Garden near the University, and Elizabeth and Johnny, as she called him, began seeing each other, on campus and off. Elizabeth was not converted to Communism by Elliott. Her political beliefs were already her own and she became more intransigent than he was in later life. Her younger sister Cecil, who graduated with a master's degree in English from the University of Adelaide, was even more of a political firebrand and carried Communist placards through the streets of Adelaide opposing the war and government policy.

Elizabeth and Elliott were alike in their beliefs but not in manner. She was lively and quick tempered, he was calm and measured; she came to decisions quickly, while he pondered every option. Her profile on campus was lower but her views were just as extreme and she spoke up for them. She was the secretary of the Radical Club and had written to the University Union asking for the club to become affiliated and given debating rights. In 1940, she was on the editorial staff of *On Dit* with Elliott and wrote a letter arguing for the continuation of intervarsity sport during the war. She warned against succumbing to war hysteria, particularly as sport taught so much about life. 'If students are to lead the community, they won't do so by playing in their own state but by meeting students from other states and seeing their point of view', she wrote.[2] It was not a popular position at a time when anything that was less than fully respectful of the war effort was regarded with suspicion. Brian Magarey, later president of the South Australian Law Society, clashed with Elizabeth over this; he wanted intervarsity sport suspended on principle because he believed that competing on the sports field showed a lack of respect for the war. While the fighting was going on, students should not be enjoying themselves, he wrote.

In 1941, at different times, Elliott and Elizabeth joined the Communist Party of Australia. The Party was reaching the peak of its Australian popularity and had almost 15,000 members nationally, even though it was illegal and met in secret. Cecil Teesdale Smith also joined around this time, as did Elliott's younger sister, Marjorie, who was studying accounting. Elliott had begun to make the acquaintance of Communists in the late 1930s when selling the Victorian anti-war publication *World Peace,* which was produced by the Movement Against War and Fascism. Each month he collected about a dozen copies of *World Peace* from a squalid address in Divett Place, a laneway in the city. He would knock on the door and collect a bundle of papers from the widow of a man who had died from injuries suffered in the First World War. *World Peace* was not a Communist publication, but there were strong ties between the peace movement and the Party and much of its membership overlapped. When the paper's distribution was taken over by Joan Finger, who was the wartime secretary of the South Australian branch of the Communist Party, Elliott began collecting copies from the Party's office in Hindley Street in the heart of the city. He read flyers and pamphlets about what the Party was doing and began to attend meetings on topics he thought were important.

Free speech was high on the list. Elliott was angry about the suppression of the Radical Club and the censorship of his views. In May 1940, all Communist organisations were declared illegal by the

2 Elizabeth Teesdale Smith, 'Abolition of intervarsity', Special issue, *On Dit,* 1940.

United Australia Party government led by Prime Minister Robert Menzies. Communist offices were raided by police, the scripts of Communist 'New Theatre' plays were confiscated and in Melbourne the office of a Communist lawyer who later became Queen's Counsel, Ted Laurie, was raided twice; on the first occasion a stapler was seized, on the second, papers.[3] Menzies also used his wartime censorship powers to suppress Communist reports on the war. One issue of the national Communist paper, *Communist Review,* appeared with Old Testament text in the place of an article that had been cut at the last minute by the censors. Yet, in the company of Communists Elliott could talk openly about changing the world. He believed, as many did at the time, that Communism was morally superior in promising an economic system that was fairer for workers. He met some extraordinary people, not just rank-and-file Communists from factory branches at General Motors-Holden's at Woodville and the Islington rail yards, but intellectuals like James (Jim) Cavanagh, who was later to become Minister for Aboriginal Affairs in the Whitlam Government. He got to know the radical Scottish trade unionist, Tom Garland, who was secretary of the Council Against War and Fascism and also a Communist. From 1937 until 1946 Garland headed the South Australian Gas Workers Union and was the state's first Communist trade union secretary.[4] In 1941 Garland stood unsuccessfully for a South Australian House of Assembly seat, with both Elizabeth and Elliott campaigning for him.

Elliott and his employers at Povey Waterhouse shared little political common ground but he admired them deeply. The decent, old-fashioned lawyers were part of a proud liberal tradition that respectfully allowed people of differing opinions to co-exist. Instead of pushing the young Communist out of the door in 1940 when he graduated, they offered him a position with the right to private practice. He gratefully accepted. 'It was an absolutely amazing thing that Elliott was there', said lawyer Max Basheer, who joined Povey Waterhouse as an articled clerk after the war. 'People looked down

3 Peter Cook, *Red Barrister: A biography of Ted Laurie,* La Trobe University Press, Melbourne, 1994, pp. 52–4.

4 Martin Shanahan, 'Garland, Thomas (Tom) (1893–1952)', *Australian Dictionary of Biography*, volume 14, Melbourne University Press, 1996, pp. 249–51.

on Communists but there was no attempt by Elliott to disguise the fact he was a member of the Party and it was very well known.'

When Germany invaded Poland in September 1939 the war overshadowed all else. In 1940 Elliott enlisted and was called up for a medical examination. His partial blindness made him unfit for military service but he was willing to fight.[5] He opposed war in general but he was a greater enemy of Fascism and he had always been acutely aware of momentous political events. As a schoolboy, he had expressed precocious anger over Benito Mussolini's invasion of Abyssinia and at university he had demonstrated against the Fascism of Spain's General Franco and the march of Nazism. But the 1939 non-aggression pact between Hitler and Stalin had confused the Communist position at the start of the Second World War and briefly silenced Communist opposition to Hitler. Despite enlisting, there was suspicion on campus about his attitude to the war. On 22 June 1941 Germany broke the pact and turned its military might on the Soviet Union. There was no longer any confusion about which side Communism, or Elliott, was on. In Russia, Stalin mobilised ten million reservists against a savage German army that was heading towards Moscow. Almost overnight, the Communist Party in Australia backed the nation's war as a people's uprising against Nazism and Fascism[6] and set out a program for Communists in the armed forces to lead reform from within.[7]

Two months before Japan bombed its way into the war with a devastating attack on the United States of America at Pearl Harbor and shortly after Germany attacked Russia, Elliott was called up. He was photographed in military uniform at Unley on 10 October 1941, where he signed the oath of allegiance to King George VI. A week later he wrote an enthusiastic piece in *On Dit* about Australia's need to fight and he encouraged students to help with munitions during

---

5 AMF enlistment records, National Archives of Australia, Canberra.

6 Stuart Macintyre, *The Reds*, Allen and Unwin, Sydney, 1998, p. 412.

7 *Communist Party Program for the Soldiers,* Beaufort Press, Sydney, 1941–42 (quoted in Beverly Symons, 'All Out for the People's War: Red Diggers in the armed forces and the Communist Party of Australia's policies in the Second World War', BA [Hons] thesis submitted to the Department of History and Politics, University of Wollongong, 1993, p. 50).

the coming holidays. He felt a personal connection to the Russian people, whom he thought of as partners in the Communist dream.

Elliott was under government surveillance. From 1940 until the 1980s, paid agents and informers spied upon him. He was reported to a series of intelligence agencies, including the Special Branch of the South Australian Police, ASIO and Australian military intelligence. The role of the South Australian Special Branch was to spy on the German community during the war, but it also kept files on trade unionists, Communists and students. A report in May 1940 concluded that Elliott was not a subject of interest to the Communist Party. This was poor analysis. By then the Party was certainly of interest to Elliott, and he to it. In 1942, ASIO took over as the main spy agency, its purpose being to gather intelligence on potential security suspects after the long-running deciphering collaboration between the United States and the United Kingdom of coded messages sent from the Soviet Union, the Venona Project, revealed the existence of Soviet spies in Australia.

Until 2008, the existence of only three ASIO surveillance files on Elliott had been disclosed in the National Archives and very little information from these was cleared by ASIO for release. It was subsequently revealed that a further 20 files existed, not all of which have been made available. Some of ASIO's information was incorrect, including in January 1942 a file stating that Elliott had dodged military training by claiming to be 'busy'. Elliott was described as a prominent Communist who, in accordance with his political views, was likely to 'advance any excuse to gain exemption from military duties'.[8] The report misrepresented both Elliott's character and his commitment to his country and it was also inaccurate because he had enlisted more than a year earlier and was already in service. He had been called up on 15 December, a week after Pearl Harbor. Five days later a correction was made which noted that Elliott Johnston was serving at the 101st General Hospital at Woodside training camp in the Adelaide Hills.

He spent his first few months of the war at Woodside, close to home and around people he knew. He made friends with a young

---

8 ASIO, 'Elliott Frank Johnston. Military Intelligence report: Persons evading universal training', National Archives of Australia, Canberra, 1942.

actor, Ralph Peterson, who was the voice of Bottomley, the bad boy of Dr Percy Pym's fourth form in the quaint but much-loved radio series *Yes, What?* on Adelaide radio station 5AD. Peterson later wrote television scripts, gags for comedian Tony Hancock and a play about boxing, *The Square Ring,* which was performed in London's West End. He worked with Elliott in the hospital at Woodside until they heard of an artillery unit in Adelaide that was seeking recruits. They applied and were transferred to the 48th battery of the 13th Field Regiment based in the foothills above Unley, where Elliott learnt how to drive (never well), how to handle a gun, and how to undertake reconnaissance for artillery positions.

As the war closed in and the separations became longer and more real, Elliott and Elizabeth decided to marry. Elliott's ASIO file includes a handwritten note copied from *The Advertiser* in March 1942: 'Miss Elizabeth Teesdale Smith, daughter of Major and Mrs Paul Teesdale Smith of South Plympton has announced her engagement to Mr Elliott Johnston, son of Mr and Mrs William Johnston of Kingswood'. They set the date for 17 April 1942 and planned a simple service before the Registrar of Births, Deaths and Marriages in Flinders Street, Adelaide. On their wedding day, Elliott was on manoeuvres in the bush near Murray Bridge but arrived at the Registry Office just in time to marry Elizabeth in front of two witnesses, his father William and Elizabeth's father Paul. The mothers were at the Teesdale Smith home on Marion Road preparing for the reception. It was a bittersweet gathering. Elliott and Elizabeth spent four days on honeymoon at one of the Teesdale Smith homes at Mount Lofty.

His regiment was bivouacked at Warradale, an Adelaide suburb off Anzac Highway and close to Marion Road, but life seemed precarious. One day a soldier in Elliott's unit was killed in an accident and Elizabeth was warned that the victim might be Elliott. The message came through her father, a decorated Gallipoli veteran who in the Second World War served again as an officer. Major Teesdale Smith took a phone call to say a van had braked suddenly, causing heavy equipment to tip over and crush a soldier. Elizabeth rushed down to Keswick Barracks but it was another soldier who had died. By September 1942, Elliott's regiment was stationed at Balcombe in Victoria and later at an artillery officer training camp in New South

Wales. Elliott became a bombardier who manned a 25-pounder gun and in late 1942 he travelled up the eastern coast to Brisbane en route to New Guinea, where Australian soldiers had spent a cruel year fighting the Japanese in conditions that were amongst the harshest of the war.

The Pacific war was raging and it was the year of bitter fighting along the Kokoda Trail. In January 1942 the Japanese had taken Rabaul on nearby New Britain island and a bloody campaign for New Guinea had begun. For the first time, the Australian mainland was under threat. Young servicemen like Elliott's close friend, Sam Kerr, were thrown into a desperate battle, with old equipment that was in poor repair. Mid-way through the year, Japanese troops landed on the northern tip of the New Guinea peninsula and began a land invasion over the cloud-covered Owen Stanley Ranges towards Port Moresby. They pushed forward with a cunning and stealth that took the exhausted Australian soldiers by surprise. But the pace of the Japanese advance outstripped their supply lines and by October 1942, about 50 kilometres from Port Moresby, the Japanese were turned and forced into slow retreat. In January 1943 the last Japanese soldier had been killed or captured at Buna and the town was back in Allied hands. Two months later Elliott arrived and was stationed at Buna.

Australian war correspondent George Johnston spent a year in New Guinea filing harrowing news reports about the treacherous conditions there and the heroism of the Australian campaign, including the terrible risks taken by dashing pilots, like RAAF Flight Lieutenant 'Pedro' Pedrina.[9] Pedro was one of the coolest pilots under pressure that Johnston had seen, flying over the air base at Rabaul with two Japanese Zeros on his tail, photographing Japanese shipping concentrations anchored in the bay. In December 1942, Pedro died just south of Buna when a Lockheed Hudson he was piloting crashed into the jungle. On board with him was his navigator and 'pusher outer', the beautiful young poet Sam Kerr, whose job had been to push bully beef, biscuits and ammunition out of the plane to the troops on the front line below.

9 George Johnston, *New Guinea Diary,* Angus and Robertson, Sydney, 1944. Johnston later wrote the best-selling novel, *My Brother Jack*, and was a friend of Max Harris, who visited him at his home in the Greek islands.

Elliott was in Australia on his way to the same northern battlefield when he heard of Sam's death. He reached New Guinea in March 1943 and would have been there earlier, but his unit missed a connection with a convoy, although their guns went on ahead. In Port Moresby the newly promoted Corporal Elliott Johnston was reunited with his weapons, but only temporarily. They were too cumbersome for New Guinea's difficult terrain, a logistical problem not anticipated by army command. With the artillery unit out of a job, its members applied for new positions. Elliott transferred to Army Education Services (AES), which became a refuge for Communists in the Australian Imperial Forces. In his memoir, the Australian Communist Ian Turner wrote that with so many other Communists transferring to the AES, the army brass claimed it was riddled with 'Commos': 'The suspicions of the brass were pretty right. Army education was an obvious point of Communist concentration and comrades all round the army tried to transfer in.'[10]

Enlisted Communists did not leave their politics at home. Meetings on army premises were banned and Elliott said he never used his position to preach Communism. However, the Party was active and had specific propaganda aims. 'First and foremost, politically, we tried to express the position of the Party as being in support of the war as an anti-Fascist war, and that involved explaining to people the origins of the war, of the struggle that had taken place in the 1930s against the rise of Fascism and the role of the Soviet Union in relation to the rise of Fascism', explained Elliott at a 1980 public forum examining the role of Communists in the Second World War.[11] Solidarity among working-class recruits was fostered and a rearguard action was fought against the propaganda that blamed food and ammunition shortages on industrial stoppages. 'Everything was magnified out of proportion, and, with an eye to the future, they [anti-Communist forces] tried to drive a split between the workers who were in the army and the other forces, and the workers who were at home. A very, very important part of our work was to combat that', Elliott said. Local committees were

10 Ian Turner, 'My Long March', *Overland*, 1974, pp. 23–40.

11 'Talk by Elliott Johnston: Communists and work in the Army in World War II', in *Communists and the Labour Movement,* State Library of Victoria, Melbourne, 1980.

set up by the AES ostensibly for welfare or entertainment but really to direct these debates. 'Once you could get a committee established in the unit, it could take up almost anything at all the lads wanted taken up. So this was a foremost thing, to try to build these committees', he said.[12]

Elliott's official job in the AES was to brief the men on the war effort and the progress of talks between Britain, the United States and the Soviet Union, and to explain their rights during and after the war. He posed careful questions and distributed material designed to make the men think about the society to which they wanted to return. At secret Communist meetings in the jungle he planned with others how to get these discussions going:

> The Army Education organisation provided magnificent opportunities for – in a non-sectarian [way], not trying to push any particular point of view – raising and discussing questions about the war, what led up to the war, the conduct of the war, the political questions that arose in the war, the questions of post-war reconstruction, the shape of the sort of country that we were fighting for, and all that sort of thing ... And of course the very conditions under which we lived made discussion a very simple thing. Fellows had very little to do when they weren't actually working, there was very little in the way of entertainment, no tellies and what not.[13]

In the final stages of the war, Elliott campaigned on particular issues that Communists believed important, like supporting the 1944 referendum to increase the wartime powers of the Prime Minister, John Curtin. Although there was no way of checking, the Party estimated it had around four thousand members in the armed forces, one-fifth of its 1945 membership. Secret networks were formed and passwords flushed out fellow thinkers. One tactic was to stroll around the camp whistling 'The Internationale' or 'The Red Flag'.

In reality the impact of Communists like Elliott was limited to low-level industrial agitation over the quality of army food or the safety of weaponry and camp conditions, such as the pilfering of

12 ibid.

13 ibid.

goods by bored troops. When cargo landed at Buna, the superior quality of the food coming in for officers caused disquiet. The rank and file soldiers would open a case and drink a can or two of orange juice, then throw the rest overboard to conceal the theft. When it began to get out of hand, the Communists met on the banks of a local river and decided to impose some rules. Soldiers could pilfer cargo, but only if a case was already broached. If they did steal food, they were not to throw the rest overboard and nothing was to be touched that was meant for the 9th Division. 'And so we went back to the waterfront and we talked to the blokes and put this to them and it worked very well, they responded to that and they understood it', said Elliott.[14]

Elliott was not in physical danger, despite Japanese bombers still flying overhead (although on one occasion he was bitten on the hand by a snake in his tent). Very occasionally he saw a familiar face from Adelaide, like Andrew Wells, later a Supreme Court judge, who unexpectedly sat down next to him at an open-air film night at Milne Bay. He also visited the grave of Sam Kerr at Bomana War Cemetery, along the coast from Port Moresby. He was to lose other friends in the war, including another of the Adelaide University poets, Paul Pfeiffer, who died in a Sunderland flying boat crash over England in 1945, and Duncan Menzies, who studied law and wrote for *Obiter Dicta* and had enlisted with the Black Watch. Lieutenant Menzies, who had fought at Tobruk, was decorated for jungle fighting in Burma and died an exceptionally heroic death as a Chindit jungle fighter. He joined the highly skilled jungle force that took its name from the Burmese word for lion; he was shot and bayoneted by the Japanese and left dying, tied to a tree.[15] All of the deaths were tragic, but Elliott had been closest to Sam Kerr and his loss was the hardest to bear. On his return to Adelaide after the war, he visited Sam's mother in North Adelaide to pay his respects.

It was April 1944 before Elliott saw Elizabeth again. After a short leave, he reported for duty at Keswick Barracks, where he was promoted to lieutenant and given additional leave to buy army

14 ibid.

15 For a moving account of the service and death of Lieutenant Duncan Menzies, see 'A Highland Chindit' by Alasdair Sutherland in *WWII People's War*, <www.bbc.co.uk/ww2peopleswar>w

gear. For the next few months he was based at an army hospital in northern New South Wales where he was the only education officer and where he enjoyed access to a large library and a gramophone. At the end of the year he returned to New Guinea, disembarking at Aitape on the north coast, which had been recaptured from the Japanese. Elliott was a member of the 6th Division, whose job was to defend the base and advance towards Wewak to destroy the remnants of the Japanese army. Part of his battalion was still fighting in the jungle and they moved slowly along the coast, securing it as they went. He would stay in New Guinea for the rest of the war.

Elliott took it upon himself to run a literacy class for soldiers who needed help to write letters home. The classes, held in a tent, included a young Aboriginal boy from Western Australia who managed a short note home to his mother. She wrote back saying how delighted she was to read her son's words. A few days later he was killed in the Australian advance towards Wewak. The nearest Elliott came to being injured was under friendly fire during an American bombing raid. He was at Wom, just west of Wewak, and had been called in to supervise the unloading of cargo. The work went on into early afternoon and the drone of US fighter planes as they passed overhead barely caused anyone to look up. But this time the bombers flew over the ocean and returned in a low swoop, strafing the beach and coast and injuring some of the men. The crew of the US planes believed they were bombing what was left of the Japanese troops at Wewak. 'It couldn't help but create some bad feeling', said Elliott, who was given the job of escorting around the camp an American officer who flew in the following morning to apologise. By the time of the Japanese surrender, in August 1945, Elliott and his brigade had reached Wewak. Three months later he was on a boat back to Sydney, demobbed and home in time for Christmas.

The intelligence service watched Elliott throughout the war, reading his letters to Elizabeth and monitoring his opinions and whereabouts. As passionate expressions of love to a young wife, they were a disappointment. 'I note that A.B. Thompson was acting secretary of Trades and Labor Council, I presume Nicholls having been relieved for campaign purposes. Will he get the job permanently now that Nicholls has gone? ... How goes the building trades amalgamation?' He floated the idea of putting his name forward as an Australian Labor Party candidate, the only time he ever considered Labor Party membership, and he explained why to Elizabeth. 'There are very few members of the Labor Party in South Australia now in the army who are either likely to stand for pre-selection, or to be elected if they stand. There may be one or two, but not many. But it is very necessary that Labor should gain the support of the soldiers and obviously this is most likely to happen if there are soldiers amongst the candidates.' His letters carried a jingoist tone that reflected the spirit of the time. 'Things, they go from better to best', he wrote home in 1943. 'In Europe they put all their eggs in the Nazi basket and here's the bloody Bolsheviks overrunning the Nazi boys and all the peoples of Europe showing every sign of delivering a very swift kick in the pants royales to the crowned heads of everywhere.' In one letter to Elizabeth he enclosed a postal note for two pounds, asking her to give the money to the 'club treasurer'.[16] It was his annual Communist Party levy. The Security Service noted that he wrote to George Shaw, the student leader from Melbourne University, the Adelaide feminist and educator, Jean Muir, who was later Jean Blackburn, and Fin Crisp.

Elliott came back more convinced of his Communism than ever, his youthful idealism having evolved into a political theory built around peace and socialism. The Australian attitude towards Communists had softened at the time Russia became an ally in the fight against Nazism and when the Curtin Labor Government took office in October 1941, the ban on the Communist Party lapsed. After the war, however, a new wave of Right-wing opposition and anti-Red propaganda was building and surveillance became more alarmist. 'Elliott and Mrs Johnston now openly attend Australian Communist Party meetings. Although these people have for years been subject to very strong suspicion regarding their connection with the Party, it is only over the last few weeks that they have openly associated with members of the Australian Communist Party', the Commonwealth Investigation Service recorded in October 1948, seven years after the Johnstons had joined. Elliott

16 Security Service report, Sgt E.F. Johnston, 11 Aust. Div. Extracts, National Archives of Australia, Canberra, 1943.

and Elizabeth attended Party meetings and used their home for Party work. They studied the origins of Communism and read the writings of Karl Marx. They were part of the peace movement and the Australian Soviet Friendship Society and managed an unofficial lending library of Soviet literature. In 1949 Elliott was the contact person for a visit to Adelaide by Wilfred Burchett, the journalist and Communist who filed the first reports to the outside world of the devastation of Hiroshima. Elliott was also a regular at Speakers' Corner in the Adelaide Botanic Garden and sold *Tribune* outside factories as the workers streamed out from their shifts. He admitted to converting Dr David Caust to Communism when they were stationed together at Woodside. He also tried to recruit teacher and historian Barbara Wall, the lifelong friend of Elizabeth's older sister Mary, with whom he was often paired at tennis. During a match Elliott invited Barbara to afternoon tea. 'He asked me to join the Communist Party', Wall said. 'I found it very difficult to say "no, I wouldn't join", but I did. I think I was probably a bit scared of what I would be letting myself in for because I didn't really know what it meant. I preferred the freedom of changing my mind.' He never asked again.

On his return from the war, Elliott went back to Povey Waterhouse. Times had changed and the firm's new articled clerk, Max Basheer, was entrusted with looking after Elliott when he succumbed to recurring bouts of malaria picked up in New Guinea six months before the war ended. Basheer would notice Elliott turn pale and fall into the familiar trembling fever and palsy. He would cover Elliott with a greatcoat and organise a taxi to take him home to Elizabeth or to the Repatriation Hospital. Over time, the symptoms receded. Basheer thought Elliott was a man of heightened intelligence and ability and he was so keen to learn from Elliott that on one occasion he carried his bags into court. He watched in awe as Elliott defended a man accused of having falsely obtained free legal aid.

Despite the kindness of his employers, Elliott knew he could not stay. Anxious that they should never be embarrassed by his political beliefs, he decided to strike out on his own. Rooms and office equipment were hard to come by, but he found a second-hand typewriter and a tiny office in a building on the eastern side of King William

Street, three doors north of Pirie Street. He hired a typist, hung out a brass plate that read 'Elliott Johnston. Barrister & Solicitor' and ignored the thuds on the ceiling coming from Huey Whitman's wrestling studio directly above.

'Depression' Communism was going out of fashion and domestic hostility towards Soviet Russia was intensifying. In 1946 Britain's wartime leader Winston Churchill made his landmark speech in which he declared that an Iron Curtain had descended across the continent of Europe. He warned that a new Soviet sphere in central and eastern Europe was being created and that Warsaw, Berlin, Prague, Vienna, Budapest, Belgrade, Bucharest and Sofia were under Moscow's totalitarian control.

In March 1949 the Chifley Labor Government had established the Australian Security Intelligence Organisation. The following year, after a landslide victory, Prime Minister Robert Menzies attempted to crush Communism altogether with the Communist Party Dissolution Bill, which was designed to outlaw the Party and dispose of its assets. Communists, Party sympathisers and those close to them were barred from Commonwealth employment and trade union office. In this climate and with ASIO silently watching, in 1950 Elliott went for the first time behind the Iron Curtain, to the Polish city of Warsaw and following that, into Russia. This was not a trip he had planned but he had stepped in at late notice to take the place of a South Australian woman delegate to the second international Peace Congress which was planned for Sheffield in England in November. The first Peace Congress, held a year earlier in Paris, had been an international event attended by the head of the World Peace Council, Nobel Prize-winning atomic physicist and Communist Frederic Joliot-Curie, the Spanish artist and Communist Pablo Picasso, and the great black American singer and civil rights activist Paul Robeson. The congress issued a manifesto of peace to all people of goodwill and declared the atom bomb was not to be used as a defensive weapon. In June 1950 a smaller peace conference was held in Melbourne and was attended by Britain's 'Red Dean', Hewlett Johnson, the Dean of Canterbury. He was a Communist supporter whom Elliott met through the Party and was photographed with Elliott's son Ian, then aged one, sitting on his knee.

The international peace movement was widely feared to be a Communist front. A few months before Elliott left for Sheffield, the Minister for Immigration, Harold Holt, had denounced the Melbourne Congress, claiming that it was a vehicle for the spread of Soviet propaganda. Elliott did not conceal his intention to go to Sheffield, and in October 1950 he addressed a peace and freedom rally in Adelaide with Wilfred Burchett and made a statement published in *Tribune*. 'I am proud to attend the World Peace Congress which will be a tremendous blow for peace at a time when desperate attempts are being made by the warmongers to embroil the world in an atomic war.'[17] Les Golding from the South Australian Ironworkers Union was also to attend. 'Atom bombs should be outlawed and so too should those who sponsor their use', Golding told *Tribune* in an article published next to a picture of a young Hiroshima girl who still needed daily treatment for radiation burns.[18] Elliott's sister, Marjorie, also went but travelled separately and arrived in Sheffield from Europe.

The Peace Council raised almost 250 pounds towards the South Australian delegates' participation in the congress and Elliott left for England on the liner *Strathmore* with other national delegates, including Ian Turner, Les Golding, and Tom Robertson from the New South Wales Building Workers Industrial Union. Also on board was one of Russia's greatest Australian supporters, the feminist Lady Jessie Street, wife of the New South Wales Chief Justice Sir Kenneth Street. Elliott filed a report to *Tribune* from India after the *Strathmore* berthed at Bombay. Police had broken up a mass peace rally in Assam, shooting dead nine people and arresting five hundred more. Elliott was upset and wrote about it. 'One of the immediate tasks of the peace movement is the organisation of the legal defence of these victims of repression', he wrote. He and the others met the All India Committee, which had organised a petition supporting the Stockholm appeal to ban nuclear weapons issued by the World Peace Council in March 1950. Most of the Indian signatures were thumbprints, reflecting the almost total illiteracy of the lower castes. Elliott saw the struggle for peace bound to the welfare

17 *Tribune,* 6 October 1950.

18 ibid., 29 September 1950.

of a nation where 600,000 people each night slept on the streets of Bombay. Individual misery needed an international solution. 'Only by ending the Cold War, by the elimination of the scandalous expenditure on armaments can the economic life of India be organised to provide a decent standard of living for the people', he wrote.[19]

In London, on his way to Sheffield, Elliott had the unexpected pleasure of meeting two wartime friends. At Buna he had worked with two education officers, one a concert pianist and the other a singer. In London, Elliott offered to deliver some luggage for a Victorian delegate and set off for Earls Court, forgetting to take the address. As he walked along the street inspecting the occupants' names on the front of each building, he noticed the name of the pianist from Buna. Over coffee in his flat, Elliott leafed through an arts magazine and saw an advertisement for an opera featuring the singer they both knew. They contacted him and were left tickets for the opera at the door and joined him later for supper.

The Sheffield Congress did not proceed as planned. In a series of dramatic developments the venue was switched to Warsaw when the Sheffield City Council objected to a Communist conference being held in its city.[20] The logistical demand of hosting 2500 delegates who needed speeches translated into six different languages was an additional obstacle. The British Labour Government of Clem Attlee saw the conference as somewhere between a Communist stunt and a military attack. It intervened by blocking the visas of delegates from Communist countries and preventing them from entering the country.[21] At the last minute more than half were turned away, some of them at Dover, including, to Elliott's absolute disgust, Frederic Joliot-Curie, the eminent scientist and Nobel Prize winner who had helped the Allied war effort as the German forces advanced into France by smuggling documents relating to his work on the atom bomb into Britain.

Before leaving Sheffield Elliott attended a protest meeting in a large hall addressed by Picasso whose sketch of a white dove had been adopted as the global symbol of world peace by the Paris Peace

19 ibid., 10 November 1950.

20 Phillip Deery, 'The Dove Flies East: Whitehall, Warsaw and the 1950 World Peace Congress', *Australian Journal of Politics and History*, vol. 48, 2002, p. 453.

21 ibid., pp. 461–2.

Congress. Elliott sat a mere few feet away from Picasso as he spoke about life and death, peace and war. He watched Picasso draw and sign a sketch of the bird, which was auctioned for 21 pounds to help fund the move to Warsaw.[22] As an old man, Elliott still has the blue-green badge from the Peace Congress bearing Picasso's dove. Shuttle flights ferried the delegates from England to Prague and then by train further behind the Iron Curtain to Warsaw. The movements of all the Australians, who included James (Jim) Healy, the federal secretary of the Waterside Workers Federation, were closely monitored at home. The Minister for Immigration, Harold Holt, declared that passports issued from 1 September 1950, which included Elliott's, were invalid for travel to Communist countries and would remain so for 12 months. Anyone flouting this by going to Warsaw would have his or her passport cancelled.

The 'peace train' to Warsaw was cheered and applauded as it passed through the countryside. In Warsaw, 2065 delegates from 81 countries were housed in two-bedroom, centrally heated workers' huts in the old Muranow ghetto destroyed by Germany during the war. The huts were built on the wreckage of old buildings and sat above street level in a sea of rubble. Elliott slept on the floor on makeshift bedding. The Congress was an uplifting event attended by scientists, politicians, priests and ordinary people. Elliott came away inspired. One of the great friends of the international peace movement was Paul Robeson, the son of a North Carolina slave. He was not a Communist but had visited the Soviet Union and spoken out against McCarthyism, the reckless campaign conducted against Communists and their sympathisers. As a consequence, his passport had been revoked, but he had sent a special recording of a song about peace to Warsaw. It was a short song and was sung in six languages, including English, and as their language was sung, the delegates from that country rose. Everyone was profoundly moved. The Chilean poet Pablo Neruda was there, as was the Soviet composer, Dmitri Shostakovich who addressed the Congress, and a Polish scientist who had worked with Einstein, Professor Leopold Infeld.

Elliott wrote an article for *Tribune*, in which he pinned his hopes for Poland's restoration on Communism. 'Warsaw would

---

22 ibid., p. 454.

make you weep. I have not driven a mile without seeing a building destroyed … but they are rebuilding the city with terrific speed and energy. The building goes on into the night. Everywhere you look there are great building works in progress.'[23] At the close of the congress he sent a telegram to Adelaide: 'Warsaw Congress great success. Breadth, strength and determination of peace-lovers to defeat warmongers. Peace will win.' Then came the diplomatic bombshell: 'Am in Moscow as guest for fortnight'. Having ignored the warnings about travel to Warsaw, Elliott was to round off his trip behind the Iron Curtain with a visit to the Soviet Union. It was a last-minute invitation and he joined a small group led by Jim Healy, who had visited Russia before, and Lady Street.

Russia and its Communist revolution were idolised in the 1950s by the Communist Party of Australia, with the Bolshevik overthrow of the Russian aristocracy accorded almost mythical status. 'It bore the hopes of mankind as the model of socialism which all countries could copy', wrote former South Australian Party secretary Jim Moss.[24] Chinese Communism was only two years old, but Russian Communism, born in Revolution and guided by leaders like Vladimir Lenin and Joseph Stalin, was living proof that workers could triumph. Elliott had a bust of Lenin on a desk in his house and he and Elizabeth read magazines from Russia touting Communism's achievements. The South Australian edition of *Tribune* ran far-fetched accounts of Soviet progress that only the most gullible could believe, including a close-up of a head of Soviet wheat bulging with grain.[25] Soviet lives were filled with industry and purpose, and *Tribune* in September 1949 announced that Russia had pioneered painless childbirth.

These fabulous achievements fuelled an eagerness in Australian Communists to see their ideology in action. Author Frank Hardy went to the Soviet Union and announced that a new civilisation had been born. 'It is based on peace and the brotherhood of man. It has released the energies and ambitions of millions in the greatest program of peaceful construction mankind has ever seen. I have

23 Elliott Johnston, 'Poles yearn for peace, *Tribune,* 1950.

24 Jim Moss, *Representatives of Discontent: History of the Communist Party in South Australia 1921–81*, Wakefield Press, 1983, p. 54.

25 'Soviet wheat', *Tribune*, 1949.

seen the beginning of Communism', he told *Tribune*.[26]

On his arrival in Moscow, Elliott was presented with flowers by two rather dour Russian women and taken to a hotel. Dinner that night ended with a warm exchange of toasts between the Russians and the Australians, who were represented by Lady Street. The next day they toured Moscow and saw Red Square, St Basil's and the Kremlin. Elliott was taken to a shop and fitted out with a thick brown coat, galoshes and a Cossack cap to protect him from the winter snow. For a few days he was a tourist abroad, inspecting the Lenin Library in Moscow, which held half a million foreign-language books, and in St Petersburg (then Leningrad) marvelling at the magnificent Hermitage Art Gallery and Museum. He watched the Red Army Ensemble sing and dance at the Tchaikovsky Concert Hall, visited a Moscow school filled with bright, well-fed girls and admired the cleanliness of the Moscow underground, where each of the 35 stations followed a different architectural style. He visited the Stalin Auto Works Palace of Culture in Moscow, which was a large factory maintained by workers, and the Kirov Palace in St Petersburg. In Tbilisi, the capital of the Georgian Republic (and where Elliott purchased an English copy of *King Lear*), the delegation spent a day at a collective farm, the symbolic pinnacle of agrarian reform. Elliott saw only industry and contentment as he watched people building fences, ploughing fields, building homes and tending produce for market. Back in Moscow he watched a Russian film, *The Fall of Berlin*, went to the Russian opera and the Bolshoi Ballet. 'These have been wonderful experiences', he wrote. Like Frank Hardy, he believed he was witnessing the flowering of Communism and he wrote an overblown account of this in an unpublished paper on the Stalinist 'miracle':

> Often in the Soviet Union I thought of the day when all over the world the nations will co-operate in this way, when cultural barriers are down, when man feels himself both a citizen of France and of the world. Through all time men have seen this vision. John Donne saw it when he wrote, 'Send not thy servant to find for whom the bell tolls, it tolls for thee'; Shelley saw it and Yeats; Christ said, 'All ye are brothers'; Stalin saw it when he wrote his thesis on the national question. Men

26 Frank Hardy, 'They live in plenty and want peace', *Tribune*, 1952.

> have fought for it and died for it, in battle, in gaols and of hunger. At times it seemed a miracle; today it is near for all men; for over one sixth of the world the vision is simple fact.[27]

But he was not completely blind to Russia's history and Elliott sought to allay his private concerns about human rights in Russia. At this time he knew nothing of the preceding decade when Stalin had been at his murderous peak and had purged millions through torture, exile or murder. But word had got out about the 1937 Moscow 'show trials', in which Communists were accused and executed for crimes against the Revolution. It was enough to provoke disquiet. Elliott's two essentials for good Communism were the existence of a sound legal system and the practice of free speech. So far, he could find excuses for shortfalls in Russia's difficult history.

> They were a very, very backward country as far as economics were concerned, and as far as economic rights were concerned. And within 20 years [of the 1917 October Revolution] they were involved in a new war in which they showed enormous courage, enormous ability and made a tremendous contribution to the defeat of Nazism. In this situation they had to rebuild their economy so I didn't think it was surprising there should be some negatives.

However, he wanted reassurance that the country was at least moving in the right direction.

He asked to meet some Moscow lawyers to find out how the law operated. He wanted proof that people were not being incarcerated on a whim and that they did not lose their livelihood without legal recourse. Elliott sat down with a translator and six Russian lawyers and he took great heart from what he heard. A legal system was in place and anyone charged with an offence was brought before the courts and tried. As additional proof, Elliott was invited to sit in on three court sessions in Moscow, where he watched magistrates deal with breaches of the law. All his concerns were allayed. Only much later did Elliott realise that he was not only duped but had played into their hands by asking the wrong fundamental questions. A legal system *was* in place and it could be shown to

27 Elliott Johnston, 'The cultural life of the Soviet people', private papers.

be working as it should. But Elliott never thought to look beyond this for Stalin's terror squads, who came in the early hours of the morning to murder or banish hapless Soviets to the Siberian gulags. He took assurances at face value and came away besotted with Russia's success. He realised his mistake much later. 'My request was defective in that it was really concerned with what was done by and through the legal system and not what could be done by Stalin. It was a great disappointment what happened', he said.

After 17 days in the Soviet Union, the delegation returned to London via Warsaw and Prague. Elliott's money was long spent and his Adelaide practice had earned nothing for two months. He was anxious to rejoin Elizabeth, but Australia House in London was pressuring the shipping companies not to return the peace delegates to Australia. The British ambassador in Warsaw, acting on Australia's behalf, had already confiscated Elliott's passport. He did not regret what he had done, even though the passport was not returned until the mid-1950s.[28] The others were just as defiant. 'We heard that our passports had been cancelled', Les Golding wrote from Warsaw. 'Well anything that happens, all we can say is that it was well worth it.'[29]

Marjorie Johnston had gone straight home from Europe by boat. Landing at Fremantle without a passport, she was allowed ashore only after union intervention. Safely back in Adelaide, she fronted a statewide campaign to turn 'peace-lovers' into 'peace-fighters'. She gave a series of talks and declared that the Attlee Government's attempt to sabotage Sheffield had failed. '[It] angered the world's people and strengthened the peace movement', she said.

For two weeks Elliott made daily visits to the London offices of the major shipping companies. He finally secured a berth on the *Orcades* and sailed home in diplomatic disgrace, first-class, in the company of an Adelaide City Councillor and later Lord Mayor, Mr James Irwin, an Adelaide solicitor, Mr C.J. Philcox, who was

---

28 In 1952 Elliott was forced to decline an invitation to a conference of the International Association of Lawyers in Berlin. L'Association Internationale des Juristes Democrates passed a motion protesting the Australian Government's ban on Elliott joining them and notified him of this from Paris.

29 Les Golding, 'Letter from Warsaw', *Tribune*, 1950.

returning from a cruise to Colombo, and a scientist, Dr Rupert Best, who had been studying the chemistry of viruses overseas. By complete coincidence, also on the ship were Vladimir Petrov and his wife Evdokia. They were in a party of five Russians who docked in Sydney on 5 February 1951 on their way to Canberra, where Petrov was to take up a diplomatic post. It was three years before Petrov, Third Secretary at the Russian Embassy, defected to the West in a Cold War spy drama that saw Evdokia intercepted in Darwin by Northern Territory police after KGB officers attempted to escort her out of the country. After his defection, Petrov informed Australian intelligence agencies that he had met and spoken with Elliott on the boat. He identified him from a photograph and told ASIO that Elliott had come up and had talked to him while they were alone on the deck. According to Petrov's account, recorded in Elliott's ASIO file, Elliott told him he should bear in mind that the Soviet Government had many well wishers and supporters among the Australian people.[30] ASIO reported that Elliott was one of only three people to speak to the Russians.

Elliott's adventure was not quite over. An influenza epidemic on the *Orcades* delayed South Australian passengers in quarantine on Torrens Island (Outer Harbor) for two days and Elliott became their spokesman. He set up a working committee to liaise between the passengers and medical authorities and his leadership was praised by fellow passengers as they disembarked. Elliott told reporters from *The News* who met him on the docks that the Warsaw conference had been a magnificent success and the peace movement would be a powerful protection against another war.

Elliott returned to his practice, but in the middle of 1951 he was asked by the Party to become a full-time organiser. A young Communist with promise was to be groomed for greatness. Without any fuss and after talking it over with Elizabeth, Elliott left the law to dedicate his working life to the Communist Party of Australia.

30 ASIO, 'Elliott Johnston', National Archives of Australia, Canberra, 13 May 1960.

CHAPTER 4

The Party and the law

On a street corner in the Spencer Gulf industrial town of Whyalla on a summer evening in 1952, Elliott prepared to address a town meeting. He was the organiser for the northern sector of South Australia, an outback landscape that took in Port Augusta, Port Pirie, Whyalla, Leigh Creek, Quorn and Iron Knob. He was hoping that the working-class people who lived around the Whyalla shipyards might be interested in what he had to say.

The Communist Party had lost half its Australian membership in four years and he did not hold out hopes of recruiting new members.[1] However, he wanted to tell people what Communism stood for and how the Communists, and not the Australian Labor Party, were the true friend of the working man and woman.

There was not a soul in sight. The chairman of the local branch stopped on his way to night shift and introduced Elliott to the empty street. 'Bugger this', thought Elliott, and began speaking about the Communist vision for a fairer Australia, wage rises, pegged prices, and the need to nationalise the Broken Hill Proprietary mining company so the profits could be used to construct a new steelworks at Whyalla. Two or three people passed by, but no one stopped as Elliott delivered his speech from beginning to end. The following afternoon he went to the pub and ordered a beer. 'Jesus, that was a bloody great speech you made last night', said the barman. Thinking he was being mocked, Elliott snapped back. 'Don't give me that bullshit, there was no one there', he said. 'No, no,' the barman said,

---

1 Tom Sheridan, *Division of Labour: Industrial relations in the Chifley years 1945–49*, Oxford University Press, Melbourne, 1989, p. 255.

'I live in the house just opposite the corner there and it was such a hot night we had the windows open. My missus and I sat there and listened to every word.'

Elliott loved the country people and got to know many of them as he hitched rides between towns. He was a travelling organiser in a large outback area but the Party could not afford to give him a car. His motorbike had broken down before he left Adelaide and he used bush goodwill to get around. He would sit in the passenger seat and draw the drivers into friendly discussion. 'Did you see the piece in the paper today about the United States letting off a bomb in the Marshall Islands?' he would ask. 'So what do you think about that?' The miles would disappear as they chatted about international affairs or the new threat of inflating prices that would erode the workers' gains. Just as he was fascinated by country people, so were they by this earnest young lawyer from the city who had thrown it all in to preach the Red gospel. At a railway town west of Iron Knob, he was midway through a speech when a man moved to the front of the crowd and held aloft an icy beer. He was not a Communist, he said, but it was a hot day and Elliott looked like a man who needed a drink.

He came across a few Communists but not many. A secret branch had been set up in Port Pirie after the Depression, where the town's tailor was the chief recruiter.[2] Other towns had small cells and occasionally someone made himself known. In Port Augusta, where Elliott ran one-man meetings at the gates outside the railway workshops, a stranger came up and offered to chair these street talks. People in Iron Knob were more receptive than others elsewhere because of a bitter strike in 1949 by the miners, who had been forced to walk 'the Hill' in their own time, the arduous half-hour climb that took them in and out of the quarry.[3] The railway town of Quorn was another important stop. Later a farming hamlet, Quorn was an important railway junction linking Adelaide to Alice Springs. The Communists in Quorn were not just railway workers but included farmers disillusioned with Labor in Canberra.

Relations between Communism and the Australian Labor

---

2 Reece Edwards, *The Knobbies*, BHP Steel, Whyalla, 1995, p. 10.

3 ibid., p. 39.

Party had become strained. They had shared platforms during the war, but in the 1950s the hardline Communist Party leader, Lance Sharkey, turned on the Chifley Government and relations soured.[4] Elliott, who had briefly considered enrolling as a Labor candidate, stood in 1953 as the Communist candidate for the state seat of Stuart in the South Australian House of Assembly. Stuart covered the northern agricultural districts of Orroroo and Burra, as well as Port Augusta and the rocket range town of Woomera, some five hundred kilometres north of Adelaide along the Stuart Highway. It was strongly Labor and he was no threat to the sitting member, Lindsay Riches, who was the mayor of Port Augusta. Communism was a sensitive issue in Woomera, home to an elite group of Australian and British scientists working in a climate of Cold War rivalry to beat the Soviets in 'the space race' and produce weapons for use if the Cold War intensified. The Communists opposed Woomera's very existence and the South Australian executive, of which Elliott was a member, had published a pamphlet, 'Rocket Range Threatens Australia'.[5] This was a few months before Britain tested its first atomic weapon at the Monte Bello Islands off the West Australian coast and a year before the Emu field trials began in the Woomera test area.

During his campaign for Stuart, Elliott avoided the Woomera Village, which was closed to outsiders. He did not even request entry, having been told by the Party not to make trouble. He ran on a curious mix of the global and the local, from the Korean War, to criticism of a plan by South Australian Liberal Premier, Tom Playford, to borrow money for a sewerage system in Whyalla. 'The scheme, when and if carried out, will be financed by loans, raised from the big monopolies. These monopolies will make the loan money out of the labour and effort of the working class, and then lend it back to them, via the government', Elliott said three days from the election.[6] He campaigned for the nationalisation of monopolies like General Motors-Holden's and BHP, he wanted a meat-processing factory for Port Augusta, a rail link between Iron

4 Alastair Davidson, *The Communist Party of Australia: A short history*, Hoover Institution Press, Stanford, CA, 1967, p. 16.

5 ibid., p. 107.

6 Elliott Johnston, 'Sewerage plan exposed', *Tribune*, 1953.

Knob and Kimba, and lower rentals for public housing. He also sought to legalise betting in country towns. 'All these need a fundamental change from the politics of the Menzies and Playford Governments, which place war expenditure and profit before the needs of the people', he argued.[7]

Other Communists ran in the 1953 state election, like Elliott's friend, Dr Alan Finger, who stood against Tom Playford in the seat of Gumeracha. However, none caused as much fuss as Elliott. On the night of the election, 7 March 1953, when the polls were counted in the booths at Woomera, Elliott had won 110 out of 558 votes, about 20 per cent of the overall vote and almost 25 per cent of the votes in the Woomera Village. At the height of the Cold War, the leading scientific group at the most sensitive facility in Australia appeared to be harbouring a Communist cell. All hell broke loose and Elliott took phone calls from the BBC in London and from the United States and New Zealand. *The News* in Adelaide ran a story headlined 'Woomera Red Vote Came From "Top Brass"'.

Elliott knew it meant trouble. He thought he might be raided and Elizabeth took papers across the road to her parents' house for safe keeping. The Menzies Government ordered an inquiry and Woomera was placed under virtual siege as Commonwealth security agents crawled over the facility as they attempted to ascertain who in a secret ballot had voted Communist. *Tribune* reported that the Menzies Government was considering seizing the ballot papers, a shocking assault on the secret polling system and a sign of how serious a threat to national security a cell of Communists in Woomera was perceived to be. Elliott was outraged. 'Menzies and his security services know very well the Communist Party has no interest in the secrets of the rocket range', he told *Tribune*. 'Our concern is to fight for a stable and lasting peace, in which rocket ranges, atom bombs, and germ warfare will have no part.'[8]

While Elliott did not fully understand the reason for the vote, he thought at first it might have been a protest against the excessive restrictions at Woomera. The South Australian Party secretary, E.G. Robertson, said he knew of no Communists at Woomera and

7 Elliott Johnston, 'Stuart candidate is staunch peace fighter', *Tribune*, 1953.

8 'Warmongers threaten democracy', *Tribune*, 1953.

distanced the Party from the result. In the end, however, the extraordinary Communist vote was believed to have been the result of a misleading 'how to vote' pamphlet circulated by the Labor Party, which triggered what Riches called 'an unintelligent Liberal vote'. Woomera was an exotic pocket of scientific personnel, transplanted from the outside world into the middle of a sprawling working-class electorate. Stuart was so firmly held by Labor that the Liberals did not even bother to field a candidate. Under the heading, 'Raise the Standard with Riches', Labor issued the ambiguous warning, 'Any other vote is a vote against Labor'. This terse message was meant to warn Labor people against voting Communist. But conservative voters confronted with the acronym CPA on the ballot paper probably thought they were voting *against* Labor and *for* the Country Party of Australia (even though it did not exist in South Australia at the time). It was almost certainly a mix-up. Nevertheless, the Menzies Government maintained security officers at the Woomera facility, reviewed security safeguards and tightened the screening methods used to recruit rocket range personnel.[9]

Elliott worked in the north for another year, spending a fortnight away, then a few days at home. He and Elizabeth submitted willingly to this disruption to their lives, as did others in the Party. When the marriage of Alan and Joan Finger dissolved, the head of the morals section, J.B. Miles, came to Adelaide to sort out their divorce. Miles declared that Finger did well as a candidate and should stay in South Australia. His wife was told to leave her children and work at party headquarters in Sydney.[10] Such intrusions into the private lives of senior Party members were accepted in the interests of the broader movement.

Early in 1954 Elliott was reassigned to Adelaide to work in the western suburbs, where the General Motors-Holden's plant and other factories around Woodville and the wharf at Port Adelaide were located. He and Elizabeth were living in their first home, bought in 1951, at 513 Marion Road, South Plympton, on the corner of Jervois Street almost directly opposite the rambling Teesdale

9 'Woomera reds vote came from top brass', *News*, 1953.

10 Jim Moss and Lucy Finger, Biography of Alan Finger, unpublished, Adelaide, 2006, p. 19.

Smith house on Marion Road. Elizabeth served as secretary of the western branch and in 1954 Elliott was elected to the state committee of the South Australian branch of the Party, where he remained for 30 years. They were Party stalwarts and Elliott held national and state committee positions, including branch chairman and member of the National Appeals Committee. When the western branch combined with the Adelaide branch to become the Adelaide electorate branch, Elliott became secretary. He was a key member of the South Australian Party and ASIO believed he was possibly the paramount person on matters of Party security and the management of its precarious legality. An ASIO 'minute' on Elliott reported that at a Party meeting in 1954, the state secretary, Edward Robertson, said that 'in the event of the Party having to go underground Elliott Johnston would have to do certain things which even I as the state secretary would not be able to ask the reason why'.[11]

In 1955, the China trip intervened. He left Australia on 21 August 1955, returning on 18 February 1957, eight days before his thirty-ninth birthday. The party to which he returned was weaker and more divided. Although Elliott had given six years to the full-time service of the Communist cause, the ground beneath him was beginning to shift. Elliott and Elizabeth, along with all thoughtful Communists, had been forced to accommodate what Stalin had done.[12] No one realised it at the time but the Communist Party of Australia was irreparably damaged.

Elliott returned from Beijing in thrall to China, although the message he brought home was for Australian Communists to find their own way. They should not blindly follow China but determine what suited the Party in Australia best. At the time, *Tribune's* coverage of China increased, an outward sign of the growing importance of Maoists and China's influence on the Australian Party. Instead of articles extolling the superiority of Soviet wheat, *Tribune* began reporting on the incredible feats of Chinese acrobats, the magnificence of the Peking opera and China's economic miracle. Elliott himself continued to praise Chinese Communism in Party

11 ASIO, 'Elliott Frank Johnston', National Archives of Australia, Canberra, 1954.

12 Stuart Macintyre, *The Reds*, Allen and Unwin, Sydney, 1998, pp. 363–77.

forums. In May 1959, ASIO reported a talk he gave about the apparent benevolence of Chinese Communism. According to ASIO, Elliott said it was 'stupid lies' to suggest that land reform in China had been imposed against the will of the people. He quoted Chinese leaders who said, 'we fought for freedom and therefore we will not take land. It must be left to all people to give of their own free will'.

It was well into the 1960s before Elliott understood that Chinese Communism was just as flawed in its practice as that of Russia. When the cruelty and stupidity of Chairman Mao's Cultural Revolution became apparent, he and Elizabeth were shocked. 'Whereas the economic policy expressed at the [China] congress in 1956 was a policy of the orderly direction of socialism, it turned into throwing all your kettles and saucepans on to the fire so you could make steel. It was just a bloody ridiculous policy', Elliott said. Even at the peak of his commitment to the Chinese experience, Elliott's sense of the absurd had never quite been tamed. During Beijing's '10 flies a day' program, he staged a private rebellion by going for long periods without catching a fly, then embarking on a manic hunt, felling 70 in an hour.

Elliott was evolving into an Australian Communist. Stalinism had not destroyed his dream, which was for an Australian version of Communism, introduced at the ballot box. In reality, this objective of an independent Australian Party was still a long way off. The CPA had been formed, unashamedly, as a sub-branch of the Moscow-based international Communist movement, the Comintern, and in the 1940s its leadership was mired in the old ways, preferring the Soviet way of doing business.[13] In the early 1950s independent policies appeared on their platform, but Soviet Communism, wrote Alastair Davidson, drove the Party until well into the 1960s: 'In the final analysis its policies emanated from Moscow'.[14]

But even token independence was enough for Elliott to make peace with his conscience. It gave him safe passage through the Party's shuddering international realignments and protected him from the tensions that surrounded personalities like Lance Sharkey, J.B. Miles, Bob Dixon, Ted Hill and other prominent Australian

13 ibid., pp. 360–3.

14 Davidson, p. 99.

Communists. He hitched his vision to the 1948 draft policy document, *The Way Forward*, which had stated: 'The Communist Party does not propose for Australia a society the same in every detail as the working class have established in Russia. The Australian people will find a way to organise a new society in keeping with our own national characteristics.'[15] It was set down that banks and major industries would be nationalised and monopolies smashed, but there would be no wholesale seizure of the means of production. Large-scale industry and transport would be in public hands and significant land holdings would be broken up, but small investors were protected and would be at least partially compensated. Communist Australia would be a planned economy, liberated from market-driven peaks and troughs. Housing, education and medical care would be free.[16] In August 1951, the Sixteenth Congress passed a motion that gave concrete shape to this separate vision. For Elliott, this was the beginning of the Australian Communist movement.

In 1957, a few months after Elliott returned from China, Lance Sharkey paid him a visit. He told him he could now best serve the Party by returning to work as a lawyer, leaving the state secretary Jim Moss as the only paid South Australian employee. Elliott took Sharkey to task over the mistakes he believed the Party had made. Sharkey in particular was an old-school Soviet supporter who ruled with a heavy hand and liked visiting Moscow, where his drinking binges were legendary.[17] Elliott told him he was wrong to have suppressed internal discussion of Stalin's atrocities and Khrushchev's speech, and he never forgave him the damage done by preventing discussion of where Russia went wrong. Sharkey talked bullshit, Elliott said, and he was glad to be returning to the law.

A strong legal system was part of Elliott's Australian Communist vision and there was no conflict for him in practising law. Instead, he began a personal mission to use his legal skills for the Australian Communist cause. He would support the Party in the usual way but he would also, as a lawyer, place himself at

---

15 Lance Sharkey, *Australian Communists and Soviet Russia*, CPA, Sydney, 1947.

16 Communist Party of Australia, 'Programme of the Communist Party of Australia: Australia's path to socialism', Sixteenth Congress, 1951, p. 29.

17 Macintyre, p. 361.

the professional service of working men and women. Like the Communist Dr Alan Finger, who used his medical practice to fight disease and improve the health of the poor, Elliott would try to raise the lot of the Australian worker. This was to become his new pathway in life.

The legal community that Elliott was rejoining had already shown great tolerance towards him and his odd beliefs. In 1941, his fifth year with Povey Waterhouse, he and Elizabeth campaigned for the Communist Tom Garland in the federal seat of Boothby, a blue-ribbon seat in the eastern suburbs of Adelaide, which was contested and won by the Adelaide University lecturer and historian, Archibald Grenfell Price. On polling day Elliott was handing out Communist how-to-vote cards outside a booth when Sir Harry Alderman, a senior barrister soon to be appointed Queen's Counsel, came in to vote. Knowing Elliott worked for Povey Waterhouse, whose offices were in the same building, Sir Harry stopped out the front for a lengthy chat. He then graciously accepted the Communist how-to-vote card and went in to the booth. 'He was a bloody good bloke', said Elliott who was grateful for the public gesture.

Elliott had graduated in December 1940 with an exemplary degree and at Povey Waterhouse he had tentatively begun court work. His first memorable court case was in defence of a young woman charged with fraud who was assigned to him through the Poor Persons' Legal Assistance Scheme. She had taken a job selling women's underwear door to door but, after a few days, had deposited the remains of the clothes at the Adelaide Railway Station, taken the money and disappeared. She was ordered to appear in court. She assured Elliott she had never meant to steal the money but had needed it to tide her over. Elliott entered a plea on her behalf of 'not guilty' and she was listed to appear in the Police Court before James Muirhead SM.

It was the dying days of the Depression and members of the public liked to sit in the old Police Court in Victoria Square, which was heated and had a large public gallery. From the bench, Muirhead gave the novice lawyer suggestions on how to phrase his questions differently. He found the accused guilty. The police prosecutor made submissions on sentencing and Elliott responded with some fervour about the woman's personal difficulties and lack of money. As he paused for breath, Muirhead tried to steer him. 'Mr Johnston, I think that perhaps the *Offenders' Probation Act* might be relevant here', he said. Elliott replied, 'I'm sorry, Mr Muirhead, I don't know that Act'. The audience in the public gallery, who heard it referred to daily, roared with laughter that a man professing to be a lawyer could know so little. Muirhead adjourned the court and his secretary handed Elliott a copy of the legislation. Elliott read with interest that if the circumstances warranted it, a magistrate could release a guilty person on a bond of good behaviour. He thanked Mr Muirhead and applied for the woman to be released on a bond. He left court with the convicted fraudster who was free to go. Thinking he had done rather well, he turned to bid her goodbye. 'Well, you nearly fucked that up', she said and walked off.

Shortly before the war, Elliott had gained his first significant client, the South Australian branch of the Federated Clerks Union. Its secretary, Harry Krantz, had been thrown into the job at the age of 21 when the previous secretary was knocked over and killed on Dequetteville Terrace by an army dispatch rider. Krantz had inherited a prickly legal problem that threatened the union's future. His predecessor had applied for the first industrial award for clerks in South Australia but after a challenge from the employers, the Supreme Court ruled that clerks were not an industry. This industrial disenfranchisement hung unresolved and meant the union could not apply for an award.

Krantz was told that David Waterhouse, a principal of Elliott's firm, could help. Waterhouse, one-armed after an accident, called in Elliott and introduced him. It was the beginning of a significant professional association and a real friendship. 'It was a joy to work with him from day one is all I can say', said Krantz, who died in March 2006. '[Elliott] still played football for the Princes' Old Collegians and he would come in bashed because of his bad sight.' They sat together in the library at Povey Waterhouse and worked out how to apply for an award. The number of clerks was growing but they worked under vastly different conditions. They met the clerks and began talks with the employers' legal representative. Some ambit claims, like equal pay for women, were struck out by the employers, but a log of claims was drawn up.

The case had been due to start at end of 1941 when the war intervened. Japan had attacked Pearl Harbor, Harry Krantz enlisted and Elliott was called up. David Waterhouse took over but, instead of fighting the case in the Industrial Court, he pursued a simple consent award which was made on 17 April 1942. It covered only 36 employers but was expanded by common rule to include most others. After the war, still with Povey Waterhouse, Elliott revived the fight to improve the Clerks Award. His ties to the Clerks Union, and the labour movement, had been strengthened in wartime by Elizabeth who had stepped into Harry Krantz's role. In 1941 Elizabeth, aged 21, was a third-year law student working part-time for her father's law firm of Harrison Teesdale Smith in Eagle Chambers. She deferred her studies and applied to replace Krantz as union secretary. She was one of the first Communist union secretaries in South Australia and ran its wartime affairs with enormous care and diligence, much to the delight of Krantz who thought Elizabeth 'a terrific girl'.

Upon his return from the war, Krantz wanted to move quickly to give his clerks an award with a career structure that recognised the huge variation in their work. In 1948 he appointed Elliott, a young lawyer just back from the forces. 'The employers had [Sir Dudley Bruce] Ross QC, who, a few months after the award, was made a judge of the Supreme Court and his junior was Frank Piper, who was also made a judge of the Supreme Court. Elliott stood up and carried the case', Krantz said.

There were about 25,000 clerks in South Australia and under the consent award they were all paid the same. The award being sought differentiated between a young clerk who recorded simple data, a skilled stenographer or typist, and an experienced manager who handled wages and accounts. The union submitted an extensive log of claims to the Industrial Court of South Australia, not all of which succeeded. On the subject of annual leave, Elliott argued before President Edward Morgan that clerks should receive three weeks paid leave, which was a week more than the norm. Summoning all his ingenuity, Elliott argued that clerical work required accuracy and concentration at a superior level and additional holidays were needed to preserve a clerk's health. 'The relevant fact was not, in my opinion, proved', President Morgan said.[18] Morgan also dismissed

---

18 *Clerks Case* (1948) 22 SAIR 46 at 88.

Elliott's claim that workers be paid no later than Thursday each week, and that radiators, electric fans and linoleum or carpet be provided as a matter of regulation. But on the substantive matter of a sliding scale that recognised different grades of clerical work, the case was a watershed. Elliott argued that clerks became more efficient and valuable over time and this should be recognised in a graded pay scale. 'The conception put by Mr Johnston is, I think, a new one in industrial jurisprudence', said President Morgan.[19] Overriding objections from the employers, he introduced a three-tiered scale into workplaces with more than five clerks, and fixed a ratio of one senior clerk to three. Senior clerks would be paid considerably more and all three grades won a margin over the minimum.

The case cemented the friendship between Elliott and Harry Krantz and sent a message to the South Australian labour movement that the young Communist, Elliott Johnston, was their man in court. Elliott argued many other cases before the Industrial Court but none that meant more to him than the case for the Clerks Union.

In 1949, having left Povey Waterhouse, Elliott and Krantz teamed up again to bring about a variation to the Clerks Award that had the effect of abolishing wartime wage-pegging. The federal government had prolonged these regulations to protect the economic stability of the post-war Australian workplace, but Elliott argued that the time for change had come. The South Australian decision drew national attention to the continuation of wage-pegging and around the nation the regulations were progressively lifted. Elliott and Elizabeth's Communism was not a problem for Krantz, who waged a constant campaign to stave off a takeover of the Clerks Union by the Right-wing Catholic 'groupers'. 'I don't think it worried me any more than I think it worried Churchill that Stalin was a Communist. Stalin killed a million bloody Huns in one day and I think Churchill would have had the Archbishop say special prayers for him. Elliott never once in the union raised his politics although it was never hidden either', Krantz said.

Elliott's cases immediately after the war reflected the times. Under the National Security Landlord and Tenancy Regulations, vacant houses were let when a soldier went to war. Their recovery

---

19 ibid., at 66.

proved to be a fraught area, with courts having to decide post-war occupancy on the basis of greatest need. Elliott acted for a railway worker from Broken Hill who was struggling to maintain possession of a building from which he ran a business. He lost and appealed, lost again and appealed to the High Court, where he was again defeated; this was Elliott's first High Court appearance. Elliott also acted for an ex-serviceman attempting to retrieve a house in the southern suburb of Colonel Light Gardens, an area developed for ex-servicemen after the First World War. His client was the son of a deceased veteran who had let the house and now the son wanted it back. Not fully understanding the peculiar set-up, Elliott served the tenant with a notice to quit and went to court against the formidable John Bray. Bray argued his client's superior hardship but this was a secondary point. His primary argument was that an Act made by the British Parliament at least two hundred years earlier had stipulated a 'notice to quit' must come from the state. Elliott raced to the court library during the lunch break but the relevant volume was out being rebound. He found the reference at the University Law School library and returned after lunch to put up a solid defence based on whether the Act applied in South Australia, and what it meant if it did. The magistrate ignored this nonsense and ruled that Dr Bray's client should have the house because he needed it more. Elliott thought it a great occasion to have met John Bray.

Elliott's long history of appearances in the South Australian Supreme Court had begun in 1948 with an attempt in *Thomson v. The Commonwealth of Australia* to overturn the rule that prevented a worker from claiming injury compensation and then suing for damages for negligence.[20] Thomson's injury was not in dispute but when he found out he had a right to a negligence claim, he retained Elliott, who issued a writ. The Commonwealth claimed it was protected by legislation from the double recovery of damages but Elliott argued that damages for negligence should proceed with a reduction of the amount awarded in workers' compensation. The case was heard by South Australian Chief Justice, Sir Mellis Napier, who upheld the Commonwealth's argument but protected Elliott's client from costs.

20 *Thomson v. The Commonwealth of Australia* (1948) SASR 116.

Elliott built his law practice on small civil matters and industrial disputes, but he also defended criminals. He acted for one Dias, a Maori who sold suit fabric (to whom Elliott had paid two pounds for a length of fabric). Dias, who was under police surveillance for consorting with reputed thieves, dropped in to see him one day to advance the money to cover his next run-in with the law. The following morning he was arrested drunk and charged with stealing a watch. Elliott argued in court that his client was too intoxicated to have answered questions adequately and Dias was acquitted.

In 1948 he had represented the Communist Party of Australia for the first time, defending five people charged in an Adelaide street protest over the price of tobacco and other goods. The demonstrators had driven through Adelaide in the back of a lorry waving placards denouncing the increased prices and accusing big business of making excessive profits. Elliott had submitted that no fines should be imposed, as the offences were trivial, traffic had not been held up and no disturbance caused. But the court had fined the defendants on the grounds of provocation at a time of industrial unrest. A year later he had again acted for the Party, this time to defend three Communists fined under a council by-law for distributing leaflets at the Chrysler factory. Elliott submitted that the fines impeded the right to free speech and that pamphlets had been handed out at the factory gates for years. He argued the traffic had not been disrupted and that the defendants were not in the way. Again, the court had overruled his argument and imposed a fine.

In 1951 Elliott had closed the King William Street office to embark on a six-year Communist adventure that took him out of Australia to Mao's Red China and Russia, post-Stalin. Now, in 1957 he was returning to the law to pick up the threads of his nascent Left-wing practice.

The Party that had paid him a modest eleven pounds a week (he and Elizabeth managed with money from her investments) provided a part-time secretary to help him get started. In July 1957, he found new rooms in King William Street, above an underground restaurant just south of Hindley Street. Two small offices were vacant on the second floor and, for the second time, Elliott hung out the brass sign, 'Elliott Johnston. Barrister & Solicitor'.

CHAPTER 5

Seeking social justice

Elliott began to wage his own 'class war'. Some Communists condemned the courts, refusing to recognise their authority, but Elliott loved the law and thought that it could be harnessed to reclaim some of the rights of the poor and marginalised. He believed in justice and this became his most trenchant weapon. He was also blessed with a patient and methodical nature. If the courts failed to hand down a just solution, he would try on appeal to extract some of the fair-mindedness he believed the lawmakers had intended. A belief in the law's ability to deliver social justice was his legacy to the Left-wing lawyers who, over the next 15 years, joined an expanding legal firm, with Elliott Johnston at the centre. When confronted by something that he felt was wrong, he would go back to the legislation. Decades later, these barristers, judges and Queen's Counsel still retained some of Elliott's faith in the law's redemptive powers.

In the 1960s South Australia was coming to the end of a long period of conservative rule under the Liberal Country League Premier, Thomas Playford. International manufacturers like General Motors–Holden's and Chrysler had become established in South Australia and the state's economic base had moved from agriculture to manufacturing. But Playford ruled South Australia like a fiefdom and his social policies were restrictive. South Australia in the Swinging Sixties was a backwater, a place where hazardous backyard abortions were procured, murderers were still hanged, lotteries were banned and at six o'clock the hotel barmen called for last orders, forcing drinkers out of the pubs and onto the streets. Industrial safeguards were in their infancy and rights to safety and compensation for injury were basic. Injury compensation was paid according to a schedule in the *Workmen's Compensation Act, 1932*, but disputed claims became full-blown court cases. Employers challenged the validity of serious injuries and, in this atmosphere, ugly and misunderstood notions about malingering and 'Mediterranean back' were bandied about like accepted science.

Elliott placed himself solidly on the side of the working man, and workers' compensation claims, large and small, became the heart of his legal practice. He sided with ordinary people, not as a matter of principle, but because he empathised with them. He made real friends in the Greek and Italian communities and understood that migrant workers dominated injury compensation claims, not because they were whingers, but because they did the back-breaking menial work that other Australians declined to do.

Many of those who sought his help were men of little means and their ability to pay was never an issue. Elliott did not consider legal fees to be relevant to justice and he regularly overlooked sending a bill. His business built quickly and in 1959 Elizabeth went back to the University of Adelaide and completed her degree. She joined him part-time, doing solicitor's work and looking after the books. In 1960, three years after he had set up his office in King William Street, the firm moved to an office on the top floor of the Rechabite Chambers on the western side of Victoria Square, close to the law courts.

Elliott accepted cases that challenged both the accepted views on malingering and medical diagnosis and responsibility for injuries and the injured. His motivation was to strengthen incrementally workers' rights to compensation and protection. In 1964, in his first significant and successful High Court appearance, he won a case that lifted the cap on workers' compensation payments. In *Mermingis v. Perry Engineering Co. Ltd*, the Full Court of the Supreme Court of South Australia decided that the injured Mermingis could be awarded a lump sum payment of thirty thousand pounds, despite the disability payments that already had been made. The employer appealed to the High Court but Elliott successfully argued that the appeal should be dismissed.[1]

The care that Elliott applied to arguments over workers' com-

1 *Mermingis v. Perry Engineering Company Limited* (1964) 112 CLR 468.

pensation illustrated his eye for forensic detail. He put assumptions to the test and challenged the court's acceptance of what constituted a disabling injury. In 1967, he was briefed by another firm to appear on appeal before the Full Court of the Supreme Court for a man who had damaged his neck ligaments in a work-related car accident and who had successfully sued his employer. The employers appealed to the Full Court against the award of damages. The Full Court found for Elliott's client and upheld the payment, acknowledging for the first time that mental injuries could be as legitimately destructive of the ability to work as a physical injury. The man was said to be a person of neurotic disposition with an ill wife who needed his constant attention. Using picturesque language, Dr Bray, now the Chief Justice, found that the man's injury triggered a subconscious desire in him to stay home to care for his wife. 'The physical injury provided, if I may use a metaphor in an area where perhaps there may have been too many metaphors, a peg or a knob on which the tendrils of the neurotic temperament could seize to produce the present impressively luxurious parasitic plant of the incapacity.'[2] Behind his florid language Bray recognised a notion of compensable work injury based on a psychological neurosis.

In a similar case in 1970, Elliott represented a Greek migrant with four children who had come to Australia with his family to make a fresh start. Four years later, at age 43, the metal end of an air hose flew off a jackhammer, striking him in the temple. He became depressed and disturbed. Elliott appealed against the insufficient size of damages and won an extra 50 per cent compensation for his client.[3]

During the 1960s, Elliott cemented his reputation as a friend of the worker. He had been practising the law, at varying levels and with notable interruptions, since 1941, and he had built a loyal clientele among the unions and the migrant community. Left-wing unions took their industrial problems to Elliott and they became the mainstay of his practice, along with referrals from the Law Society's Poor Persons' Legal Assistance Scheme.

While loved by some, he was not universally popular and

2 *Attorney-General v. Gabell* (1968) SASR 44 at 50.

3 *Pipikos v. W. Brown and Sons Pty Ltd* (1970) SASR 508.

those who disliked him included Jack Elliott, the socialist cousin with whom he should have had much in common. They fell out, according to Jack Elliott, over Stalin. In his memoir, Jack Elliott wrote that in front of Elliott he accused Stalin of murdering Lenin's followers and betraying the true principles of socialism. He wrote that Elliott (who had no idea his cousin disliked him so much) had played the dutiful Communist and defended Stalin, and that political discussion between them had ceased. His dislike of Elliott was petty and niggling. 'I had been in the army with his elder brother Ross, who had a droll sense of humour. Elliott, whatever his other gifts, had none – or so it seemed to me', he wrote.[4]

Others admired him, even lawyers representing the other side. In the *Mermingis* case Elliott came up against the employer's representative Christopher Lee, a judge of the Industrial Court and later the District Court, whose firm acted for insurers of employers opposing injury compensation claims. They took each other at their word, which saved the courts time and money. On one occasion Lee referred an injured client to Elliott even though Lee was acting for the insurer against whom the claim would be made. Many years later, at the special sitting for the retirement of Judge Lee in 2006, the unusual goodwill that existed between them was praised by the President of the Law Society of South Australia, Dymphna Eszenyi. 'I heard a story that, before your elevation to the Industrial Court, the level of mutual respect and trust between yourself and Mr Elliott Johnston, then of the firm of Johnston & Johnston, was such that whole lists of workers' compensation matters could be settled, to the satisfaction of your respective clients, between you before trial.'

Elliott's appetite for criminal work was growing and in the 1960s he began doing occasional murder trials. He ran these complex cases with a filing system made up of bulging folders tied with pink legal tape and placed with elaborate care along cupboards and on the floor. One of the early trials showed the diligence with which Elliott, an accomplished debater, could develop a practical argument in court. In *R v. Grant* he defended a man charged with

4 Jack Elliott, *Memoirs of a Barrister*, Wakefield Press, Adelaide, 2000, p. 248.

murder at a house on one of Adelaide's southern beaches.[5] Grant's wife had left him and she was staying with friends. One Sunday morning he went to the South Adelaide Football Club and drank a large quantity of beer, got a rifle and drove to where his wife was staying. He walked down the passageway, saw his wife in a room towards the end of the passage and shot her. She was grazed but not seriously injured. Her friend came running to help and she, too, was shot, again not seriously. At the end of the passage the friend's husband heard the commotion and peered around the door. Grant fired into the hinged side of the door but the bullet, which should have missed, was deflected by the two-ply wood and killed the man. On his way out, Grant shot the family dog, drove off, tried to kill himself, but survived. He was convicted. Elliott appealed to the Full Court, where he lost and appealed to the High Court. Before the High Court, Elliott theatrically waved a piece of discarded wood he had retrieved from his own home to demonstrate before Chief Justice Garfield Barwick how the bullet had been deflected through the two-ply door. 'Mr Johnston, I don't know if you know this but that piece of wood is marked "Dangerous"', Sir Garfield barked. After hearing him out, the High Court dismissed the appeal.

Capital punishment was still law and remained so until the *Criminal Law Consolidation Act* was amended in 1976. Elliott was grateful his client did not hang. He heard later that Sir Garfield thought 'Johnston had done well' but losing a murder trial when a man's life was at stake did not sit well with Elliott. 'I was pretty inexperienced in murder trials, I don't think I had had one before, and my junior was very young. I wonder whether a more experienced counsel would have been able to procure a different result. Nobody will ever know.'[6]

Odd cases came his way. Elliott defended a public servant from the Adelaide Hills who was sued by a neighbour over injuries allegedly incurred during a fight. Believing the neighbour had shot his dog, the accused knocked on the neighbour's door and a fight broke out. The other man claimed serious injury and sued. The question

5 *R v. Grant* (1964) SASR 331.

6 The last person to hang in South Australia was Glen Sabre Vallance in November 1964.

of who had started the fight was in dispute, as were the injuries, which Elliott's client believed were pre-existing. It was local knowledge that the man had on an earlier occasion been on his tractor when it overturned on steep land and rolled down the hill to a creek. In an effort to prove this, the accused hired a plane and took aerial photographs but they revealed nothing. Over lunch in his Victoria Square office while the case was on, Elliott's phone rang. Distracted, he moved around the table with the photograph in his hand. As he did so, the sun shone on the print to reveal a clear white line running from the top of the hill to the creek. Elliott and his client drove to the property later that day, parked and walked to the point on the photograph, where a clear track was visible; this was the trail the tractor had made as it tumbled to the creek. The next day Elliott won permission from Chief Justice Bray, who was hearing the case, to inspect the property and went straight to the incriminating track. The Chief Justice found that Elliott's client had provoked the fight but, more importantly, that the injuries were not proved.

Elliott was a stickler for accuracy and procedure, most of the time. He told the story of representing a woman from a town north of Adelaide who was divorcing her husband. The husband had deserted her and the case for divorce was straightforward and compelling. Under South Australian law in the 1960s, divorce applicants were required to file a document known as a 'discretion statement', in which any circumstances of adultery during the marriage were declared. The document usually remained sealed. Apologising for even having to ask, Elliott inquired whether the woman, aged in her 50s, had engaged in sex outside the marriage. Well, she said, a few months ago she had gone to the pictures on Saturday night and on her way home she had walked through a park and a man had raped her. 'Well, don't worry about that', Elliott said. 'That's not adultery. Anything else?' The next Saturday night he did it again, she said. Elliott told her to forget about that too. 'So I possibly misled the court in failing to put this in the document', he would say.

No court result was ever certain and in 1967 he defended a Greek business agent involved in a messy property sale. The result distressed Elliott and showed what a blunt tool the law could sometimes be. The Giagtzis family ran a small business in the city, Star Candy, which sold milkshakes and snacks from a shop on the southern side of what is now Rundle Mall. The shop was sold through an agent, but the purchaser, who had changed his mind, challenged the contract on the technical ground that there was only one witness to the signature, not two as required by the legislation. Star Candy sued the agent for compensation over the negligent preparation of the contract and Elliott, who acted for the agent, limited the damage payout to $10 by arguing that the agreement had been witnessed by two or three people even though only one of them had signed. It was a sad case all round, with Star Candy losing the sale through no fault of its own, then chasing damages of $11,510 from the agent, winning on principle but losing their business. The nominal damages withstood appeal to the Full Court headed by Chief Justice Bray, who nevertheless sympathised with the family's ordeal. 'The appellant has been unfortunate in its encounters with the law', he said.[7]

Elliott began to appear regularly before the Full Court and John Bray. His courtroom manner – controlled and polite – and knowledge of the law were taking him to the top of his profession. Yet he made no concessions in pursuit of advancement and his passion for Communism had not waned. His days of hectoring at Speakers' Corner in the Botanic Garden were over, but he regularly stood for office in state and federal elections, where he campaigned and handed out how-to-vote cards at polling booths, knowing full well he could never win. He did not flaunt his political extremism around the courts, but in December 1961 he was embarrassingly 'unmasked' in a media exposé. In a front-page newspaper splash, a female ASIO spy who had infiltrated the Adelaide membership portrayed him as a powerful Communist figure. The middle-aged spy, Anne Neill, whose real name was Freda Bennett, told her story to Rupert Murdoch's *Sunday Mail.* It did nothing to improve the Party's image and it named a number of people who had preferred that their Communist membership remain a secret. She had spied on the party for a decade and Elliott featured prominently in the story that ran over two weekends. It traced the connections between the peace movement and the Party through Elliott, whose picture appeared above the caption: 'Elliott Johnston ... dedicated

7 *Star Candy Store Pty Ltd v. Chaniotis* (1968) SASR 1 at 30.

Communist and a strong force in the peace movements'. According to Neill, Elliott's nomination to attend the Sheffield Peace Congress a decade earlier was opposed by some members of the South Australian Peace Council, who believed that such a well-known Communist would advertise the connections between the two. She also 'revealed' that Elliott had made up the shortfall between the money raised for Warsaw and his travelling expenses from his own pocket and that his return was celebrated with a sherry party at an Adelaide hotel. She publicly sneered at his beliefs. 'That poor Picasso bird!' she wrote of the hand-drawn dove of peace. 'It looks as though it has just managed to escape after an extremely lively five minutes with a cat and has not had time to put its feathers in order.'[8]

Elliott had recruited Neill and now she singled him out. 'Solicitor, brilliant debater and Parliamentary candidate, he was always a dedicated Communist, always a driving force in the Party', she wrote. Her exposé was more an embarrassment than anything and she wrote honestly about Elliott's vision of Australian Communism as separate from the regimes that were in place elsewhere. There seemed to be no fixed party line, she wrote, and the violent revolutionary tone of Marx's Communist Manifesto of 1848 did not seem to apply today.

But it was a betrayal and it rocked the South Australian branch. Elliott had trusted her when others had been reluctant to; he had also introduced her to his friend and colleague, prominent educationist Jean Blackburn, who was named as a Communist, along with her husband Dick Blackburn, a soil expert working for the Commonwealth Scientific and Industrial Research Organisation (CSIRO). The week after the first *Sunday Mail* instalment, Elliott was due to present a sports prize at his son's school, Forbes Primary. Sally Smith, the wife of friend and fellow Communist Graham Smith, whom Neill also named, remembers there was doubt about whether Elliott should even show his face at Ian Johnston's end-of-year speech night. 'I remember thinking they didn't want Elliott on the scene and they were arguing about whether he should go on. In the end he went', Sally Smith said.

Elliott's legal practice survived and flourished because he had

8 Anne Neill, 'Woman's dual life', *Sunday Mail*, 1961.

never hidden his Communist affiliation. He was sincere, hard-working, intelligent, and usually ready for a chat, which helped undermine the prejudice against him. He was also disarmingly quirky, with old-fashioned manners and eccentricities. He told amusing stories against himself and let his hair grow long. In his student days he was known for his attachment to a pair of bottle-green socks, an admiration for [First World War poet] Richard Aldington and Rousseau, 'and a touch of balletomania'.[9] It was hard to find a Communist who was less intimidating. His practice grew and his list of clients included anyone who needed help. One case in the 1960s involved an English actor in Adelaide who was charged with homosexual conduct. The prosecution alleged he was seen emerging from a men's toilet on the southern section of the River Torrens wiping his mouth with a handkerchief. Justice Piper (who had acted for the employers in the Clerks Award) impressed Elliott in his summing up when he paused to bring out a handkerchief and put it to his face. 'Gentlemen,' Justice Piper said to the jury, 'I often have to blow my nose and I suppose you do too sometimes'. It was an indirect plea for fairness and the actor won his case.

In 1969 he took on a sensational murder case, one that challenged public prejudice over the crime of infanticide and demonstrated Elliott's innate compassion. In the moral climate of the time, a mother who killed her baby was the worst of all murderers. Postnatal depression was not widely recognised and a range of mental illnesses were categorised simply as 'having a nervous breakdown'. A woman who murdered her child was a prime candidate for hanging. 'Mother Accused of Baby Murder', reported Rupert Murdoch's daily tabloid *The News* on 2 January, after the woman drowned her baby son in the bath at a shack on the River Murray on New Year's Day. The newspaper noted that her husband was not there to support her in court.

The woman, aged 32, had given birth to four children, but experienced an earlier unrelated tragedy when the third child, her only daughter, had fallen into a neighbour's unfenced pool and drowned. On the day of the murder, she went to the Swan Reach police station seeking help. 'Quick, quick, I think my baby is dead', she had said.

---

9 Max Harris, *On Dit,* 1939.

At the shack the policeman found the four-month-old boy dead in his cot with frothy mucus around his mouth and traces of blood on his face. The woman then called to her older son, telling him it was now safe to come home. He emerged from the bushes with blood on his head. 'I think I hit him with a bottle', she told the policeman who noticed a broken Barossa Pearl bottle on the landing.

Her husband had left early to go fishing and she had intended to bath the baby when something snapped and she lost control. 'I took him to the sink and a voice told me to get him, so I held his head under the water until he was dead', she said. 'I put him back to bed, covered his head and went on with my housework.' When her son came in, she hit him with a bottle and chased him towards the river. 'I cannot tell you any more except that I loved my baby', she said.

It was a tragedy. Elliott's defence helped the court, presided over by the newly appointed Justice Roma Mitchell, to understand its human dimension. He did not contest the killing, but called medical evidence detailing the woman's treatment at Glenside (psychiatric) Hospital after her daughter had drowned. The episode with her baby came entirely out of the blue. 'God help me,' she said later, 'He's the only one who can help me. I hope they hang me. What can you do with a person like me?'

Lawyer Peter McCusker, who joined Elliott's firm in the 1970s and later became a judge of the Industrial Court of South Australia and a Deputy President of the Australian Industrial Relations Commission, met Elliott through this case. McCusker's Irish mother taught at a Catholic college and knew the accused woman through a student. She had visited her in prison and offered to be a character witness. McCusker sat in court and saw Elliott argue that the woman must have been insane, and provide evidence relating to her diminished criminal responsibility. Justice Mitchell found the woman not guilty of murder and ordered that she be detained for medical treatment.

Elliott had taken the brief and argued against the tide with an insight that few others seemed to have. Adelaide was changing and Elliott's engagement with the law was moving into broader issues of rights and social justice.

CHAPTER 6

Red silk

By 1969, aged 51, he was among the most senior barristers in Adelaide, with experience in industrial law, personal injury compensation and criminal law. His persistent challenges to higher courts put him before his peers, who noted his ability. He had attracted glowing praise from the High Court Chief Justice Barwick, a man not easily impressed. In 1967 he acted for a hospital employee who had trapped his arm between the inner and outer cylinders of an industrial washing machine, and claimed compensation. The case went on appeal from the Supreme Court of the Northern Territory to the High Court, where Chief Justice Barwick congratulated Elliott for his contribution. 'Mr Johnston has given us a very full and frank exposition of the evidence in the case and has, if I may say so, very competently placed before us the arguments in support of the appellant's appeal.' [1]

During the 1960s, 15 Queen's Counsel were appointed in Adelaide, including Elliott's friend from Adelaide University, Sam Jacobs, his cousin Jack Elliott, a future Premier Don Dunstan, prosecutor Eb Scarfe and the future Chief Justice Len King. Elliott was due for appointment, however it was highly unlikely that a Communist would be asked to take silk.[2] But in 1967, John Bray had become the Chief Justice.

The experience of another Communist lawyer in Victoria, Ted Laurie, indicated that no Australian Communist would become

---

1 *Lambos v. The Commonwealth of Australia* (1967) CLR 180.

2 The award is known informally as 'taking silk' in recognition of the QC's silk gown.

Queen's Counsel without renouncing Party membership. Laurie, who retired from the Victorian Bar in 1982 and died seven years later, decided in the early 1960s, while still in the Party, that he wanted to take silk. As Laurie explained to his biographer Peter Cook:

> People began saying to me, other barristers began saying to me, 'When are you taking silk? Are you going to apply for silk?' In 1957, 1958, 1959, I always said, 'No, I don't intend applying for silk', because of this idea that there was something wrong in taking official emoluments and that sort of thing ... Now, you can get away with it in criminal law because you are mainly acting for criminals, or people who haven't got any money anyway, and taking silk on the criminal side doesn't help you a great deal. But in general practice the step of taking silk is very important because the Bench treats you differently.[3]

In 1961 Laurie applied for appointment as Queen's Counsel to the Victorian Chief Justice, Sir Edmund Herring. Five lawyers were interviewed and a list was sent to the Attorney-General, who forwarded the names to state Cabinet for approval. Three were named but Laurie was not among them. 'There could be no concealing the reason for refusing silk to Laurie, and no attempt was made to do so. In a brief, formal interview Laurie had been informed that he had been refused because he was a Communist', wrote Cook.

He took the advice of two senior members of the Victorian Bar that the matter would be attended to.[4] But when the Victorian Bar Council next met, it upheld the ban on Laurie. 'He had been well and truly dumped. And the trumpeted independence of the Bar and its vaunted adherence to principle were shown up as a sham', Cook wrote. Laurie regretted not going public over his rejection. 'I was a mug', he said. Four years later, when Sir Henry Winneke QC, replaced Sir Edmund Herring as Chief Justice, Laurie resigned from the Party and reapplied for silk. The former Communist became Queen's Counsel in Victoria on 16 November 1965.

Elliott did not resign from the Party to take silk and he under-

---

3 Peter Cook, *Red Barrister: A biography of Ted Laurie QC,* La Trobe University Press, Melbourne, 1994, p. 129.

4 ibid., p. 136.

went a very public trial by fire. The South Australian convention for appointing Queen's Counsel required the Chief Justice to submit a list of recommended persons, which the government of the day passed to Executive Council for approval. Chief Justice Bray asked Elliott if his name could be put forward and he agreed. This was to cause a national uproar.

Dr John Jefferson Bray, whom Elliott had encountered regularly in the 1950s and 1960s, was a reformer and jurist, a classics scholar, an intellectual, a published poet, raconteur and wit. An altogether remarkable man, he had been appointed Chief Justice by the Labor Government of Frank Walsh (which lost office a year later to the Liberal and Country League reformer, Steele Hall). Bray recognised the sensitivity of putting Elliott's name forward but went ahead anyway. On 25 September 1969, he submitted three recommendations; Elliott Johnston, F.R. (Bob) Fisher, who was the senior member of the firm of Fisher, Jeffries and Co., and R.H. (Bob) Ward from Ward and Partners. In a letter to the Chief Secretary, Ren DeGaris, Bray wrote that he had consulted other judges about Elliott. 'I have always thought it desirable to ascertain the views of the learned judges, my colleagues. In the present case, the recommendations in question had the support of all the judges in office at the time I made them', he wrote.

The recommendations of the Chief Justice were normally approved as a matter of course.[5] But the Premier, Steele Hall, dramatically refused Bray's recommendation that Elliott be appointed. He would not have a Communist Queen's Counsel. In retaliation, Bray withdrew all of the names, including Elliott's. The issue at stake was political intervention in the affairs of the law and Elliott was about to become part of legal history.

Elliott's rejection was revealed to Parliament on 27 November 1969, with a story about the 'Communist barrister turned down for silk' featuring on the front of *The Advertiser* the following day.[6] Bray issued a statement saying that judges were not concerned with

---

5 Recommendations by the Chief Justice had been rejected before. For a detailed account of this, see W.B. Fisse and D.St.L. Kelly, 'Political influence in the appointment of Queen's Counsel', *Australian Law Journal*, vol. 44, 1970, p. 318.

6 'Row erupts over rejected QC', *Advertiser*, 28 November 1969.

politics, only with legal merit. His letter, which was released, said the attainment of silk was rightly regarded as a high distinction and an honour that recognised professional skill. 'I cannot take account of a barrister's non-professional beliefs or activities, at least so long as they do not infringe the law.'[7] Because he did not support any of the nominees to the exclusion of another, he had withdrawn all three names. Bob Fisher specialised in commercial law, but he knew Elliott and held him in very high regard. He was also a great admirer and friend of Bray's and his loyalty to him guided him through the crisis. There was a great deal of publicity, but Fisher was not embarrassed. He had done nothing wrong and supported the Chief Justice.

Hall said he would rather be voted out of office than change his mind. He told Bray that if Elliott's name came before him again, it would be refused. In parliament, he detailed his objections. Elliott was a member of the Communist Party of Australia and had stood for election; he was on the Party's National Appeals Committee and its state executive and he was secretary of the Adelaide branch. He was also a recent member of the Australia and Soviet Friendship Society. Hall denied harbouring any desire to harm Elliott personally, but claimed national security was at stake. 'One could never deny the long-standing truth of the RSL (Returned Services League) slogan that the price of freedom was eternal vigilance. The State Government in this matter has exerted vigilance', he said.

Sitting opposite him in the House of Assembly was the young opposition leader and soon to be Premier, Don Dunstan, a newly minted Queen's Counsel who had fought and lost an election to Hall a year earlier. Dunstan moved a vote of 'no confidence' in the Hall Government, but Hall prevailed with a casting vote from the Speaker, Tom Stott, to cries of 'McCarthyism' from Don Dunstan, and 'Gestapo tactics' from Dunstan's deputy Des Corcoran. 'In this country people's political convictions, no matter how unpopular or distasteful, are theirs', Dunstan said. 'Any person who comes within the law may hold political convictions no matter how distasteful to the majority of parties in this country. If we proceed on this basis, then we are making this country the very kind of country which we

7 'Govt. releases letter on QC', *News,* 28 November 1969.

condemn. We have no place in this community for thought control.' Dunstan told parliament that Elliott was eminently qualified for silk and had been close to being recommended twice before. 'More than one judge spoke to me about his high qualifications for the post', Dunstan said.

It became clear that Hall's fear was not so much Elliott Johnston QC, but the spectre of 'Justice Elliott Johnston' sitting on a South Australian Supreme Court Bench, or worse, presiding over matters of state at Government House. He accused Dunstan of wanting to appoint a Communist, who might later become a judge of the Supreme Court and eventually Lieutenant-Governor of South Australia. 'Oh come off it', Dunstan scoffed. Hall goaded Dunstan. This was the chain of events the appointment of Queen's Counsel made possible, he said. 'Why does he champion him only to that stage? Would the leader discriminate and stop short of appointing him as a Lieutenant-Governor?' Dunstan dissembled and did not answer. It was a revealing exchange. Hall was able to gloat that even Dunstan drew the line somewhere with a Communist.

That night Dunstan and Hall sparred on the ABC's *Today Tonight* in an exchange neither man forgot. As the cameras rolled, Hall claimed that Dunstan's own appointment as Queen's Counsel had been political, a charge that Dunstan emphatically denied. In a show of theatrics that Dunstan must have envied, Hall whipped from his pocket a letter written four years earlier in response to the former Chief Justice Sir Mellis Napier, who recommended the appointment of two lawyers as Queen's Counsel, Sam Jacobs and Neil Ligertwood. Frank Walsh had written back saying it was 'policy of the government' that the Attorney-General, if experienced, should be a leader of the Bar and a Queen's Counsel. 'In consequence I should be grateful if you would forward to the Chief Secretary the appropriate recommendation for the appointment of the Attorney-General as Queen's Counsel.' The Attorney-General at the time was Don Dunstan and on 8 November 1965, all three were appointed.

Hall had lured Dunstan into the trap. Earlier that day he had instructed a senior bureaucrat to search the Cabinet records relating to Dunstan's appointment, and within minutes had turned up the letter, signed by Frank Walsh. Hall said Dunstan was 'foaming at the mouth' when he (Hall) read out the incriminating letter on live TV. The interview was so dramatic it was broadcast all over Australia. In his memoir, *Felicia*, Dunstan claims that Hall tried to avoid discussion of Elliott's case 'by suggesting my appointment as Queen's Counsel was political'. He did not dispute the evidence that it was.

As far as Hall was concerned, the matter was closed. Elliott's name was withdrawn and the problem was off the government's books. A flurry of letters appeared in the local papers commenting on the issue. None said Elliott was unworthy, but most agreed they could not tolerate a Communist in high office. Elliott was surprised by some of the personal support he received. 'As a Catholic priest and member of the Jesuit order I can scarcely be thought to see eye to eye with the Communist Party', wrote Father Peter Kelly SJ, a friend of Elliott from Adelaide University, who was later the Australasian Provincial of the Jesuits. 'I believe the strongest possible protest should be made against the Government's rejection of Mr Johnston as a Queen's Counsel solely because of his active membership of that Party. Even if I did not know Mr Johnston, I would regard such a rejection as unjust. But I do know him. He is a man of the highest integrity and trust.'[8]

The academic world was divided, but *The Advertiser* editorialised against the Hall Government on the grounds that intervention set a dangerous precedent. 'To deny a Communist or the holder of any other minority opinion, preferment in an occupation divorced from politics – in this case, by its very nature, particularly divorced from politics – is not democracy', it said. After a few days the heat had subsided, but not before Britain's first Communist Queen's Counsel, Dr D.N. Pritt, who had taken silk 40 years earlier and was in his eighties, observed that South Australia must be 'a terribly reactionary place. Surely a man's ability and honesty are all that matters? One would think that the Communist Party was illegal or something', he wrote.[9]

Prominent support was forthcoming from two senior colleagues, Jim Muirhead QC, later Administrator of the Northern Territory

---

8 F.P. Kelly SJ, letter to *The Advertiser,* 29 November, 1969

9 D.N. Pritt, letter to *The Advertiser,* 29 November, 1969

and the first head of the Royal Commission into Aboriginal Deaths in Custody, and Len King. 'The Government's decision is in our view wrong', they wrote in a joint letter. 'It perpetrates an injustice to an individual who by years of hard and anxious work has earned the appointment. It sets a precedent which in the years ahead may do incalculable harm to the traditional political independence of the legal profession.'[10]

The profession was in uproar. Its loyalty to Elliott and to the principle of making appointments free of political constraints was about to be tested. In Victoria, the Bar Council relinquished control when it backed the rejection of Ted Laurie. The South Australian legal fraternity took a more vigorous stand against the government's rejection of the recommendations of their Chief Justice.

The president of the Law Society of South Australia, Brian Magarey, announced that the decision had serious implications for the legal profession and the society's council (which included Sam Jacobs and Len King) was convened to consider it. The council met at the Law Society offices at 44 Grenfell Street on 1 December but came to no resolution. They were divided, and neither endorsed Elliott's appointment nor opposed it. 'Law Society Ducks Out of "Red" QC Ban Issue', said one media report; 'Lawyers Back Out of Johnston Case', said another. The conservative lawyers on the Law Society Council were genuinely worried about appointing a Communist because of the conflict between his assumed revolutionary beliefs and loyalty to the Queen. The Attorney-General, Robin Millhouse, spoke strongly against Elliott. Ted Mullighan, later a South Australian Supreme Court judge, was a junior member of the council. He remembered a conservative view supporting the government, a pragmatic group who liked Elliott but realised they lacked the numbers and went with the conservatives, and a politically naïve group, which included himself, who opposed the government's intervention, and lost. Magarey, who knew Elliott and Elizabeth from university days, tried to steer a middle ground, but admits that he was one of those who disliked Communists. 'We all thought the Commos were stupid, and we knew they were white-anting some organisations, which we didn't enjoy. I had come

10 Jim Muirhead and Len King, letter to *The Advertiser*, 11 December 1969.

back from the war, been away for five-and-a-half years, and found the place being white-anted by Commos. It wasn't a happy situation at all.' The council issued a statement recognising 'the divergence of opinion which exists as to the considerations upon which the appointment of Queen's Counsel should be based'.[11] It disqualified itself from commenting further but directed Magarey and Millhouse to approach Chief Justice Bray to seek a break in 'the present impasse as to the appointment of Queen's Counsel'.

On the quiet, the government tried to force a split in the ranks between Elliott and the other two nominees. Bob Fisher was approached by Millhouse, who sounded him out about accepting a Queen's Counsel appointment direct from the government, circumventing the procedures set out in the Regulations of 1912 and by-passing the Chief Justice. Fisher told him it was the last thing he would do; his loyalty was to the Chief Justice, not to a political party.[12]

The debate inside the profession was as much about its independence as it was about Elliott, but the controversy about what it meant to be a Communist continued. The Speaker, Tom Stott, quoted from the Communist Manifesto on the ABC's *Today Tonight* program. 'Let the ruling classes tremble at a Communistic revolution. The proletarians have nothing to lose but their chains', he read. How could a man who adhered to these principles take an oath of allegiance to Her Majesty the Queen, promising, in the words of the oath, to defend her to the utmost against all treasons and traitorous conspiracies, without equivocation, mental evasion or secret reservations? 'Mr Johnston cannot have it both ways', he thundered.

Elliott kept his silence until 3 December, two days after the Law Society Council met, when he put out a statement and appeared on *Today Tonight*. Reporter Geoff Michels interviewed him.

> *Question:* Mr Johnston what do you think of the whole issue so far?
>
> *Answer:* Well I think the fundamental point is this; that the appointment of QCs is a matter of promotion within the legal profession, that

---

11 Extract from Minutes of Law Society Council meeting, 1 December 1969.

12 A founding member of Ward and Partners, Bob Ward went on to serve as a judge of the District Court. He died in 1993.

the issues involved are competence and integrity as a lawyer, and no political consideration whatever should enter into the question.

Question: To get down to specifics, you have taken an Oath of Allegiance. Did you mean it?

Answer: Yes I did.

Question: How can you reconcile taking an Oath of Allegiance and belonging to the Communist Party of Australia?

Answer: Well I see no contradiction whatever. The Queen is the constitutional monarch, she is the titular head of the society, she represents the society, the Australian people. I owe allegiance to her and I am very happy to owe allegiance to the Australian people and their way of life. I see no contradiction between that and belonging to the Communist Party and putting forward propositions for changes in our society.

Elliott was also asked about the revolutionary Manifesto, from which Tom Stott had quoted. Elliott reminded Michels that the document was 121 years old, that feudal despotism was not the practice in Australia (as it had been in Russia) and anyway he did not support it.

But had he renounced it?

Answer: As far as renouncing it is concerned, well you can't renounce something that you have never accepted and I have never accepted this conception of violent overthrow as being a relevant consideration for Australian conditions.

Question: The Premier, Mr Hall, also referred to you on this program as being a member of an international organisation which raped Czechoslovakia. What is your reaction to that?

Answer: My reaction to that is that the facts ought to be better known. Firstly I am not a member of an international organisation at all. I am a member of an Australian political party which decides its own policies, makes its own decisions about national and international matters and owes no allegiance or obedience to anybody else at all except itself. As far as Czechoslovakia is concerned, it is well known, it has been published in every newspaper in the country that the Australian Communist Party strongly disapproves and publicly disassociated itself from the action of the Warsaw Pact countries in Czechoslovakia. We have continued that attitude; we have demanded the withdrawal of the Warsaw Pact forces from Czechoslovakia at the recent international gathering of the Communist parties. We stated the position and we argued for it.

For the first time Elliott was asked how much he wanted to become a QC and whether he would – as Ted Laurie had – give up the party for the sake of silk.

Question: Are you prepared to do this?

Answer: No, I am not prepared to do that; that would be a totally unprincipled thing to do, a selling-out of one's conscience for some political ... or rather for some gain in the legal sphere and if I were to do a thing like that I say quite frankly that I wouldn't be worthy of blackening a QC's shoes, much less wearing his gown.

Question: On a more general level, how has this issue affected you and your family?

Answer: Well I haven't done much work but apart from that it hasn't affected me at all.

Elliott confirmed that he had not requested silk but had told Chief Justice Bray he would be honoured to be recommended.

Question: Do you expect your name to be put forward again?

Answer: Well, I don't know. As you know this question of the appointment of silks is a subject of discussion between the President of the Law Society, the Chief Justice and the Premier at the present time, but, of course, I have no indication as to what the outcome of the discussion is.

On 22 December, the Law Society called a special general meeting in the Ligertwood Building in the University of Adelaide Law School to thrash out its position. The meeting was extremely well attended and the room was packed with 170 lawyers standing or sitting on the steps of the lecture room. The issue generated a great deal of heat and discussion and many of the members who attended remembered it years later. Elliott and Elizabeth thought carefully about whether to go. Elliott had until that time had a vague belief that he would never be asked to take silk. But having been nominated on merit, he objected strongly to being rejected by a conservative government because he was a Communist. He was angry at what he saw as a purely political piece of prejudice. He nevertheless decided to stay away to avoid embarrassment and to allow people to speak more freely. But on the afternoon of the meeting he had a change of heart. A member of Don Dunstan's staff paid Elliott a personal visit to pass on Dunstan's request that he and Elizabeth attend, so they did.

The meeting was not concerned with the virtues or otherwise of Elliott's becoming Queen's Counsel, which was out of the profession's hands. The meeting had been convened to decide whether the profession supported the right of the Chief Justice to recommend whom he saw fit, and for that to proceed without political intervention. But intimately woven through this argument were the perceived legitimate concerns and prejudices of individuals towards Elliott and his politics. In the crowded university lecture room the passions flowed. Millhouse reiterated his government's objections. Other lawyers spoke for Elliott, including Kevin O'Loughlin, then a magistrate at Elizabeth and later a judge in the Industrial Court of South Australia. A motion was proposed: 'That this Society disapproves the rejection of the recommendation of Mr E.F. Johnston as Queen's Counsel on grounds other than his professional competence and professional standing'. It indirectly supported Elliott and the Chief Justice by criticising the rejection of Elliott because of his politics. When a show of hands failed to confirm support, a count was called. With Elliott present, those in favour of the motion were asked to stand; then those opposing it would do the same.

It was not an easy situation. Elliott was sitting near the members of a conservative family law firm, one of whom broke ranks to support him. 'About two rows in front of me and slightly to the right were seven members of a firm who had obviously come together to the meeting, sitting together. Six of those stood against the Chief Justice and one stood in favour; I think it takes some courage to vote in those circumstances', he said. The man who stood in favour was Andrew Wilson, a family member of the firm Genders, Wilson & Bray, of which the Chief Justice had been a partner before his appointment to the Bench. Elliott was almost 20 years older than Wilson (known to his colleagues as 'Alphabet' Wilson because of his initials, A.B.C.) but they had appeared opposite each other in a drawn-out workers' compensation dispute. The case, which the insurer won, was long and hard fought, with the trial lasting for months. It could have become bitter but it never did. Elliott had impressed Wilson with his courtesy to the court and his generosity of spirit towards a young opponent.

Wilson's dilemma over Elliott, a man he liked and admired but whose politics were beyond the conservative pale, was illustrative of what many lawyers felt. Wilson was from political stock. His father, Sir Keith Wilson, had been a Liberal member for the seat of Sturt in the House of Representatives, as was his brother, Ian Wilson, and neither had any time for Communism. But Andrew Wilson knew Elliott. He did not want to write him off because he was a Communist. He remembered walking to the meeting with his father, brother and the other lawyers from the firm. Elliott was not discussed but, as the time came for the motion to be put, the tension began to rise. 'It was very emotional', Wilson said. With his father and brother sitting stonily on either side, he stood in support of Elliott. Then he sat down and the process was agonisingly repeated as those around him got to their feet. His father was angry with him and relations were frosty for some months, but Wilson was proud of what he had done. 'My father was clearly disappointed but I acknowledge his right to express his own opinion. He did not take me to task; I mean I was a man in my early 30s so he did not scold me, but there was tension between him and me', he said.

The motion supporting Elliott was carried by a substantial majority of the profession, with 110 for and 42 against.[13] Elliott and Elizabeth abstained. The Hall Government ignored the Law Society motion of implicit condemnation and the Elliott Johnston affair was all but over.

Elliott was personally heartened by the support he had received, which included letters from people he barely knew. 'You may have lost much custom by being known as a Communist and I admire you for bearing this', a stranger wrote. Nineteen years later, when Elliott retired from the Supreme Court, the President of the Law Society, Rod Burr, spoke of how much the support of others had

13 Information provided by the Law Society of South Australia 6 March 2007.

meant to him. 'I know that your Honour took great comfort at that time from the open display of support and solidarity given by your profession and the Society', Burr said.

There were a few last words. Elliott's good friend, Max Harris, had in the late 1960s become a columnist for Rupert Murdoch's new national paper, *The Australian*. In a long mid-December Saturday piece in his column, 'Browsing', Harris dissected characters and events for a national audience. Steele Hall, basically a good man, had escaped most of the prejudices of his rural background but not all, Harris wrote. Whereas Elliott, he told his readers, was a good friend of some 25 years who had a nature that was bound to frustrate. 'He is that classical irritant, the good Communist who is also a good person. Of unblemished public and private reputation, tolerant, devoid of fanaticism, contemptuous of intrigue and double-talk, he is just the sort of person to inspire frenzies of frustration and anger in the Pavlovian anti-Communists', he wrote.[14] The controversy had unfolded like a set piece, Harris wrote, like a slow-moving urban Australian farce, with each person remaining intransigent and immutable. Harris was correct, in that almost 40 years later Steele Hall's opposition to Elliott's appointment had not abated. He confirmed that his government had been untroubled by this reprimand from the profession, partly because relations with Chief Justice Bray were so poor anyway: 'They were official and frosty, I suppose you would say. There were no bad words between us but [it was] based on [Bray's] unconventional behaviour and the fact he was always thought to be a supporter of Labor.'

However, Hall's Attorney-General, Robin Millhouse, has repudiated his public stance. He is not happy with the role in which history has cast him because the views he argued publicly were not his own. He was compelled by virtue of his position to represent his government against Elliott, while privately believing Elliott's appointment should not be opposed. Millhouse, who later sat on the Supreme Court Bench with Elliott and who after his retirement became Chief Justice of the island nation of Kiribati, reveals there was a split in Cabinet between himself and Steele Hall. The list of

14 Max Harris, 'Browsing: Background to a sorry affair', *Australian*, 13 December 1969.

three names arrived on his desk without warning and Millhouse went into Cabinet arguing that all of them, including Elliott, be made Queen's Counsel. Millhouse's version was corroborated at the time by talk that Cabinet was divided over the issue, with *The Advertiser* reporter, Bob Whitington, reporting as much the day after the story broke. Millhouse now claims that he regretted not having recorded his real position. The recommendations came across his desk as a memorandum or minute, which he passed on without documenting his support. 'I have always wished that I had marked the docket to say that I recommended it. But I had been told not to mark dockets so when it went to Cabinet it was simply an oral recommendation', he said.

Millhouse lost the argument in Cabinet and for the next three weeks he had to spruik Hall's position to the press, in parliament, to the Law Society Council, and at the Law Society meeting, which he found particularly irksome: 'The general meeting of the members of the Law Society was the really difficult one. I had to go along, and the overwhelming majority was in favour of his appointment. I felt a good deal of antagonism against myself, but, again, I had to argue the Government's point of view.' Millhouse contemplated resigning. Whether from cowardice, caution or because it was not a big enough issue, Millhouse does not know, but he has always disliked carrying the can in the profession for a decision in which he did not believe. His support for Elliott was based on principle. He had no affection for Elliott, even when they sat together on the Supreme Court Bench: 'We got on all right, but we did not ever have an intimate friendship or anything like that. I don't think I ever discussed [the QC affair] with him', he said.

The sensitivities over who voted for and against Elliott at the 22 December meeting abated but never quite vanished. Some 40 years later the minutes of the meeting detailing who spoke for and against Elliott remain confidential and the Law Society council refuses to release them.

The controversy had not quite run its course. Bob Fisher and Bob Ward had also missed being appointed as Queen's Counsel. Millhouse gave up trying to by-pass Bray and in early 1970 he took a different tack and amended the Regulations governing the appointment of Queen's Counsel. Until that time, the exclusive source of nominations had been the Chief Justice (although Bray had consulted his fellow judges). On 26 March 1970, the government repealed the 1912 Regulations and widened the source of nominations beyond the Chief Justice. The new Regulations also made the consideration of the views of all senior judges mandatory. 'No practitioner of the Supreme Court shall be appointed Her Majesty's Counsel except after consideration of the views of the judges of the Supreme Court as communicated by the Chief Justice to the Governor in Executive Council and with the approval of the Chief Justice.'[15]

Two months later on 7 May 1970, Fisher and Ward were appointed but Elliott was not. In an interview with *The Advertiser* Millhouse said that, in line with the new Regulations, the Chief Justice communicated the views of his judges, and the appointments of Fisher and Ward were confirmed. Asked why Elliott was not among them, Millhouse said Elliott's name was recommended by some judges, but not by a majority.[16]

Elliott accepted this without comment. But barely a month had passed before the political ground shifted and the door to his appointment swung open. Steele Hall had declared the only way Elliott would be appointed was if Dunstan got into office. Hall had begun dismantling the Playford gerrymander by expanding the number of House of Assembly seats and giving greater representation to the city. It cost him office and on 2 June 1970, South Australia's Dunstan decade began.

Just over a fortnight later, Elliott's appointment was announced. Six of the seven available Supreme Court judges had noted his professional standing and qualifications, and Chief Justice Bray again had put forward his name for appointment.[17] His professional qualifications and experience in the law had eminently qualified him, Premier Dunstan said.

Elliott became Australia's first (and only known) Communist Queen's Counsel. It was the highest level of public recognition achieved by a serving member of the Communist Party of Australia

15 *South Australian Government Gazette*, Adelaide, 1970, 1246.

16 Eric Franklin, 'New QCs named, but not Mr Johnston', *Advertiser*, 8 May 1970.

17 Eric Franklin, 'New QC award on merit – Dunstan', *Advertiser*, 19 June 1970.

and he had arrived there on merit, as a senior member of the South Australian legal profession who did not compromise his Communist Party affiliation. In Victoria, Ted Laurie had resigned from the Communist Party in order to reapply for silk, and the other prominent Communist lawyer of the day, Ted Hill, never became a Queen's Counsel or held judicial office.

Hall was gracious in defeat. 'Mr Johnston has the support of the public because his promised elevation to Queen's Counsel was well aired at the election at which Mr Dunstan received a sound majority', he said.[18]

But there was still some nervousness in high places about South Australia's first Communist silk. Dunstan's new Attorney-General, Len King, was present at the 18 June meeting of Executive Council when Elliott's appointment came before the Acting Governor, Sir Mellis Napier. Sir Mellis expressed disquiet at Elliott's Communist affiliations and said he felt obliged to demand proof from someone whose loyalty he thought was in question. He wanted Elliott to take a special oath of loyalty to the Queen. 'I indicated that I did not agree with that but that I was prepared to ring Elliott and ask him what his attitude was', Len King said. With Executive Council still in session, King rang Elliott from another room and told him what Sir Mellis Napier wanted. Elliott refused. He did not want to *not* become Queen's Counsel because he was a Communist; nor did he expect to have to prove himself more than others. He had already sworn allegiance twice in his life and was not going to demean himself by doing so a third time.

He had sworn the Oath of Allegiance when he enlisted for the army and on admission to the Bar, and he would swear it again whenever it was customary. This was not such an occasion. King conveyed this back to Sir Mellis Napier, and Dunstan and King stood firm in support of Elliott. On 18 June 1970, Elliott received a letter congratulating him on his appointment as Queen's Counsel.

18 ibid.

Elizabeth's father Paul Teesdale Smith, a decorated Gallipoli veteran.

Elizabeth's mother, Helen Teesdale Smith, a member of the well known Waterhouse family.

Helen, Paul and Elizabeth's older sister Mary.

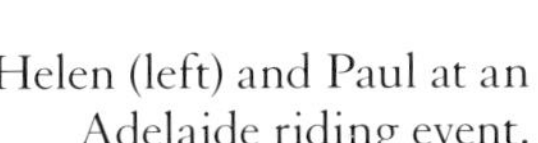

Helen (left) and Paul at an Adelaide riding event.

Elliott's parents Elsie and William with older brother Ross and his sons Robert (left) and David.

Elliott as a prefect at Prince Alfred College, front right.

Woodlands hockey team, Elizabeth second row, centre, and sisters Cecil, back right, and Mary, front right.

The tree-lined entrance to Maryland, Marion Road, South Plympton, the Teesdale Smith family home.

The Teesdale Smiths:
Cecil, Paul, Malcolm, Helen, Mary and Elizabeth at Maryland.

Helen and Paul outside the stables at Maryland.

Elizabeth's younger brother Malcolm, known as Mick.

Elizabeth and Mick Teesdale Smith.

Elizabeth in her university days.

Elliott and Elizabeth on their wedding day, 17 April 1942.

Elliott with Ian,
later known as Stewart.

Elizabeth and Stewart.

Stewart and Elizabeth, Maryland.

Stewart with grandfather Paul at Maryland.

Stewart at Maryland, his own private Arcadia.

Marjorie Johnston during her brief marriage to Max Schmidt.

On a Communist trip to Soviet Russia in late 1950.
Elliott is third from the right.

Lady Jessie Street thanks their Russian hosts on behalf of the Australian delegates.

Elliott on his return from Warsaw and Russia, February 1951. The picture appeared in *The News*.

Elliott with fellow Communist Jim Healy, secretary of the Waterside Workers Federation.

The modest offices of Johnston & Johnston at 345 Carrington Street, Adelaide.

Elliott in 1969 at the height of the QC controversy. (Courtesy of *The Advertiser*)

Elliott (right) with his friend Josko Grubic at the Coorong.

A field visit during the Van Beelen appeal, Elliott pointing. Sam Jacobs (sunglasses) is on the right and Kevin Borick (beard) on the left. The two judges are in hats.

Elizabeth and Elliott visit the Parthenon on their way to the UK for an appeal to the Privy Council.

Climbing the steps of the Parthenon.

Relaxing in Greece.

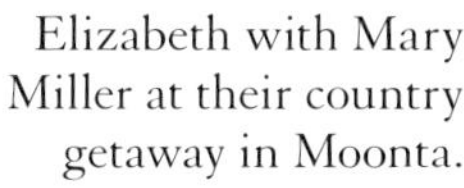

Elizabeth with Mary Miller at their country getaway in Moonta.

Elliott addresses a May Day rally in the late 1970s.

Andrew Collett, Paul Heywood-Smith and Elliott at a Sturt football match at Thebarton Oval in the late 1970s.

Communist campaign poster by Adelaide artist Jim Cane. Elliott stood against Mick Young in 1980 when the Fraser Government was in power.

THE NEWS

Phone 51 0351 Adelaide: Friday, November 28, 1969 5c

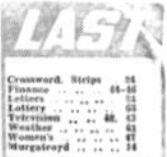

GOVT. RELEASES LETTER ON QC

Dr. Bray request: Storm grows

In response to a request by the Chief Justice, Dr. Bray, the Government today released the text of a letter the Chief Justice sent to the Chief Secretary over the Government's Queen's Counsel decision.

The Chief Justice said in his letter that the decision to withdraw the names of all lawyers recommended for appointment as Queen's Counsel was his alone.

This is the latest development in the furore that has followed the Government's decision not to appoint Mr. Johnston a QC, "because of his affiliations with the Communist Party."

Today's picture of Mr. Elliott Johnston.

The letter, written last Friday, was released today by the Government following an earlier statement by Dr. Bray.

The Chief Justice's statement read as follows:

"The judges, of course, are not concerned with any political considerations and take no sides in any political controversy.

"They are concerned only with the recognition of legal merit.

"But, in order to avoid any misunderstanding and to dispel any misconceptions I have asked the Government to release the text of a letter I wrote to the Chief Secretary concerning the matter and this, I understand, it has agreed to do."

Supported

The Chief Justice's letter to the Chief Secretary read:

"I refer to my letter of 25th September, 1969, making certain recommendations for silk and to my recent interview with the Premier and the Attorney-General.

"The responsibility for making recommendations to His Excellency the Governor in Executive Council for the appointment of Queen's Counsel is, of course, mine.

"But in exercising that responsibility I have always thought it desirable to ascertain the views of the learned judges, my colleagues.

"In the present case, the recommendations in question had the support of all the judges in office at the time I made them.

"The attainment of silk is rightly regarded as a high professional distinction and a recognition of professional skill and professional honor.

"In making recommendations I can have regard only to professional considerations.

"I cannot take account of a barrister's non-professional beliefs or activities, at least so long as they do not infringe the law.

"The recommendations were carefully made, both with respect to the proper proportion of silks to juniors and with respect to the individual preeminence of the nominees.

'Only choice'

"I must regard them as a whole and I cannot and do not recommend any nominee to the exclusion of any other.

"I fully realise that it is my duty only to recommend and that the responsibility of advising His Excellency to accept or reject the recommendations rests elsewhere.

"Since the recommendations are not acceptable as a whole, I consider that my only choice is to withdraw them altogether and that I now do.

"I should add, in case there is any misunderstanding, that although, as I have said, the judges all concurred in the initial recommendations, the decision to withdraw them is mine alone.

Meet soon

"I might add that, as foreshadowed at the interview, I have seen the nominees and informed them that the recommendations have been withdrawn."

The Premier, Mr Hall, said today the Government's decision to refuse to appoint Mr. Johnston was final.

Mr. Johnston would not be appointed a QC by his Government even if the Chief Justice resubmitted the name, Mr. Hall added.

The Law Society of South Australia has called a meeting of its 20 council members for Monday to consider the matter.

The president, Mr. B. A. Magarey, said the council would have to consider the implications of Cabinet's decision.

He was not aware of any previous occasion when appointments as QC were influenced by political considerations.

Yesterday's furore in Parliament culminated in a censure motion by the Labor Opposition Leader, Mr. Dunstan.

The Government survived the motion on the casting vote of the Speaker, Mr. Stott.

In a statement today, the Premier said yesterday's decision was one that must be made by the Government.

• Cont. P. 61.
• See: Public divided — P. 6.

THE LIVING SAINT P.7

THE NEWS

Adelaide: Thursday, October 18, 1979 15c

LAST

WEATHER Fine. TEMP. (at 1 pm): 24.1C (75F). Sunset 6.33. (Details, Page 38.)

Terror hold-up in Italy

MAFIA AMBUSH ADELAIDE QC

CALABRIA

ASPROMONTE MOUNTAINS

Reggio

SICILY

Mountain bandits' shotgun attack

Mafia terrorists, armed with shotguns and sticks, held up and robbed Adelaide Queen's Counsel, Mr Elliott Johnston, and his wife in Italy.

Mr and Mrs Johnston were ambushed on a lonely back road near Calabria in the southern part of country.

Three masked men stopped the couple and another Australian, Isabel Cortside, from Victoria.

They forced the trio out of their hire car and ordered them to hand over 100,000 lire ($110), their passports and other travel documents.

Mr Johnston . . . forced from car

By Mike Safe

The bandits fled in another vehicle.

Mr Johnston, 61, is one of Adelaide's most distinguished legal men.

There is no report that he or his wife, Elizabeth, were injured in the hold-up.

The bandits struck in a remote section of the Aspromonte Mountains, a region often frequented by Mafia-linked bandits.

Return

The Australian Embassy in Rome and the Foreign Affairs Department are making inquiries into the attack.

A legal associate of Mr Johnston said in Adelaide today the couple had been holidaying in Italy.

They had been away for nearly a month and were scheduled to return in 16 days.

"At this stage, we know very little," the associate said.

"One of our people heard a report on the radio this morning and we're waiting for further news."

Mr Johnston was made a Queen's Counsel in 1970.

Controversy surrounded his appointment because of his connections with the Communist Party.

Two front pages, a decade apart.

Australia's first Communist Supreme Court judge. (Courtesy of *The Advertiser*)

Justice Johnston visits Communist China in December 1983.

Elliott on his retirement from the Supreme Court in 1988. (Courtesy of *The Advertiser*)

Barbara Wall, Elizabeth's cousin Pauline, Elliott and Elizabeth at Gilles Street.

Elliott at the Royal Commission into Aboriginal Deaths in Custody. (Courtesy of *The Advertiser*)

With friend and fellow Commissioner Pat Dodson.

Old friends – Elliott and Chancellor of the University of Adelaide, John von Doussa.

Elliott receives an Honorary PhD from the Chancellor.

Brian Withers with Elliott at the
60th anniversary of Johnston Withers.

Elliott speaks to old friends and
comrades.

Elliott in his nineties.

Celebrating his 90th birthday with Lowitja O'Donoghue, Andrew Collett, Mick Doyle and Robyn Layton.

Elliott and Stewart at Gilles Street in 2010.

CHAPTER 7

The Dunstan decade

The 1970s ushered in the beginning of a golden time, a period of more than a decade when Johnston & Johnston, headed by Elliott and Elizabeth, blossomed into a leading Left-wing practice. The arrival of the new Labor Premier, Don Dunstan, whose pink shorts were the outward sign of a man ready to release a state from convention, meant that Elliott's time had come. His firm became central to a wave of reform that washed through Adelaide. The city metamorphosed into not quite the 'Athens of the south' that Dunstan envisaged but a socially enlightened city, where shopping hours were relaxed, police powers were curbed and the Adelaide Festival Centre was built. Social change was backed by legislation to permit homosexuality; rape within marriage became a crime; anti-discrimination legislation was introduced; and, although no one had been hanged for 12 years, capital punishment was abolished.

For the lawyers who joined Elliott, this was the experience of a lifetime. John (Jack) Lewis, later a magistrate and a District Court judge, joined the firm at the end of the 1960s as a partner because Elliott's egalitarianism extended to the belief that all his lawyers should be equal. (He saw this later as 'a rather silly idea' because he needed to know a person first.)

Lewis joined an articled clerk, Fazio Di Fazio, who became a Judge of the Industrial Court of South Australia. Di Fazio's entry into Elliott's firm in 1965 had been watched by ASIO, which already had files on his father, Raffaele Di Fazio, an Italian barber who attended Communist Party meetings. In 1969 ASIO reported that Di Fazio had made it clear he was not a Communist and that he did not share Elliott's opinions.[1] None of the other lawyers were Communists, but in 1970 Elliott's Maoist sister, Marjorie, began managing the books.

In early 1969, he brought in a second partner, Robyn Layton. Attractive and smart, she was the first of Elliott's young radicals whose special interests shaped the firm's reform agenda. Layton, who was then married to a young lawyer, John Bannon, later Premier of South Australia, arrived when the firm was still located at Rechabite Chambers. Layton remembers getting a card that read 'Happy International Women's Day' with an inscription in handwriting she could not read. Layton, who had completed her articles, concluded it was from Elliott. She had never heard of International Women's Day[2] but she rang and asked if he was looking for a solicitor. No, he told her, but he wanted a partner, so could she come in for a chat? She was in her twenties and part of a new generation who, through their behaviour, beliefs, music, language and dress were challenging the social and political conservatism of the post-war decade. They believed in their right to express themselves socially and sexually in ways their parents could not, and they were making their voices heard. She began as a probationary solicitor and quickly became a partner. 'He knew I was interested in civil liberties because I belonged to the Council of Civil Liberties. He knew that I was married to John Bannon so he would have assumed a Leftist streak from that, and it would be true as well in my own right. I think he knew a lot of those things before I rang him up', Layton said.

Elliott gathered around him people who were more or less anointed for the role. He liked to take young lawyers under his wing. By now a distinguished-looking man with greying hair, he would sit having coffee with criminal lawyers like Derrance Stevenson and Peter Waye at an outdoor café in King William Street, near the courts. Younger lawyers would come up and talk to him about cases of interest. The causes within Elliott's orbit came

1 ASIO, 'Elliott Frank Johnston', National Archives of Australia, Canberra, 1969.

2 The Marion and Adelaide Electoral Branches of the Communist Party of Australia had resolved in March 1969 to send out cards celebrating International Women's Day as part of an equal rights campaign.

to include the Vietnam War, sex discrimination, apartheid in South Africa, industrial democracy, women's rights, native title and legal representation for Aboriginal offenders, who were adrift in a criminal system they barely understood.

From 1965 when Australia announced it was sending combat troops to fight with the United States in Vietnam, opposition to the war and to conscription spread through the Left into the trade union movement and on to university campuses. Many Adelaide academics supported the moderate voice of the anti-war movement, the Campaign for Peace in Vietnam (CPV), which was chaired by the Flinders University lecturer in philosophy, Professor Brian Medlin. In 1969, with an end to conscription in sight, the movement evolved into the Vietnam Moratorium Campaign (VMC), which was dedicated to nationwide protests against the war. Smaller groups, including the Radical Alliance and the Students for Democratic Action, which had close links to the Communist Party, were active on the campuses. They opposed not just the Vietnam War but also the 'imperialist' United States of America (where in May 1970 members of the Ohio National Guard killed four students in an anti-war student protest at Kent State University). Their methods went beyond peaceful protest into civil disobedience and active support for the Communist north, the National Liberation Front.

Elliott and his firm became the local heroes of the anti-Vietnam radical protest movement, a friend to those who fell foul of the law. In the late 1960s and early 1970s Elliott, John Lewis and Robyn Layton acted pro bono for most of those arrested, including Elliott's son Ian, who as a teenager had permanently adopted his second name, Stewart. Elliott personally opposed the war. 'The Communist Party had from the very beginning been against the war. I don't know if that's how [support for the protesters] came about or not. From then on I think we acted for 97 per cent of the people charged with offences', he said. In May 1969, after a sit-in in Currie Street, Elliott appeared for 35 of the 60 demonstrators who had been charged. Colourful media reports described bearded, long-haired supporters, some wearing slogan badges. The magistrate had to warn against laughter in the court. The penalties were not harsh and the courts usually heeded Elliott's pleas for common sense and meted out punishments that would not jeopardise the future careers of demonstrators, many of whom were students.

So-called draft dodgers, young men avoiding National Service on principle after they had been selected in the conscription ballot, sought his help, among them Flinders University drama student Kim Dalton.[3] Dalton had resisted his call-up and Layton successfully argued in court that his national service papers were void because of a minor irregularity in the way they had been served. Waiting in the corridors outside the courtroom with fresh papers were the federal police. Layton did not know it but Dalton had rounded up supporters from the university, who arrived en masse at the Magistrates Court. As she was getting instructions, Dalton suddenly took off and lost himself in the crowd. The federal police suspected Layton of aiding his escape and a solicitor from the Commonwealth interviewed her about a potential charge of obstructing the course of justice. She refused to answer his questions. After Elliott complained to the Commonwealth Director of Public Prosecutions, the matter was dropped.

The anti-Vietnam demonstrations grew in intensity and on 18 September 1970 a massive street protest in Adelaide involving five thousand people became the most violent the Australian peace movement had seen. The VMC organisers led the march to the city's busiest intersection, at the corner of King William Street and North Terrace, directly outside Parliament House and Government House, and occupied it. It turned ugly when police rode in on horseback and made arrests. Police and protestors scuffled, abuse was hurled, and in the course of the demonstration 141 people were arrested, including Stewart Johnston, Professor Brian Medlin and a future Labor Premier of South Australia, Lynn Arnold.

Elliott and his partners examined each case for new grounds with which to defend the rights of the activists. Brian Medlin's case received enormous publicity. An Oxford graduate, poet, and a self-styled romantic figure with boots and long black hair who strode around Flinders University campus where he was the Foundation Professor of Philosophy, Medlin was the charismatic head of the

---

3 In 2006 Kim Dalton was appointed the head of television of the Australian Broadcasting Corporation.

intellectual protest against the Vietnam war. A friend of Don Dunstan, of Chief Justice John Bray and an old friend from Oxford days of the writer Iris Murdoch, he helped organise the September rally. Elliott acted for him at a trial heard by Elliott's cousin Don Elliott SM. In the course of the evidence there was a dispute about the use of police force. Medlin, who claimed he had been picked up bodily by the police and put struggling into a police van, caught Elliott off guard by grabbing and lifting him bodily from behind to demonstrate what had happened. Despite character evidence from Bray, Medlin was convicted and imprisoned. He refused to appeal; he wanted to go to prison to make the point that those who opposed the war would face the consequences.

Stewart Johnston was also arrested on minor offences. In court, Jack Lewis promised to contest them all. Police withdrew all but one charge and Stewart was put on a bond.

The case of another protestor, Timothy Klar, went on appeal to the Full Court of the Supreme Court presided over by Chief Justice Bray. Klar was charged with failing to obey a police order and wilfully obstructing the intersection of King William Street and North Terrace. He was convicted in the Magistrates Court in October. The magistrate, who knew that another demonstration was planned for December, ordered that Klar be imprisoned with hard labour for 14 days. The sentence would be suspended only if Klar agreed to enter into a good behaviour bond in the sum of $250 and agreed to keep the peace and 'not engage in any activity which involves a breach of public order'. Klar refused because he would be barred from the next demonstration. Layton secured his release on bail and a few months later, with Elliott leading, she persuaded the Full Court that the penalty was invalid.[4]

This upsurge of energy on campuses was part of the 1970s ethos of personal liberation and freedom of expression that challenged legal understanding of what was acceptable public conduct. Protesters were routinely charged with offensive behaviour for swearing, with the courts having to redefine which words would offend. In late 1971 Kim Dalton was convicted by the Magistrates Court after a counter-culture pop festival at the sound shell at Elder

4 *R v. Wright*; ex parte Klar (1971) 1 SASR 103.

Park on the banks of the River Torrens. He was charged with indecent language over a poem he had recited containing the words 'fuck', 'fucked' and 'cunt'. He pleaded not guilty in the Magistrates Court but was convicted. Layton took his case on appeal to the Full Court, which quashed the conviction on the grounds that Dalton had not been properly informed of what he was alleged to have said. The point was a matter of law and Dalton's appeal was successful but the court also considered whether genuine offence had been caused. Chief Justice Bray decided that the question of whether the words used by Dalton were indecent depended on the circumstances and the context in which they were spoken. They could be used, for instance, in friendly conversation as 'intensives or expletives or in their literal significance'.[5] In relation to this question the Chief Justice agreed with the reasoning of Justice David Hogarth, who said he had heard all three words thousands of times during six years in the army. Justice Hogarth said the words could be viewed as uncouth or offensive but Dalton had not been charged with offensive language (the charge was indecent language under the *Police Offences Act*) and it was not an offence to be uncouth. Besides, he said, in some circles it was now de rigueur to use such words in private conversation, for example, when asking someone to pass the butter.[6]

It was the common-sense approach of Bray's court that allowed this enlightened shift in standards to enter case law, and the Chief Justice was probably more significant than anyone in allowing public morality to move on. To fight the tide was clearly ridiculous. Justice Hogarth said in the Dalton judgment that it was difficult to take the matter seriously when experts were put on the stand to testify on the significance of the word 'fuck' in literature. 'Certain of this "expert" evidence was of a surprising character, and indeed led me to wonder whether the witness in question, who deposed to one of the appellant's poems having an allegorical significance more profound than appeared on the surface, may not have been lampooning current methods of literary criticism. If this was his intention, I am far from saying that he was not justified in so doing; but the witness box is

5 *Dalton v. Bartlett* (1972) 3 SASR 549.

6 *Dalton v. Bartlett* (supra) at 555.

not the place in which it should be done', Justice Hogarth wrote.

At the same Elder Park concert in 1971 a skit was performed that led to a charge of indecent behaviour, for which a man was convicted and fined $100. With Elliott advising and supporting her, Layton acted for him on appeal and the Bray court found itself considering the indecency or otherwise of an untitled sketch intended to satirise sexual innuendo in advertising. The man had no speaking part but appeared on stage wearing a tube 1.5-metre-high made of hessian and wire, wrapped in newspaper, with a cone on top with a hole in it. He was called Spunky. A bogus advertising eulogy for the 'Spunky' product was recited and, in the words of the Chief Justice:

> During the reading the appellant bobbed up and down, at first slowly but with gradually increasing tempo corresponding to the increased tempo of [the] delivery. Some girls danced around the appellant as he was doing this, with their arms touching the outside of his costume in a manner said to be suggestive of adoration. At the climax of the speech the appellant emitted a stream of shaving cream through the hole in the top of his costume from a pressure can in his hand. The appellant admitted that his costume represented a penis but said it also represented, *inter alia*, a cigarette or a missile ... There was no real doubt that, whatever else the appellant was symbolising, he was also symbolising a penis in a state of erection being worked up to ejaculation. So much is common ground.[7]

The case was heard a month before Dalton's indecency trial and the Chief Justice upheld the conviction but reduced 'Spunky's' fine to $15. In terms of reforming public morality, the Chief Justice was not ready to declare that contemporary standards of propriety were not offended by 'the simulation, however unrealistic, of an erect penis five or six feet high in a state of ejaculation in a public park on a Sunday afternoon'[8]. But he likened the offence to the sort of thing put on by undergraduates during university saturnalia and said there was no evidence that anyone, including the police, had been offended. 'The interests of society are best served by treating this episode as the triviality which I think it is', he concluded.

---

7 *Prowse v. Bartlett* (1972) 3 SASR 472 at 473.

8 ibid.

These were colourful times, involving creative civic protests like flag-burning, sit-ins and street theatre, and, on one occasion, the attempted payment of a fine with a cheque stuck to the head of a dead pig.

In 1974 Lindy Powell became part of the firm's increasingly interesting mix. She replaced Jack Lewis, who had been appointed a magistrate. Extraordinarily lively, very funny and clever, Powell was a University of Adelaide graduate and judge's associate to Justice Roma Mitchell, who had tried to steer her into family law. Powell chose Elliott's firm instead. She had three years earlier married Stewart Johnston. They were children of their times and had clashed with police in Rundle Street during a civil rights demonstration against the all-white South African Springbok rugby union team which toured Australia. Stewart was arrested again, this time trying to save Powell from being dragged into a police van. Powell, who in 1994 was appointed Queen's Counsel, had broken from the marchers to perch on the back of the motorbike of a clearly hostile policeman and from the seat of his bike had given a celebrity wave. The furious policeman dropped his motorbike and Powell fled but was pulled out of the march and hauled off to a van. As Stewart tried to drag her back, Powell was punched in the face: 'This fist comes around the side and I'll never forget it. It had a wedding ring on it and it really punched me in the jaw. Next thing I know I am on my back on the footpath in Rundle Street and they are dragging Stewart away.' Jack Lewis again defended Stewart on charges of hindering police in the exercise of their duties and offensive language. Both charges were dropped because of the lack of evidence.

Powell arrived at the firm just as her short marriage to Stewart was breaking up. It was delicate because Elliott and Elizabeth had welcomed Powell into the family with open arms, and now they were working together as lawyers. Powell says Elliott and Elizabeth were upset and relations were cool for six months, and then got back to normal. At no time did Powell feel that she was not welcome.

The firm had changed dramatically from the early days when Johnston & Johnston had a small office in the city. In 1970, just after Elliott had taken silk, they moved from Rechabite Chambers to an old terrace building at 345 Carrington Street, bought by Elliott and Elizabeth and just within walking distance of the courts. In 1970

Brian Withers, who became a mainstay of the firm and whose name endured in the firm's later business name of Johnston Withers, had joined Elliott and Elizabeth, Robyn Layton, Faz Di Fazio and Jack Lewis. Withers met Elliott after briefing him as counsel in a case of alleged prostitution at a massage parlour at Glenelg. In court Elliott had asked just enough questions to undermine the vice squad's evidence. Over a victory coffee, Withers told Elliott he was looking to move from his current position in the office of Peter Waye. As it happened, Elliott needed someone to take over 400 or so files that had been gathering dust since his appointment as Queen's Counsel. Withers, later a Master of the Supreme Court, also entered the firm as a partner. 'Everybody was a partner except the articled clerks and everybody was part of it', Withers said.

As Queen's Counsel, Elliott was available to be briefed at the top of the profession and he already had notable criminal experience, including in the 1960s a major murder trial. Elliott in 1966 had defended a man who was jointly charged with murdering a former prison mate. The decomposing body of Keith Pascoe had been found in an outcrop of rocks at Trigg Point, a beach between Port Noarlunga and Moana. Pascoe, who was identified from a heart-shaped tattoo on his right hand, had been kicked in the ribs and shot in the head. Elliott's client, Young, and his friend, Radan, were charged and they turned on each other.

Elliott, with Derrance Stevenson as his junior, methodically defended Young, a hairdresser from Mile End. Radan claimed he saw Young shoot Pascoe and admitted helping to bury him in the sand while he was still alive. He claimed Young had threatened him and his family, while Young claimed he was being framed. The trial dealt with complex science relating to paint chips, material found on shoes and in the boot of a car, and striations that linked Young's rifle to the bullet. Justice Roma Mitchell, presiding in her first criminal trial, sentenced them to death after a jury had found them guilty.[9] Ted Mullighan was the junior lawyer who defended Radan and he watched Elliott quietly unpick the prosecution's case. 'He was extraordinarily thorough and he turned over not just every stone but

---

9 The sentence of hanging handed down by Mitchell J was commuted to life imprisonment by the Walsh Labor Government.

every piece of gravel as well. He was unfazed by judicial irritability or anything like that. He was focused', Mullighan said.

With this background, Elliott was briefed in the early 1970s in the highly publicised trial of Frits Van Beelen, accused of the murder and rape of a schoolgirl. It was long and complex and it was Elliott's first major Crown brief. On 16 July 1971, 15-year-old Deborah Leach was found dead at Taperoo beach in Adelaide's north-west. She had come home from the local high school the day before, changed, and had taken her dog for a walk along the beach, north of Largs Bay. Her parents came home to find only the dog and they reported her missing. At midnight the police were combing the beach and shortly before dawn some of her belongings were found. Minutes later, her partially clothed body, covered with seaweed, was found on a small dune. It was determined later that she had been drowned and then raped.

The police had a single lead. A car had been seen parked at the beach and by chance three men from a nearby factory who had gone fishing in the Port River noted three letters of the number plate, when they came ashore.[10] By complete coincidence the detective heading the investigation a few days later had seen the same car from a window in the Angas Street police station overlooking Victoria Square. He ran downstairs and saw the car was parked outside the Post Office. Frits Van Beelen was picking up his wife from work. He admitted having been at Taperoo Beach on the day of the murder but denied the crime. He was an unemployed carpenter and claimed he had just been driving around. Police took a jumper from his house that became crucial in the case against him because they found on it red and black fibres that matched those on the girl's singlet.

Van Beelen was convicted but appealed successfully and the case was re-tried. Elliott was briefed to appear for the prosecution and at the second trial Elliott questioned Van Beelen extensively on

10 The men remembered the letters (RCC) for reasons that greatly amused Elliott. They were English and Irish migrants who conducted a long-running friendly dispute about the virtues of the Catholic versus Protestant religions. When the police asked the men how they remembered the letters but not the numbers from the plate, they conferred privately then confessed that the letters 'RCC' had been the subject of a joke.

the details of evidence given at the first trial about what had happened that day. Van Beelen said he had bought the local paper and had read it looking for job advertisements; he admitted that he had walked along Taperoo Beach but he had not seen the girl.

During the retrial, the defence, led by Kevin Borick, called a witness from England who attacked the forensic link between the fibres from the girl's singlet and Van Beelen's clothing. The expert claimed another test could decide the question more precisely. Hairs from the singlet and the jumper were placed in a liquid inside a thin glass tube and left to react. If the fibres did not match, they would disintegrate at different rates, but when Elliott returned to the laboratory the six strands were precisely the same length. The jury again convicted Van Beelen and he again appealed, but the Full Court with Chief Justice Bray presiding rejected an attempt to introduce new evidence.

In 1974 after a petition for mercy had been lodged with the Governor, Van Beelen again sought leave to appeal and came before the Full Court of the Supreme Court to argue that another man, known only as 'S', had murdered Deborah Leach. His lawyers claimed that 'S' had confessed to the crime before Van Beelen's arrest and that 'S', who limped, had been seen near the beach behaving oddly and with the legs of his trousers wet. Police who took the initial statement from 'S' had dismissed his evidence because he was mentally unstable and had a history of confessing; however, they had not informed the court. The appeal was refused on the grounds that it would be inadmissible as hearsay and, furthermore, that wet trouser bottoms were not sufficiently incriminating. But the case went on appeal to the High Court and subsequently to the Privy Council on the basis that the confession by 'S' should have been led during the trial.

In early 1975, Elliott left Adelaide for London and the Privy Council accompanied by Elizabeth and barrister Kevin Duggan, who was his junior.[11] The trip at taxpayers' expense was an enriching experience for Elliott, and he set up office in a beautiful room in the Privy Council on the corner of Whitehall and Downing Street.

11 Kevin Duggan became a Queen's Counsel in 1979 and a Justice of the South Australian Supreme Court in 1988.

On 11 March 1975, in line with Privy Council convention, Kevin Borick, who was counsel for the appellant, stood when the council was in session, announcing his presence and that of the counsel for the respondent, who was Elliott. In a long series of exchanges with a member of the Privy Council Lord Wilberforce, Borick made his case for special leave to appeal. The Privy Council then adjourned to discuss whether it would hear the appeal and returned to announce that it would not. Elliott dined out on the fact that, during his only appearance before the Privy Council in London, a legal rite of passage steeped in Dickensian ceremony and odd rituals that included giving money to an assistant tipstaff to secure a decent office, he did not say a word.

During the hearing, Elliott lodged at the Dukes Hotel in St James's Place, an historic hotel with suites named after various dukes. Duggan was nervous about the cost and when he mentioned it, Elliott offered to move out, but the South Australian Agent-General in London assured them that government people 'always stayed there'. For years after Elliott and Duggan addressed each other by the name of their suites; Elliott was the Duke of Cornwall, Duggan the Duke of Brunswick.

More than three decades later the Van Beelen case was still the subject of legal controversy. In 2001 an ABC *Four Corners* investigation into the work of South Australian forensic pathologist Dr Colin Manock cited it as controversial because it was the first in Australia to rely so heavily on forensic evidence. The timing of the murder of Deborah Leach, which had had to occur in a window of about 30 minutes before Van Beelen had picked up his wife from work, was called into question. In 1988 Ted Mullighan provided an opinion for the Legal Services Commission on the safety of the verdict after a woman had become suspicious that her former husband was the murderer. Mullighan found no credible new evidence that would exonerate Van Beelen or unsettle the jury's guilty verdict. Elliott, who rarely prosecuted for the Crown, privately believed that the test on the fibres placed Van Beelen's guilt beyond dispute.[12]

In 1971, not long after Withers had taken over Elliott's files,

12 Van Beelen had been convicted of a sexual offence at a neighbouring beach a year earlier but this was not admitted into evidence during the trial.

Elizabeth left to join the Crown Law Office. Dunstan had an ambitious reform agenda and Elizabeth saw a once-in-a-lifetime chance to participate in the overhaul of consumer protection, equal opportunity and anti-discrimination legislation, and Aboriginal land rights. Following her departure, the firm became Johnston & Partners for a time, then in 1975 changed to Johnston, Layton, Withers & Co., and in 1979 to Johnston Withers McCusker & Co. Two more of the core group around Elliott had joined in the 1970s; Peter McCusker in 1972, and Paul Heywood-Smith, an intellectual who was prone to radicalism on issues on which he held strong beliefs. Heywood-Smith had done articles with Johnston & Johnston before leaving for the United Kingdom to work in Westminster for a conservative legal practice and later a shipping firm. He returned to Adelaide in 1976. Elliott knew that Heywood-Smith had been arrested in Adelaide five years earlier during the Springboks protest and, as if this was the only credential a man needed, he welcomed him into the firm. Heywood-Smith had joined the Communist Party in the United Kingdom for a short time but was not a member in Australia.

Each member of the firm contributed colour and politics, and Elliott loved the atmosphere in the Carrington Street office, where drinks in the kitchen on the way to the car park after work became a daily ritual. Other colleagues and friends would drop in at the end of the day, including on occasions Jack Elliott, Roma Mitchell and John Bray. Elliott loved the friendships, the mentoring, the conversations, the stimulation, and the sheer pleasure of being part of a group of clever people who shared his broad vision.

The lawyers were not well paid, but there were huge fringe benefits. In the 1970s the firm bought Ormerod Cottages, four units in a heritage building on the Royal Circus in the seaside village of Robe overlooking Lake George. They leased out three of them and used the fourth to open an office in Robe. Everyone had a week away on rotation. 'We would take some files down and have a very pleasant week away. They were different days', said Withers.

They bought a boat at Goolwa to explore the Coorong and the lakes at the River Murray mouth. Elliott was as poor a sailor as he was a driver but he was enthusiastic. On a trip from Goolwa across the edge of Lake Alexandrina, Elliott, Heywood-Smith and the secretary of the United Firefighters Union, Mick Doyle (later a commissioner with the South Australian Industrial Commission) moored the boat outside Yabby City, a restaurant run by Coorong fisherman Henry Jones. Elliott leaped into the dinghy to take them to the shore, sunk it and sent them all into the water. They arrived for dinner dripping wet.

It was such a convivial time that Elliott would not have taken silk had he been required to leave it in order to join South Australia's new independent Bar. In 1964 a handful of lawyers, including Howard Zelling, Jack Elliott, Robin Millhouse and Chris Legoe, formed the South Australian Bar Association, an independent Bar of barristers who practised exclusively as counsel briefed by others.[13] It was the beginning of a tradition of specialised advocacy that became mandatory in 1979 when the Chief Justice, Len King, advised the President of the Law Society that all future Queen's Counsel would be required to leave private practice. That meant a firm like Elliott's with an in-house QC, who was both a lure for clients and a mentor to the younger lawyers, was being phased out. Elliott regretted the change and would have sacrificed silk if he had been forced to choose. 'I just loved the firm so much', he said.

His reputation attracted unusual clients. In 1973, the Paul Dainty Corporation brought The Rolling Stones to Australia on tour. Dainty was nervous about their reputation as drug-takers and sought legal help. The Stones' singer, Mick Jagger, had initially been banned from entering Australia because of previous drug convictions, but in the end the authorities had relented. Joe Cocker had been charged with drug offences in Australia only a few months before and Dainty wanted a lawyer to accompany The Stones on their Adelaide leg in case a legal problem arose. Layton, then 28, spent two days with them as they prepared for their concerts at Memorial Drive. She reported back that the problem was not the behaviour of the band but that of the roadies. Layton found Mick Jagger to be the brightest and most interesting of The Rolling Stones, who were disciplined, professional and well rehearsed. Jagger, in particular, kept himself very physically fit and was an athlete.

---

13 John Emerson, *History of the Independent Bar in South Australia*, University of Adelaide Barr Smith Press, Adelaide, 2006, p. 15.

Elliott's firm was also asked in the late 1970s to act for an Irish Republican militant, Philip McCullough, a friend of the IRA martyr Bobby Sands, who had been apprehended on a visa violation while fund-raising for the IRA in Australia. How he knew about Elliott was never quite clear, but when Peter McCusker went to the Adelaide City Watch House to see him, McCullough wanted Elliott Johnston. McCusker assured him he had been sent by Elliott and McCullough was mollified. He had been arrested for failing to disclose on his visa application a criminal record relating to an explosion in Belfast that had destroyed a telephone booth, and he was to be deported. McCusker secured his release from prison and McCullough spoke at a meeting of the Irish–Australian club in Adelaide before disappearing underground. He was smuggled out of Australia by an Irish network and put on a KLM flight to Amsterdam. Before leaving, he visited an Irish pub in Adelaide, the Brecknock Hotel in King William Street, where Elliott engaged him in a long and respectful discussion. Elliott told McCullough that he understood why the IRA was pursuing a military strategy, but that the problem only would ever be resolved through a political solution.

By far the greater number of the firm's clients were unions, who had sought Elliott out because of his success with Harry Krantz and the Clerks Union. In the 1970s the Amalgamated Metalworkers Union brought in a flow of workers' compensation and industrial work and Elliott passed most of it to the younger partners, McCusker, Withers and Layton. Lindy Powell was allocated the Moulders Union, a tough bunch of foundry workers with a reputation for stoicism. They were initially unimpressed with being traded down from Elliott to a young woman, but Powell was so obviously interested in the manufacturing process that their resistance crumbled. She loved getting to know them. 'No one could ever accuse a moulder of whingeing. They got a real injury. And even when they got a real injury they often didn't whinge', Powell said. When she moved house and asked the union if they could find her a mould for a tiered fountain, they offered her John Dowie's *Three Rivers*, a major centrepiece of public art in Adelaide's Victoria Square. 'Forget your front yard, how big's the back?' they asked. (She gratefully declined.)

Brian Withers generated the highest income of all the partners and cheerfully worked at the core union work and workers' compensation cases. The firm did not charge solicitor–client costs and took as payment the fees recovered from the insurers. Withers took over the Amalgamated Metal Workers and the Clerks unions from Elliott and represented hundreds of injured workers, many of them Italian and Greek. Work flowed through the door because of the firm's reputation as a friend of the Left and most of it was union-referred. By the 1980s the firm represented 19 unions, more than any other South Australian legal practice. 'There was no other firm that I know of in Australia with as many union clients and they were from the very Right-wing through to the extreme Maoists. We had the lot', McCusker said.

The office was a legal partnership but it had the character of a family practice, with Elliott as the wise patriarch. A client of Powell's who was angry about the way his insurance claim had been settled took to the streets wearing a sandwich board denouncing Powell as a running dog lackey in cahoots with the insurance company. Powell, young and inexperienced, was devastated to see him marching up and down in front of the Supreme Court defaming her in large print. Panicked, she raced in to see Elliott and asked him what to do. 'Any publicity is good publicity,' he said, 'now sit down'.

One of the hallmarks of the Dunstan decade was the emergence in Adelaide of a distinct restaurant culture, and restaurateur Barry Ross and chef Cheong Liew were experimenting with east–west fusion cuisine at Neddy's, around the corner from Carrington Street. The firm's lawyers would gather for Friday lunch in the old vine-covered courtyard and stay all afternoon, eating strange and exquisite food. Adelaide was being transformed, and the firm was in the thick of it. When Cheong Liew and Barry Ross asked Lindy Powell to incorporate their business, she named the trading company Chongo Bongo, in recognition of their hippy spirit.

Elliott was being briefed from outside as a QC but he helped the others when he could. A year after she joined, Lindy Powell had carriage of the case of a man arrested in Melbourne Street in North Adelaide for charging $1 to tell fortunes using tarot cards. He was convicted in the Magistrates Court but he appealed to the Supreme

Court. The case was argued on the question of whether 'pretending' to tell fortunes involved deliberate deceit. Powell researched the case back to fifteenth-century England and decided that, if the accused believed he could tell fortunes, it was not an offence. The client had no money but Elliott agreed that his firm would conduct an appeal. On Powell's second day in the Supreme Court, the door opened and Elliott came in. At that time one of Adelaide's best-known Queen's Counsel, Elliott had found out the night before that Powell was conducting a Full Court appeal on her own. He had come to court to be her clerk. He bowed to the Bench and sat down at the Bar table in the usual clerk's position, handing Powell books, smiling and offering nods of encouragement. Powell remembers a probing question from Chief Justice Bray that she began to answer one way, until Elliott gave her the thumbs down. 'On the other hand ...' she said, and Elliott's thumb shot up. 'The ridiculous thing was everybody in the court knew what was going on and everybody in the court maintained this wonderful façade that he was my clerk and he's giving me the nod about what I should and shouldn't do. It was so endearing', she said. The case was written up in the legal reports with comments from Chief Justice Bray that gave a warm nod of encouragement in her direction. 'It is only out of deference to the able and earnest arguments of Miss Powell, for the appellant, that I add a few words', the Chief Justice wrote.[14] The appeal was dismissed.

The firm's profits were allocated by Elliott, who presided over a modified Communist distribution model that took account of everyday bourgeois realities. If someone was cash-strapped because of a new mortgage, it would be considered at the partners' meetings, where profit shares were basically recommended by Elliott, and agreed to by the others. He divided the money according to their needs and no one complained because it was at his expense. 'Now,' he would say after announcing a proposed distribution, 'is everyone happy with that?' When Robyn Layton was pregnant, Elliott suggested she should continue to receive a share of the profit for two months after she had given birth. Paid maternity leave was unheard of at the time. His commitment to these ideals was so genuine that

14 *Hartridge v. Samuels* (1976) 14 SASR 209.

the arrangement did not trigger bad feeling. As Powell said: 'We all had a good income, we were happy with what we had. Working with the Johnstons was a lifestyle decision. So basically it was all a bit Communist and we accepted that.' After Elliott left the firm in 1983, modern accounting practices, client–solicitor costs and formal partnership agreements were put into place.

Elliott, who was aged 52 when he was appointed Queen's Counsel and 60 when the firm was in its heyday, still stood as a Communist candidate for elections, state and federal, and donated much of his money to the Communist Party of Australia. He knew he had no hope of winning a seat but he still wanted people to know what he and the Party stood for. Over the years his interests had widened and the single-minded service that had been the mark of his early years had mellowed as the promise of Communism withered.

Amateur football, in particular the South Australian National Football League (SANFL), was his other obsession. He was a lifelong supporter of the Sturt club, based at Unley Oval close to where he had grown up, and he followed its fluctuating fortunes week by week. He still attends Sturt's matches at Unley Oval with Withers and others. In the 1970s to his great pleasure, he was the prime source of legal advice for the state football code, headed for more than two decades by his old friend, lawyer Max Basheer. In 1978 Basheer was appointed Chairman of the SANFL, a post he held until 2003. Elliott was the league's principal counsel and advised it during club transfers, including the legal wrangle in the Federal Court over the transfer of the two Williams brothers (who later became Magpies coach Stephen Williams and AFL Port Power coach Mark Williams) from West Adelaide to Port Adelaide, where their father Fos Williams had played and coached.

A large part of his SANFL work in the 1970s was concerned with the construction of Football Park on part of the reclaimed swampland that had been developed into the suburb of West Lakes, behind the sand dunes at Tennyson. It was proposed that lights about 60 metres high be erected to allow games to be played at night. Their installation became a six-and-a-half year legal and political saga. The SANFL went to court after the City of Woodville Council withdrew permission for their installation. The dispute dragged on through a Royal Commission, with the first match under lights not played until 1984, a year after Elliott was appointed a judge.

In the mid-1970s Elliott represented a General Motors-Holden's (GM-H) employee in a case that became a watershed in protecting employees from unfair dismissal over their union activism. On 20 November 1974, union official Ted Gnatenko, who had ties to the Communist Party, was sacked by GM-H for misconduct after he had presided over a union meeting inside the plant at Elizabeth. At a meeting outside the factory following his sacking, Gnatenko urged the union not to strike on his behalf. He took action for unfair dismissal in the South Australian Industrial Court, with the proceedings issued by Elliott and Layton. GM-H countered in the Supreme Court. GM-H wanted the proceedings struck out because its workers were covered by a federal award, which, it argued, prevailed over the unfair dismissal protection offered by state legislation. After the Full Court of the Supreme Court had upheld the GM-H argument (and made an order for prohibition that stayed the proceedings Elliott had instituted), Elliott began proceedings in the Federal Industrial Commission. GM-H contended that the Federal Commission had no jurisdiction because Gnatenko's claim was not an interstate dispute.[15] Elliott argued that, if that were the case, GM-H could sack every union delegate in the country, provided they did so one at a time. The Commissioner attempted to mediate and asked the parties to confer in his chambers in private, and to abide by his decision. Elliott, who believed the decision could go either way, jumped at the chance, but GM-H refused. The Commissioner then amended the award retrospectively to provide that, where state legislation permitted proceedings to be instituted for unfair dismissal, those provisions could be applied to the federal award. The case, which ran for more than two years, descended into legal technicalities, but the issue remained very much alive. Gnatenko, an educated man with a good work record, would address unionists in four or five languages. He attended hearings flanked by supporters.

Back in the Supreme Court, Elliott sought a stay of the earlier order, which had not yet been made effective by a sealed order of

---

15 *R v. Industrial Court of South Australia; ex parte General Motors-Holden Pty Ltd* (1975) 10 SASR 582.

the court. The Full Court held that it should set aside its earlier order for prohibition. Meanwhile, GM-H had lodged an appeal to the High Court and to the Full Industrial Court against the retrospectivity of the Commissioner's amendment. Elliott was unable to appear in the High Court appeal and Ted Laurie came from Victoria to take the case, with Layton as his junior. Laurie endured relentless questioning and challenges from the Chief Justice, Sir Garfield Barwick, and Layton, dispirited, reported to Elliott that they were likely to lose. She was wrong. The High Court dismissed the GM-H appeal in a vote of six to one, with only Chief Justice Barwick dissenting.[16]

The final hurdle was the Full Industrial Court, where Elliott felt on shaky ground. GM-H argued convincingly against the principle of retrospectivity but Elliott faced the attack head on. He explained to the court why the Federal Industrial Commission had felt that this exception was justified, and the court agreed. It taught him a lesson: get the weakness in your argument out into the open and deal with it. With the amendment shored up, the Full Court of the Supreme Court, which had held over its orders awaiting the Full Industrial Court decision, dismissed the application for orders and Gnatenko was able to return to the Industrial Court, where GM-H was ordered to re-employ him. The case was of great significance to the ordinary worker and unions became better informed about their rights.

Elliott continued to push incrementally the standards of protection and compensation that injured workers could expect. He challenged the unwritten belief that injury in the workplace was unavoidable in some jobs and that the responsibility for avoiding accidents was too amorphous to be legally defined. He would sit with the other lawyers in the kitchen at the end of the day, deciding which cases would best test these assumptions. The High Court's readiness to hear such arguments was indicated by Justice Lionel Murphy, who said as much in the case of *Raimondo v. State of South Australia*.[17] Raimondo, an experienced painter, was injured while painting the ceiling at Hillcrest Hospital. A plank had fallen from two supporting trestles on his head. He was awarded $95,873 in

---

16 *R. v. Clarkson; ex parte General Motors-Holden Pty Ltd.* (1975) 134 CLR 56.

17 *Raimondo v. State of South Australia* (1979) 23 ALR 513.

damages, which were halved because of contributory negligence on his part. The employer successfully appealed to the Full Court. Raimondo appealed to the High Court but failed. In his dissenting judgment, Justice Murphy condemned Australia's industrial safety record as poor by international standards and in need of upgrading. He lamented the current practice that allowed employers not to be in breach of their common law duty when their employees followed unsafe practices. 'Acceptance of this contention represents a lowering of what seems to me to have been the previously accepted common law standard', Justice Murphy commented.[18]

In 1977 Elliott had pursued a work injury case against agricultural machinery company, John Shearer Ltd. A Sicilian factory welder had injured his back trying to lift a heavy trestle that had one leg stuck to the floor. When the trial judge found John Shearer not to be liable, Elliott took the case on appeal to the Full Court of the Supreme Court, which heard Elliott's argument that the trestle had sunk into the tar on the foundry floor, making it more difficult to lift. The court, headed by Justice Zelling, held that the worker was exposed to unreasonable risk because the employer knew the tendency of trestle legs to become embedded in the tar on the floor.[19]

Another back injury case defined the higher duty of care employers owed to their workers. In April 1978 a welder named Turner was repairing the damaged jetty at Wallaroo, a grain port on South Australia's Yorke Peninsula. The welder was using a generator driven by a diesel engine that ran out of fuel while he was on scaffolding, 18 metres above the jetty. Annoyed, the welder climbed down and tried to lift a 44-gallon drum of fuel that was lying on its side. In doing so he badly hurt his back. Elliott's claim against the employer, the South Australian Department of Marine and Harbours, was that there was no work safety practice covering what the welder should have done and no warning against lifting the heavy drum. While a single judge of the Supreme Court found the department guilty of negligence, the Full Court upheld the department's appeal. On Elliott's advice, Turner appealed to the High Court, which in 1982 handed down a judgment defining the duty

18 ibid., at 521.

19 *Crisa v. John Shearer Limited* (1980) 27 SASR 422.

of employers to take reasonable care to avoid exposing an employee to unnecessary risk of injury. This included the risk that injury may occur through inattention or misjudgment by the employee while performing the allotted task.[20]

The decision flowed into the workplace in the form of pre-emptive action by employers and their insurers, who began to realise that planning for work safety was their concern. Nurses working with geriatric patients and in nursing homes were trained to use lifting devices, as hospitals sought to minimise the risk of back injury, and in factories forklifts became more widespread. Mechanical devices and other protections were used to minimise exposure to legal liability. It was a fundamental concept that was finally being recognised because Elliott had pursued it. The way he put it to the court, protecting a worker from injury was the right and sensible thing to do.

One winter's day in June 1979 Elliott ran into a good friend and fellow lawyer Derrance Stevenson in the Supreme Court library. Stevenson, who had juniored Elliott in the murder trial following the discovery of a body at Trigg Beach, near Moana, was a witty, elegant and attractive man who wore an earring in his left ear and an extravagant opal ring. He was a homosexual who led a colourful private life that included a sexual relationship with David Szach who was 25 years younger. Two days after Elliott had chatted with Stevenson in the Supreme Court library, Stevenson, then 44 years old, was violently murdered at his modernist, architect-designed home and office on the southern edge of the city.[21] His body was found face down in a large chest freezer with a basket of frozen food above his head and bags of frozen food on his buttocks and lower back. The freezer lid had been glued shut and detectives had to force it open. An autopsy report found Stevenson had been shot in the back of the head with a .22 calibre rifle.

The next day Szach, whom Stevenson had brought home for sex three years earlier when Szach was 16, was arrested in Coober Pedy, 940 kilometres north of Adelaide, and charged with murder. Szach had inexplicably gone to the police station at Coober Pedy to ask about his missing friend. 'I have a homosexual relationship with

20 *Turner v. State of South Australia* (1982) 42 ALR 669.

21 The building, with a landmark inverted roof, was demolished in 2008.

Derrance and he's missing, and he's the only person in the world I have and I want you to find him', he told Coober Pedy police. Szach was driving Stevenson's 260Z red Datsun car and a unique opal that belonged to Stevenson was in his possession, as were a briefcase and glasses that Stevenson used for outdoor vision. While Szach said he had left Stevenson's home at no later than 6 pm the previous night, an accountant who worked nearby gave evidence that he had seen Szach leave, wearing glasses, at 6.40 pm. Szach gave differing accounts of his movements, altered the times and made an unsworn statement that he had returned to the house at 8 pm and had left half an hour later without seeing anyone. Witnesses put him at Port Wakefield just after midnight and at Coober Pedy by 10 am. It emerged that Stevenson had informed Szach a day earlier that their relationship was over and he had bought him a bus ticket to Coober Pedy, which Szach had cashed in.

Szach pleaded not guilty and it was a case few lawyers wanted to touch. Stevenson's trial would attract media attention and there was a natural repugnance among lawyers to defend someone accused of murdering one of their own. Elliott took the case. He did so without considering Szach's possible guilt, even though he was a personal friend of the victim. 'Really, you just take the case and defend the person as best you can', he said. He argued unsuccessfully at the trial that the conversation Szach had with the police in Coober Pedy was inadmissible because the police had failed to tell Szach that a body thought to be Stevenson's had already been found in the freezer. Elliott also introduced evidence about an unidentified man who had gone to the offices of the Legal Services Commission the morning after the murder. He wanted help and asked twice if anything he said would remain confidential. He mentioned Stevenson and said, 'When I left him last night, he was in no condition to act for anyone'. The man was never heard from again but Elliott called the Legal Services Commission officer as a witness.

Elliott attempted to convince the jury there were too many mysteries for a conclusive finding of guilt. But Szach, who still protested his innocence 30 years later, was convicted and gaoled for 14 years. Szach appealed against his conviction, but the appeal was dismissed. As with the Van Beelen trial, the timing of Stevenson's death relied on scientific evidence from forensic pathologist Dr Colin Manock, whose reliability was later questioned. In March 2007 a Family First member of the South Australian Parliament, Dennis Hood, said Dr Manock's handling of the Stevenson case had become an issue and asked the Attorney-General, Michael Atkinson, to re-open the Szach case. The request was refused, as was a similar request in 1995. Szach, who in his forties fell ill with motor neurone disease, argued in 2007 that he was a victim of a miscarriage of justice and that he had not been involved in Stevenson's murder. 'Personally, I doubt that', said Elliott, who privately believed that the motive was Stevenson telling Szach their affair was over.

Elliott headed a busy law firm, but his habit of working for little and committing others in the firm to do the same prevented him from being well off, let alone rich. The beautiful dinner plates and antique furniture at the Johnston home in Gilles Street were from the Teesdale Smith side of the family, not acquisitions of the Johnston marriage, and in the early days ASIO singled out for mention the poor-quality furnishings in the Johnstons' house, where the sofa had protruding springs. In the early 1970s Elliott and Elizabeth had moved from Crafers, a suburb in the Adelaide Hills, and rented a property in Rose Street at Wayville before buying Gilles Street in the city, and moving there in August 1972.

He was still a serious and committed Communist and worked with humility and purpose for a Party that was divided and in decline. In 1971 when the Communist Party had to move out of the People's Bookshop at 180 Hindley Street, Elliott loaned the $500 deposit needed to secure the purchase of 27 Wright Court, its new headquarters. He steered the sale through and advised them on obtaining a bank overdraft.

In the 1980 federal election, Elliott stood again for the seat of Port Adelaide, where Mick Young, later a minister in the Hawke Cabinet, was the sitting member. Long-haired, coat tossed over one shoulder and with a Communist agenda updated to include multiculturalism, the liberation of women ('sexual and economic equality for women and homosexuals'), a nuclear-free future and the removal of foreign bases like Pine Gap from Australia, Elliott gamely took on the Fraser Government.[22] By then the Communist Party of

---

[22] J. Wishart, *Let's Get Rid of Fraser,* Communist Party of Australia pamphlet,

Australia was staggering along, beaten and bloodied after the forced reappraisal of Soviet Russia, the split in allegiances between China and the Soviet Union, and the final blow of the 1968 Warsaw Pact invasion of Czechoslovakia. In a speech during the campaign he revealed the depth of his continuing commitment to the Party and what it still meant to him. Tonight was not the night to talk about the past but about the present, he said during a 30-minute speech. He acknowledged that there was no worthy model for socialism, not Cuba, not China, and not Russia. Echoing a belief that first emerged in China 25 years earlier, Elliott explained that every country had to find its own way, according to its own circumstances and traditions. He was much more emphatic now about how Communism had to let the light of democracy shine in. 'Experience teaches us that it must never be overlooked that socialism means human liberation. It is inconsistent with the repression of ideas or the right to express ideas, or the right to organise to promote ideas', he said. Capitalism's grip could only be prised open at the ballot box, by a majority movement, which knew what was at stake. 'We realise of course that in the struggle the established classes will resort to every sort of tactic', he said in reference to the dismissal of the Whitlam Labor Government five years earlier by the Governor-General. 'But we are convinced that no model of socialism which does not include a dedication to personal freedom will ever inspire the Australian people to battle for it.'[23]

The only career progression left was an appointment to the Bench, but after the imbroglio that his appointment as Queen's Counsel had prompted, an invitation seemed unlikely. Apart from his politics, Elliott did not believe he was eligible because he had limited experience in commercial representation. Nothing stood in the way of his taking on big commercial cases but he was rarely asked, and he avoided some cases on principle. 'I never took a case against a worker acting for an employer, if it was a matter involving his work', he said. But he was open to anything else he found interesting, and in the 1970s his load of commercial briefs had increased, although with some wariness on the side of big business. A solicitor

---

Adelaide, 1980.

23 Elliott Johnston private papers.

he knew rang him in the early 1970s and hinted that a brief was in the offing but he must first be 'looked over'. Amused rather than offended, Elliott attended a lunch and heard later he had passed the test. He was subsequently briefed in *August Investments Pty Ltd v. Poseidon Ltd and Samin Ltd*, appearing for Samin. Poseidon was a well-known South Australian mining company with nickel interests in Western Australia, and the case involved a purported takeover of Samin by Poseidon. The offer was to exchange two fully paid shares in Poseidon in return for 15 fully paid shares in Samin. August Investments applied for an injunction to restrain Poseidon from proceeding with the takeover scheme on the ground that, if carried out, it would amount to a reduction in the capital of Poseidon in a manner not authorised by the companies' legislation of the day. The trial judge refused to grant an injunction, a decision upheld on appeal by the Full Court. The High Court refused leave to appeal.

Two years later Elliott again had his credentials quietly looked over before he was briefed. The company in this case was the Melbourne-based Myer group and Elliott represented it between 1973 and 1975 in a dispute over an application to build a shopping centre at Queenstown, near Port Adelaide. In June 1972, Port Adelaide Council had granted Myer planning approval to develop a regional shopping centre on land at Queenstown. In the meantime, the South Australian Government had enacted planning Regulations that effectively prevented the development. Later, in October 1973, the council again granted planning approval for the proposed development. A key element of the case was the complex issue of whether the Regulations had been validly made.[24] Myer was eventually allowed to proceed but the delay had been so long and costly that the shopping centre was never built. Elliott later learnt that the briefing solicitor had rung Myer in Melbourne to warn them of his Communist connections. It was one of the longest cases he did.

In 1979 Elliott worked closely with the politically conservative Mount Gambier trucking magnate Allan Scott, who showed no apparent reluctance to hire a Communist Queen's Counsel. While on holiday in Italy with Elizabeth, Elliott received a call requesting

---

24 *Myer Queenstown Garden Plaza Pty Ltd. v. Corporation of City of Port Adelaide and the Attorney-General* (1975) 11 SASR 504.

that he act for Scott against the Bank of Adelaide. Scott, who died in 2008 and was one of South Australia's richest men, was the fourth largest shareholder in the bank. The bank was in financial trouble because of poorly judged real estate investments in Queensland made by its subsidiary, Finance Corporation of Australia. The ANZ Bank proposed an effective takeover structured in an arrangement that avoided the provisions of the Takeovers Code, although it required the approval of the Supreme Court. Scott objected. He wanted the Bank of Adelaide, a pillar of the Adelaide establishment, to remain independent, and Elliott, with corporate lawyer Tony Johnson, went to court on his behalf to argue that the strict provisions of the Takeovers Code should apply.

In an act of brinkmanship, the ANZ notified the court that, if the arrangement was not approved by a certain date, its offer would be withdrawn. Elliott, Tony Johnson and Allan Scott were summoned to see the Liberal Premier, David Tonkin, and his Cabinet. They heard, in effect, that if the ANZ withdrew, there was a likelihood of a run on the Bank of Adelaide. No one was convinced this was true, but the risk of being wrong was too great and Scott withdrew his objections and allowed the ANZ to take control.

Elliott's name had become well known nationally in the 1970s through his prosecution of Medicare fraud. The Commonwealth Attorney-General instructed Elliott to prosecute some of the early cases against South Australian doctors charged with exploiting the new universal health system. It was very public work and the case of the Adelaide doctor who was convicted of 119 counts of Medicare abuse was widely reported. A government scheme that promised everyone high-quality health care resonated with Elliott's core beliefs and its abuse was abhorrent to him. Ted Mullighan, who defended one of the accused doctors, found Elliott unusually determined in the way he prosecuted those accused of Medicare fraud. Elliott had a sense of moral outrage over their conduct; he thought what they did was plainly wrong.

Had he not been a Communist, it is almost certain Elliott would have been called to the Bench any time from the mid-1970s. Peter Duncan, the Attorney-General in the Dunstan Government after Len King had been appointed to the Supreme Court, discussed with Dunstan and other ministers Elliott's possible inclusion on the Bench. Duncan, who was South Australia's youngest minister at the age of 28, discovered that Dunstan, who was ready to defy convention in other ways, was not prepared to put Elliott on the Bench, ostensibly because he lacked experience in the commercial area. However, Len King said that Elliott was ruled out by Dunstan because he was a Communist. King, who was Attorney-General from 1970 until 1975, decided with Dunstan soon after Elliott took silk that his politics disqualified him from higher office. 'Dunstan and I both agreed in 1970 that whilst it was appropriate, and in fact justice required, that Elliott be appointed a Queen's Counsel, in view of the Communist Party's attitude to changing the legal order by other than constitutional means, it was not appropriate for that Party to exercise the authority of the state as a judge. That was talked about in 1970 and nobody ever suggested that Elliott should be appointed while I was Attorney-General', Len King said.

King thought that Dunstan's prime concern was avoiding another public backlash, but Dunstan's aversion to Communism went deeper. Dunstan had fallen short of supporting the idea of a Communist judge when argument raged in Parliament over Elliott's future as a Queen's Counsel, drawing scathing comment from Steele Hall. During his television appearance with Hall, Dunstan was also reluctant to contemplate Elliott's making the leap from Queen's Counsel to judge. 'Look here, this is a matter of Queen's Counsel', Dunstan had said to Hall. 'What could he do as Queen's Counsel? What could he do? Use the Bar as a barricade?'

In fact Dunstan had declared himself an enemy of Communism at the outset of his political career. In 1953 the young endorsed Labor candidate for Norwood promoted himself in a campaign leaflet as an 'Anti-Communist Unionist' who had wrested the South Australian chapter of Actors and Announcers Equity from Communist control.[25] Once in office and confronted by the reality of putting Elliott on the Bench, Dunstan encountered the limits of his own willingness to flout convention. The lingering remnants of anti-Communist prejudice held him back. Elliott would not become a judge during the Dunstan decade.

25 Don Dunstan, 'Don Dunstan: Your endorsed Labor candidate for Norwood', South Australian State election pamphlet, ALP, Adelaide, 1953.

CHAPTER 8

Justice Elliott Johnston

In the late 1970s Elliott shored up his credentials as a labour hero with an electoral challenge that restored Dunstan's seat of Norwood to the Australian Labor Party. In the 1979 election (which was lost by Dunstan's successor, Des Corcoran) Labor's Greg Crafter was defeated by a handful of votes. Crafter, who had won the seat six months earlier in a by-election after Dunstan had resigned, wanted to challenge the result on the basis of irregularities that included an advertisement placed by his rival, Liberal candidate Frank Webster, in an Italian newspaper. Webster, his hair styled like Dunstan's, appeared under the heading '*il vostro deputato*', which meant, 'I am your representative'. Crafter, a lawyer, considered this to be defamatory, but he had to cast doubt over a sufficient number of votes to change the result before a challenge could proceed.

The South Australian branch of the Australian Labor Party asked Elliott to prepare a claim and lodge a petition. But the legal argument was not clear cut and the state ALP executive feared the potentially ruinous effect of costs. One of the partners, Peter McCusker, and Elliott visited ALP headquarters, where Elliott indicated that, in his view, there was some likelihood of winning. 'If that's your view Boss, that's good enough for me', said Deputy Opposition Leader, Jack Wright, and walked out of the room.

It was a tough case and Crafter would join Elliott at Carrington Street with McCusker, junior barrister John Doyle, a young lawyer Ann McLean, Kathleen McEvoy from the University of Adelaide Law School and a handful of volunteers. They worked long into the night to prepare for the trial in the Court of Disputed Returns, but two weeks before it was due to begin, Elliott withdrew. The Derrance Stevenson trial needed his full attention. At late notice, he asked Ted Mullighan QC, to take the brief, and Mullighan appeared with Doyle (who later became South Australian Chief Justice) as his junior. In the trial heard by Justice Roma Mitchell, at least 80 votes were found to be in doubt, more than enough to justify the proceedings, and she found that the words, '*il vostro deputato*' only could mean 'your member of Parliament' and that they had defamed Crafter. The decision led to a second by-election, which Crafter won by 800 votes.

During the six months Corcoran was in power, Elliott's candidature for the Supreme Court had again been canvassed at Cabinet level. The then Attorney-General, Chris Sumner, had asked about Cabinet's attitude towards appointing Elliott. Sumner, who was a close friend of Robyn Layton and John Bannon from Adelaide University days, said that the Corcoran Cabinet did not have the stomach for it. He raised it informally but in a serious context and was told 'it just wasn't on'.

Elliott's standing only continued to rise. He had contributed to the development of the profession, which stood him in good stead for appointment to the Bench. In the mid-1970s, he had founded the Australian Society of Labor Lawyers with Sumner, Victorian lawyer Gareth Evans, and Jesuit priest and lawyer Father Frank Brennan. It provided a forum for lawyers committed to working-class values and progressive movements and was dedicated to legislative and other reforms.[1] In 1971, Elliott was also a founding member and the first chair of the Aboriginal Legal Rights Movement in South Australia, and he was active in the South Australian Law Society, where he sat on the newly established Criminal Law Sub-Committee. He chaired this committee in the late 1970s and presided over discussions about criminal law, including the divisive issue of whether a man could be guilty of rape if the woman was his wife. In 1982 the Legal Practitioners Disciplinary Tribunal was established and Elliott, the senior barrister, was the chairman.

---

1 Sumner recalled protracted debate between Gareth Evans and Elliott over whether to call the new organisation the Society of Labor Lawyers or the Society of Labour Lawyers. Elliott wanted Labour Lawyers because it defined it as separate from the ALP. Both won, with the South Australian body using Labour, while nationally it was Labor.

Elliott never intended to become a judge. He felt useful where he was, a servant of the working classes at the Bar, who would accept a bottle of whisky in lieu of payment. He took cases that cemented his position as a guardian of the Left. Aged in his 60s, he still was making his mark. In April 1983 he obtained a judgment that clarified the obligation of doctors to inform patients of the likely effectiveness of medical procedures.[2] Elliott represented a young woman who had undergone a tubal ligation at the same time as she gave birth by Caesarean section. She asked whether her husband should have a vasectomy, but was told there was no need. Two years later she had another child and sued for negligence on the ground that her doctor had failed to warn her that the operation of tubal ligation might not fully protect her from becoming pregnant again. She won in a decision that went on appeal to the Full Court headed by Len King. While the case went against her, the judges set out the responsibility of doctors to inform patients of known risks. It sent a message to the medical community that they could not 'play God' in deciding what their patients should be told.

One of Elliott's last cases was among his most significant. This was the High Court decision in *Commercial Bank of Australia Ltd v. Amadio*, a decision which forced banks to behave more ethically in the future management of mortgages. It involved two Italian migrants aged in their 70s whose son, Vincenzo Amadio, ran a troubled building company. The company was insolvent, but the Commercial Bank of Australia allowed it to maintain the appearance of liquidity by selectively honouring cheques until March 1977, when it closed the account. Later that month, the account was re-opened and the overdraft limit lifted to $270,000 to allow Amadio to clear the debt. The account was to be secured by a mortgage over the house owned by Amadio's parents, who were elderly Italian migrants with a limited understanding of written English. Amadio told his parents that the mortgage was for $50,000 and would last for six months. However, the Commercial Bank had drawn up a deed that included a guarantee securing all the company's current and future debt against the house. The branch manager went to the parents' home to have the mortgage signed and the father men-

2 *F v. R* (1983) 33 SASR 189.

tioned his belief that it was only for six months. The bank went ahead, knowing the family was being misled and had received no independent advice.

Amadio's company went into liquidation owing $239,000 and the bank demanded its money from the elderly Amadios, who sued on the ground that the bank had acted unconscionably. The bank succeeded before a judge of the Supreme Court of South Australia but the Amadios appealed to the Full Court of South Australia, and won. The bank appealed to the High Court, where Elliott argued that it had taken advantage of the couple's limited understanding of written English and their reliance on their son.

The High Court agreed and set aside the mortgage agreement, removing the couple's liability for their son's debt.[3] The judgment was broad enough to put the banking community on notice and it became mandatory for mortgagees to have access to independent advice. Elliott did not know the Amadios. He argued the case on appeal but he was passionate about a principle of fair dealing being established. 'Look, this is an important matter', he had blurted out to the Full Court in an emotional outburst that nailed the Bank's unethical conduct. 'These people didn't know the Bank had mortgaged their house to that amount and the manager of the branch went to their house and sat there with them while they signed it, without saying anything.' This was one of the last, most interesting and most important cases that Elliott had argued. Twenty-five years later the Chief Justice of the High Court, Murray Gleeson, cited the Amadio case as one of the landmarks in equity jurisprudence.[4]

In 1982 when John Bannon, who had been a minister at the tail end of the Dunstan years, swept into office, Sumner again put Elliott's name forward as the state's most senior silk. 'He really was the de facto leader of the Bar, the senior statesman who was older than some of the others. South Australia is not a big place, so when you were looking at any appointment on merit, there were only a certain number of people who qualified. Elliott was top of the list', Sumner said. This time, the response in Cabinet was warm.

---

3 *Commercial Bank of Australia Ltd v. Amadio* (1983) 151 CLR 447.

4 Murray Gleeson, *Australia's Contribution to Common Law*, Singapore Academy of Law, September, 2007.

Support was not unanimous, but there were no strong objections and the Chief Justice, Len King, also endorsed it. Bannon was keen to have Elliott as a judge and his only reservation was the wisdom of appointing him so late in his career. 'We felt he was totally qualified and should have been made judge years ago, under Dunstan. Chris [Sumner] was confident there was no question he would take up the opportunity and that really should be the end of the matter. So in the end it was "let's get on with it, let's get four good years out of him" ', Bannon said.

Supreme Court justices were entitled to a pension after five years service and Elliott was appointed in June 1983, aged 65. His birthday was in February, which meant he would reach the mandatory retirement age of 70 a few months short of qualifying for a pension. Bannon confirmed that Cabinet at least discussed paying a pension or an ex gratia payment to Elliott so that he was not disadvantaged in relation to other judges. 'I think the argument very reasonably was that normally a judge would be appointed with much more than five years to go, so it was an unusual situation. In Elliott's case, he had not been considered for political reasons, not because of the legal and judicial situation. We weren't sure how we would tackle it but we were prepared to discuss or negotiate that because we did not want it to be a barrier to him accepting the position', Bannon said.

Elliott took the phone call from Sumner inviting him onto the Bench while he was in Canberra, where the Commonwealth was briefing him over the prosecution of the pathology company, Gribbles, for an alleged breach of Medicare. In Adelaide the next day, Sumner asked if Elliott would like him to look into an arrangement that would allow a pension to be paid. Elliott shook his head and said it was not the proper thing to do and never mentioned it again. With retirement looming, and having parted with large amounts of money and foregone others, Elliott lacked the sense of personal entitlement that drove many others. He agreed to consider the Bench. More than a week later, Sumner ran into Elizabeth in the foyer of the State Government Insurance Commission (SGIC) building on the corner of Wakefield Street and Victoria Square. He asked whether Elliott had made up his mind yet. Elizabeth, who was working with the Crown Law Office, shook her head in exasperation. She told him she was sick of it and wished he would decide.

Elliott would be the first Communist appointed to such high office. He never had believed such an honour would be his. Now it had been offered, he was in torment over whether to accept. He was still first and foremost a Communist and he would have to resign from the Party. He had given to the Communist cause physically, financially, socially and intellectually for more than 40 years, as had Elizabeth. He had stood for political office about a dozen times; he had served for 27 years on the state executive and had chaired the South Australian committee from 1970 until 1975. He had attended every national conference from 1948 until 1976 (except while in China) and he had been a delegate to the national conference from 1946 until 1974. He was on the national executive from 1970 to 1974 and he had campaigned as a Communist candidate, attacking the Fraser Government just three years earlier. However, he also appreciated that his appointment was historic, and that it would enhance the Party's status in the eyes of the community. He knew it would be of advantage to the Party if a long-standing member could achieve something as a judge.

It was important to Elliott that he was not being forced to give up his politics because he was a Communist. Political neutrality was a prerequisite for all judicial appointments and it would have been the same had he been a Liberal. 'On appointment, a judge must sever any association with any political group because you must be seen to be impartial. Whether they are or not is another matter, but they must be prepared to be', said Sam Jacobs QC, a former acting Chief Justice who in 2001–02, with other retired judges, had written a book on codes of judicial behaviour.

Some time later Elliott rang Sumner and accepted. He was the first member of the Communist Party of Australia to take silk and he was now the first to become a judge. Elliott told his law partners, none of whom was surprised. He hated leaving the firm, which was now called Johnston Withers. Jack Lewis was long gone and in 1978 Robyn Layton had joined the Industrial Court, aged 33. The strength of the firm was Brian Withers, Lindy Powell, Peter McCusker, Paul Heywood-Smith and Andrew Collett, a lawyer with a background in Aboriginal affairs who was articled to the firm in 1976 after opening country offices for the Aboriginal Legal Rights Movement at Port Augusta. In 1982 Ann McLean and Carmel Kerin were invited to become partners and were appointed just after Elliott left.

While it may not have felt so to Elliott, it was a good time to move on. Adelaide was changing and a burst of modernity was gathering pace. Lawyers like Powell, who had once relied on him, were now successful solo practitioners. Elliott was engrossed in briefs from outside the firm and it was getting harder to see him. What had been a joyful and collaborative workplace was naturally starting to splinter. Elliott was already past normal retirement age and there were small signs that he was losing his touch. During a trial in 1983, he made inappropriate remarks to a jury. 'As for [the prosecution] evidence, I suggest to you that is a lot of crap', he told the jurors, attempting to speak a language they understood. Called to account over lunch, he returned and amended the record, apologising for using what he called 'an un-Parliamentary expression'. 'Actually, what I meant to say was that the evidence lacked cogency', he explained. It was an amusing anecdote that was mentioned at his farewell, but it had caused private consternation.

The courtroom was also changing around him. Elliott's style was ponderous and long winded. He was not a great rhetorician; he was a debater and a clear but complex thinker who would ask tangential questions that showed a sublime disregard for the patience of others. During the Van Beelen trial he asked a single question that covered a page-and-a-half of court transcript, canvassing every scenario and locking in a long string of assumptions before reaching the question. The bewildered witness asked him to repeat it. He was comfortable with silence and would deliberate on his feet, the clock slowly ticking as the questions took form. But courtrooms were becoming more technologically complex, and pressures of time and money were stripping them of colour. The old style of courtroom theatre with its codified courtesies and small amusements was being phased out. A good advocate still had to be commanding, but more was at stake. Costs spiralled as firms adopted strict business models and billed in blocks of minutes. Marketing and business development specialists were brought in to plan corporate strategies. None of this meant much to Elliott but the lure of lifestyle and Left-wing causes might not have kept Johnston Withers afloat.

On 30 June 1983, before the Full Court of the Supreme Court and wearing a horsehair wig borrowed the night before from John Bray, Elliott joined the Bench. Lindy Powell and Brian Withers convulsed with laughter as they saw Elliott drive out of the car park at the back of 345 Carrington Street on his way to the Supreme Court. Reversing out, he hit the gatepost on the left and, straightening up, hit the post on the right. Then he straightened up again and gave the left post a final nudge before negotiating the exit. Powell looked at him and thought – apart from the fact that he was a terrible driver – that it was symbolic of him wanting to go, yet not wanting to.

He had already farewelled the Communist Party in a letter in which he said the very thought of resigning from the Party brought him 'much mental and emotional upset'. But he accepted it had to be. He told the Party his central reason for becoming a judge was because Communists had to be seen to take up all positions in society and to occupy them responsibly. 'It is my dearest wish that my discharge of the office will bring credit to the movement which has, for more than forty years, shaped and taught me', he wrote.[5] He made special mention of the pleasure he had in participating in a recent case that had cleared the Communist Party of Australia of the slur of being a subversive organisation.

In 1981 Stephen Rix, a young Communist working in the Department of Trade and Resources in Canberra, had been refused an ASIO security clearance. A young Catholic from a social justice background, he had joined the Party a year earlier. ASIO claimed the Party was a subversive organisation under the meaning of the legislation. Elliott conducted Rix's appeal to the Security Appeals Tribunal against ASIO, which did not have to appear. Still cloaked in secrecy, ASIO was given a separate hearing before the tribunal, headed by a Justice of the New South Wales Supreme Court, Gordon Samuels. Against this invisible opponent, Elliott called as a witness the former Party secretary Eric Aarons, who took over as secretary after his brother Laurie retired in 1976. Aarons gave evidence that the Australian party was independent of China and

5 Elliott Johnston, letter of resignation, *Tribune*, 6 July 1983.

Moscow, and believed in democracy, not revolution. The tribunal believed him and declared the Communist Party of Australia was not subversive within the meaning of the *Australian Security Intelligence Organisation Act, 1979.* It said the use of the word 'revolutionary' did not imply violence and, as Elliott long had argued, the Party was not tied to Moscow. 'The CPA is regarded as pursuing an independent line internationally. It maintains fraternal links with Communist or Marxist parties overseas but there is no evidence that at this time it is subject to influence or direction by, for example, the Communist Party of the Soviet Union', the tribunal found.[6] It was an exceptionally sweet victory.

When Elliott presented his commission to the Supreme Court the language of the other speakers was warm and genuine. Attorney-General Sumner praised Elliott's willingness to take on difficult cases, and for treating his clients with humanity. He described Elliott as the undisputed leader of the Bar, a lawyer who had defended working-class rights and who was a leading barrister in criminal law and murder trials. He noted that Elliott had acted for the Myer Corporation and for Allan Scott, and, in 1980, had delivered a textbook exposition on the fair and accurate report of judicial proceedings. (He had won a libel action for a man who was denounced as 'an animal' in a 1977 report in the *Truth* newspaper headed 'Woman – My Rape Ordeal', which was based on details of allegations of which the man had already been acquitted.[7]) Sumner told the court that when the High Court last sat in South Australia, Elliott held five of the short list of briefs. Two were for employer negligence, one was for damages in a building matter, the fourth was a point of criminal law arising from the acceptance of statements by accused persons, and the fifth led to the ruling on the bank's duty of disclosure in the *Amadio* case. In recognition of Elliott's private struggle, Sumner paid tribute to the sacrifice Elliott was making in leaving the Communist Party. 'I appreciate, and the Government greatly appreciates, that your decision to accept probably confronted you with certain dilemmas', he said. He also drew attention to the absence of notoriety attached to his appointment.

---

6 As reported in *Tribune*, 22 June 1983.

7 *Bunker v. James and Downland Publications Ltd* (1980) 26 SASR 286.

'The overwhelming support which your appointment has received, particularly from the legal profession, but also I believe from the South Australian community, has been a source of satisfaction to me, as I am sure it has been to you', he said.

Elliott's responded gallantly. There seemed to be no point, he said, in trying to do what John Bray had told him to, which was to say he was unworthy but would do his best. 'It seemed to me that my unworthiness was such a well-advertised fact it hardly needed my recommendations, as it were, and that one will do one's best has long been regarded, and correctly been regarded by lawyers as the weakest of all possible guarantees', he said. He thanked everyone, from the court staff, to Elizabeth and Stewart, and his late father-in-law Paul Teesdale Smith, a former Deputy Coroner. He thanked his law partners for their wit, their compassion and their 'stead-fast and unwavering rejection of any connection between wisdom and age'. He also paid tribute to the Aboriginal community from whom he had learnt much. He spoke of the pain of leaving not just the Communist Party of Australia but also the labour movement, and thanked all of them, including his former fellow Communists, directly from the Bench: 'The taking of a step which was inevitably followed by other steps, by the severing of relationships which long had existed was a very serious step for me and caused me a good deal of heartburn. I want to express to the members of the Party from which I have just resigned, and to wider sections of the labour movement, my profound thanks for what they have contributed to the shaping of my ideas and to my life.'

At the conclusion of his remarks, the Court filed out. They were acting Chief Justice Roma Mitchell and fellow justices Howard Zelling, Andrew Wells, Keith Sangster, Sam Jacobs, Michael White, Christopher Legoe, Brian Cox, Robert Mohr, Roderick Matheson and Robin Millhouse. As the most junior justice, Elliott was last to leave and he paused, turned around to look at the packed courtroom and gave a small farewell wave. Said Powell: 'I've never seen a judge do it. All the rest filed off and he turned. It was absolutely lovely.' The appointment went through without a ripple. At 65, there was nothing left to prove.

Justice Roma Mitchell, who sat on the Bench with Elliott for three months before her retirement in September 1983 said later that, while 14 years earlier many members of the profession had opposed Elliott taking silk, now not a single voice had been raised in protest. 'The comments from all sections of the community were eulogistic. He had proved himself as a barrister beyond reproach', she said.[8]

The transition from barrister to judge was not smooth. All judges must accommodate privately the weight of the responsibility handed to them. To risk having errors exposed on appeal is bad enough, but what keeps even the most experienced judges awake at night is passing sentence on a convicted prisoner. This was never going to come easily to Elliott. It caused him great personal anguish, which he concealed from most of his colleagues. He first had to find a new way of thinking. He was accustomed to offering help without passing judgment. He saw the best in people, to the point of being thought gullible, and he believed in giving everyone the benefit of the doubt. In a speech at a 1988 symposium, Elliott conceded it would be naïve in a world where people killed, sold heroin and cheated on their taxes to suppose that some people did not cheat on claims for personal injuries. But it was a reluctant concession.

> Personally, I do not think that there are many total frauds. Of course, there are people who tend to be self-pitying, people who find some social or family compensations in being a little worse than perhaps they are, people who give themselves the benefit of the doubt about whether they can work, people who do not like the job anyway. In short, people who for all sorts of reasons consciously or unconsciously tend to exaggerate to some degree ...[9]

He had to learn detachment. He could encourage parties to settle but he could not help them. He was sorely tested in two early cases that upset him because he could see the damage that was being done. One was a family dispute among four sons of a Greek migrant who had purchased land in Adelaide for growing vegetables. The land became valuable and was the subject of a bitter dispute between the sons after the father had died because he had

8 Dame Roma Mitchell, 'A tribute to the Hon Elliott Johnston AO QC', *Flinders Journal of Law Reform*, vol. 2, Adelaide, 1998, p. 180.

9 Elliott Johnston. 'The whiplash injury – some legal aspects', speech for Law Society of South Australia symposium, 1988, Elliott Johnston private papers.

secretly transferred ownership to one of the sons and his wife. The other three sons alleged that their father had promised the land to all four. They instituted proceedings, claiming that the land had been held in trust for them. Although the decision had no legal significance, Elliott was upset by this Greek family tragedy. In the Full Court judgment on the case, he had to decide on the grounds of legal principle. Fairness was not the criterion, he said, and the result might unfairly affect some members of the family. The decision he was forced to make against the three sons went against the grain of what he believed.[10] Their claim failed but they succeeded on appeal.

He was similarly troubled by a disputed insurance claim following a fire in a factory owned by Hart Manufacturing on Goodwood Road in Adelaide's inner south. The insurance company claimed it was arson and refused to pay. Elliott rejected what he thought was spurious argument by the insurance company relating to an area of the factory floor where petrol was supposedly used as an accelerant. He found in the factory owner's favour. His decision was appealed to the Privy Council but settled along the way. The case worried him because he thought an injustice had occurred.

But the difficult business of sentencing the guilty was the hardest thing for him to grapple with, and he struggled. His natural compassion was at odds with locking people up, even when the benefit of the doubt was not his to give. He started out hampered by a lifetime of generous thinking and without having come to terms with the implications of sending someone to prison. One of his earliest cases involved a married couple, both drug addicts, who were charged with armed robbery. It was a hopeless, nasty crime. They had held up a chemist with a loaded gun and then panicked, throwing the gun out of the car. The jury found them guilty and Elliott sentenced them to two-and-a-half years. The Crown appealed against the sentence. It was more than doubled to six years. Elliott, chastened, began to face the reality of his new position. He genuinely believed that prison would not help the couple, but the sentence he had handed down was too lenient, and he knew it. He made up his mind to behave sensibly.

For the next four years he negotiated a fine line between his

---

10 *Glouftsis and Others v. Glouftsis and another* (1987) 44 SASR 298.

natural reluctance to send people to prison and community expectations of law and order. A sentence that was too lenient risked appeal and his reputation quickly would be in tatters. He quietly devised, for each case, a length of time delicately poised at a point just ahead of what was so lenient that the Crown would appeal. He did not necessarily think this was correct and sometimes gave longer than the bare minimum, but he was determined to avoid any further appeal. He fell into step with his fellow justices. There were no more appeals against soft prison sentences and in his final year one of his sentences was challenged as being too harsh. It was one of the worst cases Elliott confronted. It involved an Aboriginal youth from New South Wales who made contact with his alcoholic father at Elizabeth in Adelaide's north and, after a night of drinking, murdered an elderly woman, whom he had robbed and strangled with the string of her violin. The circumstances were sad and hopeless, but a terrible crime had been committed and Elliott's sentence of almost 20 years withstood appeal. On a visit some time later to Yatala Labour Prison, he saw the murderer who greeted him respectfully. They had a long talk about the young man's uncertain future.

In late December 1983, six months after joining the Bench, Elliott made a politically risky decision to accept an invitation from the Chinese Communist Party to visit China. Had it become public, the trip would have been a fresh controversy for the Bannon Government, which had shown faith in appointing him. China was still not a mainstream destination for Australians and this was not a tourist trip. Elliott went as an invited former student at Chairman Mao's international Communist school. It was a political manoeuvre by the Chinese Communists to improve their relations with Communists in other countries. 'The Chinese clearly wanted to rebuild the relationship with the Australian party that had been severed since the CPA split in 1963', wrote Bernie Taft, who went on the same trip. 'Whatever their political intent, to revisit China after so many years was an exciting prospect for me.'[11] Elliott received the invitation through Taft, who rang to invite him and Elizabeth. Elliott had privately vowed not to return to China until Mao Tse-

11 Taft, p. 300.

tung was out of office, but Mao had died in 1976 and Elliott agreed to go.

The Johnstons, Bernie Taft and his second wife Eileen Chapman spent just over a fortnight in China and visited Beijing, Shanghai, Hangzhou and Wuxi. They mixed politics with sightseeing, visited a factory in the north, took a boat trip on the Huangpu River in Shanghai and saw the Qin Dynasty terracotta soldiers that had been unearthed only a few years earlier by a peasant digging a well. They saw people they had known 30 years ago. None of their old Chinese friends had fared well and they heard sad tales of banishment, hurt and exile. In human terms, Mao's rule had inflicted tremendous personal suffering and since his death and the arrest of the Gang of Four, the devastated country had struggled to free itself from a blighted period of its history. The remnants of Mao's regime were painfully visible.

Elliott was visiting China as a former student of the international school and there was a moment of awkwardness when he and Bernie Taft were taken to a meeting with prominent Chinese Communist Party officials to talk about the progress of Australian Communism. Embarrassed, the South Australian Supreme Court justice stayed silent and Taft took the questions.

A few weeks after they returned to Australia, Elliott and Taft fell out. On the return trip Elliott and Elizabeth spent a pleasant night at the Tafts' home in Melbourne and parted good friends. However, a few weeks later seven of the eight members of the Victorian state executive of the Communist Party of Australia, including Taft, resigned *en bloc* to form a new group, the Socialist Forum. In July 1984, Taft wrote to Elliott and Elizabeth to justify his position. Taft had been a member of the Party even before Elliott, but he wrote that Communism had no future in Australia. He hoped they would remain friends. 'Over the last few weeks, I thought you may have wondered why we did not talk about the possibility of the group leaving the Party whilst we were in China together. The simple reason is that in January I did not know or anticipate that things would come to a head at the time they did and certainly not in the manner in which it happened. At that stage, I still had hopes that we would be able to come to a common decision to transform the party.'[12] Elliott was not a member of the Party but Elizabeth was, and both were unimpressed. They were disappointed at the Party's obvious continuing slide towards oblivion but they also felt duped. Elliott never forgave Taft.

Elliott's tenure as a justice of the Supreme Court was limited to four years and seven months and during this short time the plight of individuals continued to move him. He heard the case of a woman who, in breach of quarantine laws, had brought bean and tomato seeds and garlic bulbs into Australia from Greece, concealing them in her handbag. She was caught, and fined $1000 by a magistrate. She came before Elliott on appeal, challenging the fine as being manifestly excessive. Elliott, who had little to do early on the Bench, took off on a tangent over the right to charge people where they were apprehended. She had been intercepted at Tullamarine airport but convicted in Adelaide. The issue on appeal concerned the interpretation of the Commonwealth's *Quarantine Act*. Elliott studied legislation dating back to Henry VIII about the difficulties of bringing to justice 'traitors, pirates, thieves, robbers and murderers on the high seas'.[13] He set aside the conviction. The Crown appealed and the Full Court quashed Elliott's excursion into mediaeval law.

He behaved more conventionally in another case of smuggled food. This case involved a member of the Adelaide City Council who had visited Scotland on holiday and who had attempted to smuggle in a tin of haggis. The councillor was charged and convicted by a magistrate under federal legislation, which meant he no longer could serve on the council. The councillor was represented by Ted Mullighan who appealed and argued before Elliott that the magistrate had not foreseen the implications of conviction. Elliott sent the case back to the lower court, which delivered a guilty verdict without recording a conviction.

Elliott was not able to continue his fight for justice from the Bench. He had to be guided by what was legally correct and not what, in other circumstances, he thought was morally right. But he did have the power to rectify legal wrongs emanating from lower courts. In *Begg v. Daire,* Elliott overturned the conviction of

12 Elliott Johnston private papers.

13 *Tsorvas v. Van Velsen* (1984) 37 SASR 490.

a man found guilty of begging; the man had gone from house to house in the suburb of Wayville asking for money to buy medicine. Elliott found the magistrate was wrong to ignore Begg's intention to pay the money back.[14] In *R v. Romeo,* Elliott, with other judges, reduced a prison sentence for a man who had sold heroin to a police informer, from 10 years with eight years non-parole, to seven years with five years non-parole. The lower court had not been told that the informer had earlier been caught with heroin and amphetamines and had trapped the other man in order to reduce his own sentence.[15]

He handled sensitively an appeal from the Magistrates Court against the conviction of a young music student who had been caught on a drunken dare trying to break into a bookshop with a crowbar. The student had planned to steal a book to prove he had entered the shop but was arrested, as a consequence missing a professional music engagement the next day. Although this was a university prank, it threatened the student's future as a touring musician. Elliott found the matter was not trivial but that there were extenuating circumstances. He quashed the conviction. However, the student had to pay costs and compensation, and was placed on a good behaviour bond. The student had been in custody for three weeks while the court obtained a pre-sentence report, which Elliott noted was not in keeping with the justice of the case.[16]

At times Elliott inserted observations he thought were important into his judgments. In December 1983, a case came before the Full Court on appeal from the Children's Court. A boy, aged 14 years, had been arrested with his brother at a country railway station. The boy was questioned and charged with possessing an implement for housebreaking, in this instance, an adjustable spanner. The admissibility of incriminating statements the boy had made on the night was in doubt because the police officer had not contacted the boy's father to have him present. The appeal succeeded and the case collapsed. Elliott offered his views on whether the statement the boy had given could have ever been considered voluntary. He believed

14 *Begg v. Daire* (1986) 40 SASR 375.

15 *R v. Romeo* (1987) 45 SASR 212.

16 *W v. Marsh* (1983) 35 SASR 333.

it would have taken some degree of effort to impress upon a young boy being interviewed by a police officer in the early hours of the morning that he had the choice to remain silent. 'The defendant was in strange surroundings separated from his older brother, in threatening or at the very least highly uncomfortable circumstances. It is one thing for a youth in this situation to say that he understands the words of the caution, another that he really appreciates in a practical sense that he has a choice to answer or not', Elliott wrote.[17]

He never forgot that these were crimes affecting people. In a troubling case of incest, he expressed some hope that family ties might survive. On the Full Court with Len King and Robert Mohr, he heard an appeal against the two-year sentence given to a father, 56, for the indecent assault of and incest with two of his daughters, one of whom was 12. Elliott found that a moderately higher sentence may have been possible but the sentence as it stood was not wrong. 'I remark that it would appear that it is, at least, very possible that after the respondent has served his term of imprisonment the family, or some members of it, will come together again', he concluded.[18]

In another case he used common sense and found that part of a suicide note left in a car that was titled 'Last Will and Testament' was clearly meant as a will and should be treated as such. In a similar vein, he dismissed an attempt by a woman charged with prostitution to argue she was not in a brothel, when the motel where she had agreed to have paid sex had rooms with unmade beds, a stream of people who were coming and going, and walls lined with advertisements for escort agencies that answered a call at the press of a button.

Following a change to the *Juries Act* in 1985, Elliott was appointed to conduct one of the first Supreme Court cases in the criminal jurisdiction to be heard by a judge alone. A prominent footballer, who had been charged with rape and whose identity might have influenced a jury, asked that a judge alone hear the trial. The case was assigned to Elliott. It was then an unusual situation and Elliott had to instruct himself, as he would have instructed a

17 *T v. Waye* (1983) 35 SASR 247.

18 *The Queen v. Drewett* (1983) 35 SASR 344 at 348.

jury, about how to treat evidence given during the trial. He included in these instructions his view of the human capacity to lie about money, power and sex. Sexuality was a complex part of the human make-up and it provoked lies because of the intensity of emotion it aroused. 'It may well be that people in general are more prone to tell lies or colour the truth about matters sexual than about many other subjects. But not necessarily so, and in particular in my experience not more so than about matters of money, business and power', he remarked. He found the footballer not guilty.[19]

On the Full Court, he was commonly with the majority, but on occasions he struck out on his own, as in a long and careful treatise on riparian rights. If nothing else, it demonstrated his capacity for detail. The case was a suit against two landowners who had dammed a spring-fed creek on their property, preventing it from flowing in summer into the land of their neighbours, one of whom was a dairy farmer. Elliott considered that the case was of great importance to the rural community and he believed that Howard Zelling had referred it to the Full Court for that reason. In a rare departure from the views of the Chief Justice, Elliott argued against the view that this unproclaimed watercourse, known as Bull Creek, was not governed by the *Water Resources Act, 1976*, which meant there were no restrictions on the rights of individuals to divert and take water. In his long dissenting reasons, Elliott agreed that individuals had common law rights to water from unproclaimed creeks but that the continuance of water flow was a matter for the Crown and was not a riparian right.[20] He was not upholding the landowner's right to block the flow of water, but he believed the only authority that could order it unblocked was the South Australian Government.

Elliott stood up for principle in the case of the minor conviction of a woman found guilty of contempt of court in Tanunda, in the Barossa Valley. It was a small injustice but Elliott thought her case was no less important because of it. The woman was in court when her child was sentenced and she had abused the magistrate. 'That's just ridiculous', she called out. The magistrate ordered that

19 *R v. G* (1987) 45 SASR 102.

20 *Reid v. Chapman* (1984) 37 SASR 117 at 130–134.

she be detained, adding that he was 'too annoyed to deal with you now'.[21] She was held in custody while a complaint was prepared, then brought back to court where she apologised. The magistrate found a charge of contempt was proved and dismissed it without conviction or penalty. She appealed, arguing she had been given no chance to defend herself. Elliott agreed and said she should have been told she was to be charged and given the right to respond. 'The indispensable requirement of natural justice is that the defendant shall have the opportunity of putting submissions, whether as to fact or law, before any decision of guilt is arrived at', he said.

Another of Elliott's useful abilities on the Bench was a talent for lateral thinking and the capacity to work through obstacles. He was on the Full Court that had to decide whether a Special Magistrate, and later Justice Derek Bollen on appeal, was correct in denying a serious sequential offender a non-parole period. The man, a persistently dishonest alcoholic confidence trickster, had committed a spate of 70 theft-related offences, in which he defrauded shopkeepers at the rate of up to $2000 a fortnight. His trick was to buy goods worth up to $60 then present a cheque for about $150 and claim the balance in cash. He ranged over many suburbs in one day. 'He must be almost as compulsive a thief as he is an alcoholic', said Justice Michael White, who concluded that the man's greed for money outstripped his need for alcohol. Justice White agreed with Elliott (and with Justice Derek Bollen on the first appeal) that the head sentence of six years was richly deserved and the man may have actually got a discount through the sheer quantity of his offending.

Justice White wrote that he considered a non-parole period should not be set; however, he was persuaded to think otherwise by 'the clear and cogent thinking' of Elliott Johnston. Elliott had looked into the offender's background. Aged 28, the man had been a juvenile offender and his adult convictions included house breaking and larceny. He had been in custody until mid-1984 (this was 1986) and was out on parole when he committed the offences. Elliott noted that between mid-1976 and April 1980 the man had a clean record, other than a single charge of drunkenness and buying liquor out of hours. He also knew from a report to the court that the man

---

21 *G v. Moss* (1984) 37 SASR 9.

sought treatment for his alcoholism. He concluded it was fair to believe a non-parole period would not help, given it had not done so in the past. But *not* to fix a non-parole period made the sentence fully punitive with no access to rehabilitation and it would almost certainly turn him out to offend again. Elliott proposed setting a long non-parole period of almost the same length as the sentence. Justice White agreed, saying that it would be up to the prisoner whether to accept the suggested offer of a long parole period. If he was genuine, he would accept parole; if not he would reject it.[22] The man's outlook was not promising but Elliott convinced the others he should be given another chance to reform.

Elliott retired in February 1988, on his seventieth birthday, but stayed until March to finish writing judgments. On 26 February, 48 years after completing his law degree and 47 years after becoming a Communist, Elliott's peers farewelled him from the Supreme Court Bench. It was a mark of how much times had changed that certain things were now said. The price Elliott had paid for his beliefs, one of glory delayed rather than glory denied, had short-changed him as a judge and was now freely admitted. Of the Queen's Counsel furore which had so divided the profession, the Chief Justice Len King said that he had thought it strange at the time but now found it barely comprehensible.

Elliott was the fifty-first justice appointed to the South Australian Supreme Court and he was the last of the generation of judges who had joined the Bar before the end of the Second World War. He had appeared before 30 of the 50 Supreme Court justices who had preceded him and was an articled clerk in appearances before another three. Yet his time on the Bench had been exceptionally brief. The average period served was 16 years and Elliott was there for four-and-a-half. 'It is a tenure which, I am sure, all here today would agree was too short', said Sumner, who had welcomed and who now farewelled Elliott. 'The fact is that your Honour's appointment to the Bench came later than most because successive governments, Labor and Liberal, were reluctant to recommend your appointment because of your political beliefs and in particular your membership of the Communist Party. You were eminently well-

22 *Flentjar v. Wright* (1986) 42 SASR 246.

qualified for appointment well before, in fact, you were appointed.'

Sumner praised Elliott for maintaining a lifetime's habit of finding the best in people and for his respect for and belief in the goodness of ordinary Australians. In doing so, he touched on the great mystery of Elliott Johnston, which was the naivety that bound him to a cause, even (although Sumner did not say this) when all hope was lost. He had held on to the ideals of his youth, while others had quietly put theirs aside. Almost 50 years later this marked him as a man of principle. 'Although you have had to fight for unpopular causes in your professional and political life, you have been secure in your personal value system and have never given way to the attractions of an offhanded, detached, uncaring cynicism which seems to afflict many people as they leave the idealism of youth behind. For you, your ideals remain as important now as they always have been', Sumner concluded.

Elliott's response was short and gracious. He commended the capacity of judges to disagree with each other without rancour or harm to their relationships. He was more convinced than ever of the need for judicial independence and stressed how essential it was for judges to take no part in political or social debate. He referred to the difficulty he had with sentencing, but only in general terms. There were three victims before a court, he said: the victim of the offence, the community whose peace and equanimity was wounded by a breach of its laws, and the person in the dock, who was often a victim of intellectual or other incapacities. To make those three things match up had been a very hard task indeed.

The President of the South Australian Law Society, Rod Burr, praised Elliott's enduring attachment to ideals that were formed at university. Burr quoted the words of the Jewish rabbi and scholar, Chaim Potok, on what it meant to live a life of significance. 'A man must fill his life with meaning. Meaning is not automatically given to life. It is hard work to fill one's life with meaning. A life filled with meaning is worthy of rest.'

Elliott, he told the Supreme Court, had earned his rest.

CHAPTER 9

The Royal Commissioner

Elliott looked forward to becoming a Communist once more. Elizabeth in retirement was managing The People's Bookshop at the new Communist headquarters east of the city, close to where they lived. He had kept in touch with the Party's internal affairs from the Bench and planned to return as a rank-and-file member.

But just before leaving the Bench, Sumner passed on to him a federal invitation to join the recently formed Commonwealth Royal Commission into Aboriginal Deaths in Custody. The commission, established in August 1987, was an initiative of the Hawke Government, which was troubled by the number of Aboriginal offenders dying in custody. Their deaths were often poorly explained and seemed suspicious.[1] The former South Australian lawyer, Jim Muirhead, headed the commission and he had recommended Elliott for the job.

Even though Elliott's law practice had primarily been in industrial and criminal law, he was eminently suited for a leading role on Aboriginal issues. While he had grown up barely seeing an Aboriginal person, their plight, including the fight for land rights, was on the agenda for all Australian Communists. The Party's policy was well ahead of prevailing social attitudes and as early as the 1940s *Tribune* showed pictures of Aboriginal slave gangs chained together at Fitzroy Crossing in Western Australia.[2] In the 1950s it was Communist policy to improve the position of Aboriginal people, with the South Australian branch campaigning against the British

1 Elliott Johnston, *Royal Commission into Aboriginal Deaths in Custody: National report: Overview and recommendations*, AGPS, Canberra, 1991.

2 'Aboriginal Slave Gang in Chains', *Tribune,* 11 March 1949.

nuclear tests at Maralinga, traditional Aboriginal lands in the north-west of the state.

In the 1960s, Elliott had begun getting to know Aboriginal people who were referred to him through legal aid and he started to understand their struggle. They submitted to white man's law without comprehending it and the consequences of this silent submission were becoming apparent in Australia's prisons. In the 1970s, Justice Roma Mitchell wrote that the correctional problem presented by South Australian Aboriginal people was 'that they form a component of the prison population out of all proportion to their numbers in the community'.[3] They were in prison for trivial offences like public drunkenness, indecent language or offensive behaviour. Andrew Collett, who was articled to Elliott's firm in 1976 and became one of its core group of lawyers, analysed the Port Augusta court lists for 1972 and found that Aboriginal people were massively over-represented for minor offences.

In 1971, Elliott and Elizabeth had attended a meeting called to discuss the need for a legal service to advise Aboriginal offenders. In Sydney two years earlier, activists, including Paul Coe and Gary Foley, had established Australia's first Aboriginal Legal Rights Service at Redfern and attracted federal funding. Foley visited Adelaide and spoke to about 60 people in the refectory of the University of Adelaide. The group decided that Aboriginal people should meet independently and decide what to do. Three months later, the Aboriginal Legal Rights Movement (ALRM) was formed and Elliott was elected its first chairman. He did not seek the role but accepted it on the understanding that he would stay on until an Aboriginal person was ready to take over.

The ALRM had no money, but it squeezed into the small office of the Women's Council at 248 Pirie Street. While they waited for funding, Robyn Layton coordinated a list of lawyers who would act pro bono for any Aboriginal person charged with an offence. Magistrates would spread the word to ring Layton, who would find someone able to get to court in time.[4] A $22,000 grant from

3 Justice Roma Mitchell, *First Report: Sentencing and corrections*, Criminal Law and Penal Methods Reform Committee of South Australia, Adelaide, 1973.

4 The list of about 12 lawyers included John Doyle who became South Australian Chief Justice in 1995.

the McMahon Government in 1972 was enough to appoint a solicitor, Syd Tilmouth (who came to the job interview with his dog), an Aboriginal field officer, Tim Agius, and a secretary, Joanne Willmot. Layton's list was no longer needed.

The impact of the ALRM was profound. It was credited with improving relations between Aborigines and police and, indirectly, for the establishment of Aboriginal sobriety groups. 'It contributed to the raising of the status of Aborigines in their own eyes, and in the eyes of the community', wrote the biographer of Ruby Hammond, a prominent Indigenous woman who in 1977 succeeded Andrew Collett as executive secretary.[5]

Elliott's firm began to help Aboriginal people claw back rights they never knew they had. They discovered they could plead 'not guilty', contest charges and sue for compensation. Collett dealt with an Aboriginal stockman in Port Augusta who had fallen from a horse and injured his knee, and had been sacked with no wages. It was among the easiest workers' compensation cases ever won and it began to alter Aboriginal people's perceptions about their entitlements. Until then, almost no workers' compensation had been paid to Aboriginal stockmen in South Australia.

Even with Elliott as chairman and Collett as executive secretary, the ALRM was an Indigenous initiative under Indigenous control, an organisation 'run by Aborigines assisted by white people whom they themselves chose'.[6] The shortage of professionally able individuals in the Aboriginal community reflected their disadvantage and it was a sensitive issue. 'The failure of the education system to come to grips with the special education requirements of Aboriginal people meant that Aboriginal professional staff with law qualifications were not available', Edmund Wanganeen wrote in his history of the development of the ALRM in South Australia.[7] In 1980 when Jim Stanley from Palm Island indicated he would stand, Elliott withdrew. He had presided over the ALRM for nine years

5 Margaret Forte, *Flight of an Eagle: The dreaming of Ruby Hammond*, Wakefield Press, Adelaide, 1973, p. 5.

6 ibid., p. 5.

7 Edmund Wanganeen, *Justice Without Prejudice: The development of the Aboriginal Legal Rights Movement in South Australia,* South Australian College of Advanced Education, Adelaide, 1986, p. 14.

and he had won the undying admiration, love and respect of many Aboriginal people.

His standing in the black community had been confirmed in a landmark case that led to the acquittal of an Aboriginal activist charged with a street offence during a brawl at Port Adelaide. On a Saturday night in 1974, he was sitting with Elizabeth in their Gilles Street lounge when an Aboriginal woman, the late activist Val Power, rang to say there was trouble at Port Adelaide. A brawl had started at the New Exchange hotel, where Aboriginal people and seamen gathered to drink. Windows were smashed and bottles and furniture were thrown as the fight spilled into the street. Up to 300 people were caught up in it and 17 were arrested, 16 Aboriginal and one sailor. While the fight was in progress, Power addressed the crowd and urged black people 'to stick together in defence of their rights'.[8] She ran to a phone box and rang the federal Minister for Aboriginal Affairs, South Australian Senator, Jim Cavanagh. Still on the phone, she leant out and told everyone to stay together and not be pushed around. The police ordered her to leave, but she refused and was arrested. Power was convicted of loitering in the Port Adelaide Magistrates' Court, but Elliott took her case on appeal to the Supreme Court before Justice Zelling who, after referring a legal question to the Full Court, acquitted her. Zelling noted there had been collaboration between the police in the preparation of their notes. When Elliott had questioned them separately, their stories were not the same.

Aboriginal people knew Elliott was someone special. 'Elliott Johnston had been the legal friend of the poor and the oppressed in South Australia since he first put up his plate. He had probably done more work for less money than any other lawyer in Australia', the biographer of Ruby Hammond wrote.[9] He walks on water that man, said the chair of the ALRM in South Australia, Neil Gillespie.

In April 1975, Elliott's growing expertise in Indigenous affairs was beginning to be recognised nationally. He was invited by Senator Cavanagh to be one of three people sitting on the Laverton Royal Commission in Western Australia. Elliott joined West

---

8 *Power v. Huffa* (1976) 14 SASR 337.

9 Forte, op. cit., p. 156.

Australian Supreme Court Judge Gresley Clarkson, who was the chair, and an Aboriginal man, Ernest Bridge. Bridge came from the north of the state and Elliott would fly to Perth from Adelaide. They would meet at their hotel. Bridge, a successful businessman, became the first Indigenous cabinet minister in an Australian government.

The incident at Skull Creek that led to the Laverton Royal Commission was a sign of the strained relations between white and black Australia. On the night of 5 January 1975, violence broke out between 22 police and a large group of Aboriginal men, women and children who were passing through Laverton, about 300 km from Kalgoorlie, on their way to Warburton. Two vehicles carrying 76 Aboriginal people to a traditional gathering pulled into a creek. Within minutes, 25 people were arrested in a scuffle that provoked allegations of police assault. Although the mêlée was over in a few minutes, a great deal of disquiet followed the incident, with the police and Aboriginal people arguing over what had occurred.

The Royal Commission sat for more than a year as it tried to sort out the truth behind the conflicting claims, with Elliott travelling extensively between Perth, Kalgoorlie and Laverton. In its report, the Royal Commission found fault with police who had arrested without justification 21 Aborigines, falsified official records and tried to hinder the inquiry. But it also emphasised the difficulties police faced, including unprovoked Aboriginal hostility. The findings did not lay blame on either side but took a conciliatory line that race relations must improve. Australian society was to blame, not these particular individuals. In its report the commission concluded: 'It is obvious that many of the problems develop out of the historical development of the relationships between Europeans and the Aboriginal people whose way of life and culture has been affected. The problems lie at the door of the whole society and not just at the door of the police force or any other section of society.'[10]

Elliott had already given a great deal of time and thought to Australian racial disadvantage when Chris Sumner rang to invite him to join the Royal Commission. He understood the complexity

---

10 Gresley Clarkson, Ernest Bridge and Elliott Johnston, *Laverton Royal Commission: Final Report*, West Australian Parliament and Commonwealth Parliament, Perth, Canberra, 1976.

of black–white relations, particularly Aboriginal legal issues. He accepted the position without hesitation.

But first, there were personal matters to attend to. In March 1988, three days after he finished writing his judgments, he underwent triple bypass heart surgery to correct a serious health problem diagnosed a year earlier. He also had to deal with the painful issue of his continued estrangement from the CPA. It would be further prolonged by his latest appointment. He knew he was joining the Royal Commission, although he could not say so publicly and he wanted to advise the Party in advance of any announcement. On 4 May 1988, Elliott wrote to the state executive to say he had intended rejoining, but now could not because the restrictions on a royal commissioner were the same as for a judge. He wanted them to know that this was no change of heart over Communism, far from it. '[While on the Bench] I have followed *Tribune* and many of the documents of the party. I remain convinced of the importance of the CPA now and in the future for the welfare of our country and the Left movement, whether as an independent party or as an important element in the position of a wider movement.' After an outstanding career in the law, 47 years after he had joined the CPA, Communism was still his anchor. 'My position remains as it was at the time of my resignation in 1983 (although my views on a number of matters have developed and changed, as I am sure have yours). I send my warm personal greetings to all my friends in the movement. I will watch your changes with great interest. I hope that my own conduct will reflect credit on the Party, which has, more than any other single factor, shaped my own life and my own outlook.'[11]

Elliott joined the Royal Commission into Aboriginal Deaths in Custody believing that Aboriginal people were badly treated in prison and died as a result. The catalyst for its establishment had been the sad and lonely death of John Pat, a 16-year-old boy who had died on 28 September 1983 of internal head injuries in the police station lock-up at Roebourne, a small Aboriginal community near Karratha in West Australia's north-west Pilbara. The fatal injury had occurred a few hours earlier in a brawl outside a Roebourne hotel. At the police station Pat was assaulted and placed semi-con-

11 Letter to the CPA, 4 May 1988, Elliott Johnston private papers.

scious in a juvenile cell. He was found dead during a routine check. His death became a symbol of the brutal disadvantage experienced by Indigenous Australians.

Jim Muirhead had been appointed sole commissioner a few months earlier but quickly appreciated that the number of deaths was too great for one person to deal with alone. Other commissioners were then authorised to examine deaths in geographically defined areas. Elliott joined at this stage, along with Daniel O'Dea, Hal Wootten QC, and Lewis Wyvill QC. The terms of the commission were also broadened and changed as the figures were examined and understood. The commissioners realised that the number of deaths in custody was virtually the same for black Australians as it was for white. The problem, which was largely hidden, was the dramatic over-representation of Aboriginal people in prisons and police holding cells, and their much poorer health. There was already quite a disproportionate number of Aboriginal people in prison custody, but it was infinitely worse in police custody. This realisation changed the commission's thinking. Without fanfare, the Royal Commission into Aboriginal Deaths in Custody, which was set up to report on the deaths of 99 Aboriginal and Torres Strait Islanders who had died in custody between 1 January 1980 and 31 May 1989, broadened into an examination of how their Aboriginality brought them into custody in the first place.

In early 1989, Muirhead unexpectedly resigned to become the Administrator of the Northern Territory, and in April Elliott took his place. He became head of the Royal Commission and its driving force. A week later Elliott issued a statement emphasising the Commission's commitment to investigating the social, cultural and legal factors that caused Aboriginal disadvantage. Elliott Johnston's National Report with its overview and 339 recommendations was his greatest single contribution to making Australia a better place.

Each death was examined in detail and documented. People were interviewed, documents were subpoenaed and post-mortems were re-examined by pathologists. The hearings were public and legal counsel represented the families of the deceased. Aboriginal people for the first time had a voice; the Royal Commission received input from the Aboriginal Issues Units formed in each state to channel information from Aboriginal communities, organisations and individuals.

Muirhead had been due to hear most of the Western Australian cases and Elliott, accompanied by the commission's secretary John Gavin, visited the Western Australian Premier, Peter Dowding, to ask about the appointment of a replacement commissioner. But Dowding was reluctant to bring in someone to examine deaths that had already been dealt with by the coroner. Elliott was frustrated by this, but the next morning Gavin suggested a commissioner be brought in to look solely at the underlying issues. Dowding agreed and walked over to the window of his office while he thought about whom to appoint. 'What about Pat Dodson?' Elliott said in a deliberately toneless voice. Dowding whipped around. 'What an excellent idea, I'll do that', he said. Pat Dodson became the first Aboriginal person appointed to the Royal Commission and the only commissioner with a brief to look at the bigger racial picture.

All of the commissioners had the power to sit anywhere and Elliott, who had relatively few cases in South Australia, inquired into most of the deaths in the Northern Territory, and in Western Australia into the death of John Pat. The circumstances of his death at Roebourne account for 300 pages of the report. Elliott had looked at the troubled life of an unemployed youth with a record of drinking offences in a town with a fraught history with alcohol. Damaging patterns of drinking had formed years earlier and were modelled on the pastoral industry's practice of long periods of abstinence followed by binges. 'That's when it started in the 60s, all through the 70s right up until now. All the Aboriginal people spoiled, even the new generation coming on', a woman elder told Elliott.[12] His report on John Pat included the extraordinary decision by Roebourne police to use a dead kangaroo to test evidence by simulating the conditions leading to Pat's death. They dragged a kangaroo carcass from a police van and kicked it, and a witness described the beating. 'He could clearly hear the doors of the van closing and the sound of kicking the kangaroo and its head hitting the ground with what he said was a sort of dull thud', Elliott

---

12 Elliott Johnston, 'Inquiry into the death of John Peter Pat', in *Royal Commission into Aboriginal Deaths in Custody*, AGPS, Canberra, 1991, p. 287.

wrote.[13] He attempted to finalise the account of Pat's death in a way that would give some hope to Pat's mother, Mavis, who had said to him, 'I don't know what's going to come out of the Royal Commission but I hope it makes everything all right for Aboriginal people'. Elliott wanted the report to at least explain what happened to her son, and 'to that extent ease some of her anguish'.[14]

In late 1990 the five commissioners gathered in Adelaide to compile the final report. Reports on the individual deaths were published separately, but the final report was to be a joint exercise. The commissioners began with a chapter on the role of coroners and agreed on a recommendation that every future death in custody should be investigated. That took three days and it was clear that at this rate the final report would be never be finished. From then on they collaborated only on the recommendations, settling on 335 of the 339, with the final four added later by Elliott. During this critical phase of deliberations Elliott sat with Dodson to his right and he would lean his head on his hand and glance at him when a recommendation was made. He would see Dodson give a little nod of assent. 'I thought it was wonderful. He personally agreed with every one of the recommendations', Elliott said.

While the series of final reports in March 1991 found that none of the 99 deaths was caused by murder or manslaughter, the care of some prisoners had been negligent. Although the report identified no common thread of abuse, neglect or racism, it made a series of practical recommendations, which included the decriminalisation of public drunkenness and the establishment of non-custodial facilities for intoxicated people. Offensive language should not trigger an arrest and custody should become a last resort. Police handover procedures should be tightened so an officer coming on duty would know who was in the cells and what state they were in. Some of the recommendations suggested simple compassion, like placing an Aboriginal prisoner in an institution close to family and recognising kinship obligations by allowing them to attend funeral services and burials.

But it was the overview in the National Report that turned the

13 ibid., p. 177.

14 ibid., p. 37.

findings of the Royal Commission into a seminal political document, one where the importance of racial history and the need for self-determination were placed before the Australian people in a constructive and reasonable way. The immediate problem was the grossly disproportionate rate at which Aboriginal people were being jailed. The real problem was why this was happening. Elliott reminded Australians that Aboriginal land had been taken without a treaty, agreement or compensation, and with bloodshed. The loss of land meant the destruction of the Aboriginal economy and of Aboriginal culture. Aboriginal people were never treated as equals and they daily suffered the ignominy of racist attitudes and policies that were nakedly racially based.[15] 'The view propounded by this report is that the most significant contributing factor is the disadvantaged and unequal position in which Aboriginal people find themselves in society – socially, economically and culturally', the overview said.[16]

Elliott's stewardship of the Royal Commission turned a political response to deaths in prison into a broad social document that addressed the inequality residing in Australia two decades after the 1967 referendum whereby Aboriginal people became nominal citizens. The report was a plea for Aboriginal self-determination and not a judgment on white Australia, with the solution lying in Aboriginal people taking control of their own lives.

Elliott's singular contribution to the outcomes of the Royal Commission – although he claimed no special credit for it – was his addition of the final recommendation, which flagged reconciliation as the way forward. It read in part 'that all political leaders and their parties recognise that reconciliation between the Aboriginal and non-Aboriginal communities in Australia must be achieved'.[17] He included it almost as an afterthought and to him it seemed a natural extension of what had gone before.

The Minister for Aboriginal Affairs, Robert Tickner, tabled the 11 volumes in the House of Representatives in Canberra on 9 May 1991, saying it would provide an agenda for the coming decade.

15 Elliott Johnston, *Royal Commission into Aboriginal Deaths in Custody: National report: Overview and Recommendations,* p. 10.

16 ibid., p. 15.

17 ibid., p. 108.

Tickner spoke sensitively about the 99 deaths, men who had hanged themselves using strips of sheeting or blankets, football socks, a length of electric flex, a belt, the sleeve of a jacket, a shirt, a shoe-lace, a bandage, a pair of jeans. One man slit his own throat with a razor and another drove a paintbrush through his eye. The findings were supported by the Shadow Minister for Aboriginal Affairs, Dr Michael Woolridge, who had worked as a doctor at the Northern Territory settlement of Hermannsburg. He said it gave the nation an opportunity to move forward and, if good came out of it, the Liberal Party would support it. But he criticised the commission for not singling out the impact of poverty on imprisonment rates so that the significance of their Aboriginality was made clearer. 'My experience as a doctor is certainly that if one were to compare a group of non-Aboriginal people in similar poverty, one would find a much higher imprisonment rate than in the normal population', he said.[18]

The report had other critics. Some militant Aboriginal people thought police and prison officers were exclusively to blame and should have been held more to account. Conversely, an individual finding by Commissioner Hal Wootten rebounded harshly on a young regional nurse, Sophie Heathcote. She had been on duty at Wilcannia, a small Aboriginal town in western New South Wales, on a night in June 1987 when an Aboriginal man, Mark Quayle, was brought in suffering from acute alcohol withdrawal. He was suffering delirium tremens and had what his family called 'the dings'. Quayle was entrusted to her medical care, but when he began wandering outside she phoned the police, who took him away in a panel van and put him in a cell. By morning, he had hanged himself. Commissioner Wootten found that Quayle's death was indirectly the fault of Heathcote, the doctor she had consulted by phone, and the two constables who put him in a cell. Wootten wrote in his report that their uncaring conduct, which treated Quayle as less than equally human, showed an attitude towards Aboriginal people that was widespread. Heathcote, who spoke about the consequences on the ABC's *Australian Story* in 2000, said she was caring for other patients on the night and could not control Quayle. She had believed

18 Australia, House of Representatives, *Debates*, 9 May 1991, viewed 31 October 2007, <www. parlinfoweb.aph.gov.au >.

that police would keep an eye on him and she did not intend that he be locked in a cell. As a consequence of a coronial inquiry and the Royal Commission, she was deregistered as a nurse and spent four years fighting through the courts to be reinstated. She told the ABC that she supported the Royal Commission but not in the way it went about Quayle's case. 'I didn't always feel that they dealt a particularly fair deal or a particularly honest deal', she said.[19]

The relevance of the Royal Commission's conclusions has endured for almost two decades, twice as long as Tickner predicted. They are still the benchmark cited in courts and in government submissions and, in the absence of other objectives, forged a pathway to reconciliation. Pat Dodson thinks that Elliott's genius lay in the way he brought compassion to social, cultural and legal settings: 'The report was far-ranging because of the social factors. It set out an image that says, if you take just a narrow approach to the criminal code, that's not going to give you much insight into the nature of the problem. You need to look as broadly as possible to the social circumstances of people, their opportunities and where those opportunities are being denied.'

The dispatch of the Army into the ravaged Indigenous communities of central Australia by the Howard Government in 2007 distressed Elliott. In 1991 the leaders of both political parties had supported the commission's report and its approach. But under John Howard, the impetus towards reconciliation, made even more urgent by the 1997 *Bringing Them Home* report into the impact of the separation of 'the stolen generation' of Indigenous children from their families, was lost. Elliott was disappointed and angry because the objective of Aboriginal self-determination had been thrown out the window, the Aboriginal and Torres Strait Islander Commission (ATSIC) dismantled and Aboriginal people were back to being told what to do. The catastrophic social breakdown, fuelled by the abuse of alcohol, drugs and petrol, had flourished for years and the damage was incalculable. He was angry that alcohol was still a problem, when its gravity and impact had featured so prominently in the report of the Royal Commission. His report had 11 recom-

19 Sophie Heathcote, 'The trials of Sister Sophie', *Australian Story*, Australian Broadcasting Corporation, 7 September 2000.

mendations on alcohol and 17 on alcohol and drugs.

In 1998, Flinders University permanently honoured Elliott's contribution to public life, in particular to Indigenous law, in the annual Elliott Johnston Tribute Lecture. Each year during South Australia's Law Week, a distinguished person speaks on a topic relating to Indigenous people and the law. The inaugural lecture at the Adelaide Town Hall was given by Jesuit priest, lawyer and academic Father Frank Brennan, who spoke of Elliott's service to the Communist Party, as well as to the law and Aboriginal Australia. 'We are pleased to know that he became a very respectable post-Communist contributing much to the life of the nation. I do not know whether he classes himself as an ex-Communist', Father Brennan said.

Elliott's work as a Royal Commissioner was part of a lifelong campaign to ensure that ordinary people were heard and treated well. Relations between black and white Australia had to be conducted with respect, and between equals.

CHAPTER 10

Elizabeth: A splendid thing

Elliott overshadowed Elizabeth, but only in the public eye. He was the Communist activist and campaigner, the prominent lawyer, the controversial Queen's Counsel, Supreme Court justice and Royal Commissioner, and he had left a bigger footprint. Elizabeth preferred it that way. She was the great love of his life, his comrade, best friend and wife, and she had fought for social and political change as hard as he had done. As it turned out, she was a member of the Communist Party longer than he was.

They were an intriguing couple. Professionally, they were independent and Elizabeth had a close circle of women friends. She was strong-minded and had inherited her family's belief in hard work. Together they brought a dash of radicalism to their mainly middle-class set. While they took pleasure in the trappings of wine, food and travel, their Left-wing missionary zeal burned on into their old age. The real question might not have been how they stayed true to their beliefs, but how they survived the sheer tedium of years of Communist Party meetings, fundraising and conferences.

From the time Elliott came back from the war, they were never apart for long. They were married for 60 years and together raised Stewart, whom they adored. They shared in each other's brilliant careers and believed in Communism until the end. A handful of other young women from educated Adelaide families became Marxists in the 1940s, but Elizabeth outlasted them all. Her father, Paul Teesdale Smith, had encouraged her in her teens to think about the relative virtues of capitalism and Communism and she made a choice for life. For 50 years she was an energetic grassroots worker who handed out leaflets, roneoed brochures and was a mainstay of fundraisers. She was at the centre of Communist family days, picnics and the annual *Tribune* fair, where members baked cakes and sold eggs, fruit, cakes and jam and homemade toys and cut hair. Like Elliott, she built a prominent career dedicated to social reform without leaving the Party. If anything, she became more uncompromising as she got older and was described in an ASIO file note as a more 'diehard' Communist than Elliott.[1] She stayed in the Party until it collapsed around her.

She was sociable, but could be short-tempered and blunt. A crusader for public policy reform, she wanted wealth and opportunity spread more equitably. Born in Adelaide on 1 October 1920 into a bright and liberal family that set great store by discussion and debate, she was educated from 1924 to 1938 at Woodlands Church of England Girls' Grammar School at seaside Glenelg. It was a privileged education in a street lined with giant Norfolk Island pines; her mother would pull up in a small horse-drawn trap in the middle of the day to bring Elizabeth and her older sister, Mary, their lunch. They would come home in the care of their nurse or on the Glenelg tram. Elizabeth, the second born, was smart and energetic and, like Mary and younger sister Cecil, she was a skilled athlete.

Their mother was Helen Waterhouse, daughter of one of Adelaide's wealthy old families, headed by businessman, financier and philanthropist Arthur Waterhouse. A former chairman of the Bank of Adelaide, he erected a number of significant city buildings and donated works to the Art Gallery of South Australia; he was the son of Thomas Greaves Waterhouse, a successful businessman in the early days of the colony. Helen's mother, Laura Morgan, was the daughter of William Morgan, a former South Australian Premier. The Waterhouse family had significant holdings in the Adelaide Hills and in 1913 built a new home at 73 Lefevre Terrace in North Adelaide, opposite the open parklands. The house, still standing as the Princes Lodge Motel, was a landmark building with stables and a stylish Marseilles tiled roof.

Elizabeth's mother, Helen, and her aunt, Lorna, introduced hockey into Australia. As teenagers in the late 1890s, they were sent

1 ASIO, 'Elliott Frank Johnston', National Archives of Australia, Canberra, 12 January 1965.

to board at Cheltenham Ladies College in the English Cotswolds, where they fell in love with this wonderful new game.[2] The first recorded match in Australia was played when Helen Waterhouse obtained permission from the Adelaide City Council for a hockey game on 22 August 1901, in 'Paddock 6 (north from the drain and the inner fence in Tynte Street, North Adelaide)'. The Waterhouse girls from North Adelaide – Helen, sister Joyce and Lorna, as captain – played a team from Glenelg.[3] A few years later Helen played hockey for South Australia. This athleticism passed from Helen Waterhouse to the Teesdale Smith girls, and at Woodlands Elizabeth played hockey and tennis, in her senior year captaining both of the 'A' teams. At university in her first year she represented Adelaide in tennis and swimming and won a Blue for hockey.[4]

Her family's great passion, however, was for horses, hounds and hunting. After the First World War, the Adelaide Hunt Club was swamped with young women who wanted to ride to hounds and in the 1930s Elizabeth and Mary were among the first, and the best, to do so. Hunting was an elitist English tradition enjoyed by the Adelaide aristocracy, with the hunts in Adelaide hosted by significant old families like Peter Waite at Urrbrae, Sir Lancelot Stirling at Strathalbyn and Walter Reynell at Reynella House. This was Elizabeth's milieu. Her mother rode to hounds, while her father Paul Teesdale Smith was master of the Hunt Club from 1924 until 1928 and helped reinstate the hunt after the First World War by bringing in a strain of hounds from Hertfordshire. With the support of families like the Downers, the Tolls, the Crozers, the Bickfords and the Tennants, Teesdale Smith helped to establish hunting at Buckland Park, north of Adelaide near Virginia.[5]

Paul Teesdale Smith was the son of a wealthy engineering family and had fought a long and debilitating Gallipoli campaign with

---

2 Helen Jaensch, *Hat Pins to Bodysuits: Women's hockey in South Australia: The first 100 years*, H. Jaensch, S. Jones and V. Nairn, Adelaide, 2003.The British Navy is credited with introducing men's hockey to Australia in the late 1800s but the first recorded games were by women in Adelaide a few years later.

3 ibid.

4 Sisters Mary and Cecil played hockey for South Australia and Australia. Like Elizabeth, Cecil won a university Blue.

5 John Daly, *The Adelaide Hunt: A history of the Adelaide Hunt Club,* The Club, Adelaide, 1986, p. 69.

the 9th Light Horse Brigade, winning the Distinguished Conduct Medal. From the front, he wrote detailed and thoughtful letters to Elizabeth's mother, Helen, who became his fiancée and before the end of the war, his bride. Read as a whole, his letters were an intimate record of his part in the Gallipoli campaign and were first-hand evidence of the valiant ANZAC spirit. They also showed the rapid maturing of a man, barely 19 years old when he left for the war.

His pride in being a member of the Australian cavalry in the Gallipoli campaign and in defence of the Suez Canal was largely expressed as an earnest desire not to worry those back home. He described brutal military engagements as 'stunts' and wrote how glad he was not to have spent the war years in a law office, because then he would have seen the worst of men, whereas at war he saw nothing but the best. He wrote without sentiment about people he knew who were killed or wounded. 'Did I tell you I saw my death in the paper?' he wrote in 1915. 'It isn't often it occurs, when a live man sees he is dead. The trouble occurred from there being two or three P.T. Smiths in Light Horse Regiments and some brainy idgit jumping to the conclusion it was *ego ipse*.'[6]

In August 1915 he was part of the campaign that included the battle of the Nek, where half those who fought were killed or wounded. His letters also describe his role in the battle for Hill 60 in the Sari Bari range, the last major assault of the Gallipoli campaign in which the 9th Brigade suffered a casualty rate of around 50 per cent. He wrote of scrambling through trenches where men were dead and dying and being humbled by the bravery of others. 'One chap whose legs were badly mangled by a bomb was being pulled along and got a bad shaking on a corner near us, [he] asked them to stop. They waited a bit and then he said, "Go on sport, don't mind me"', he wrote.

By the time Teesdale Smith returned to Adelaide in 1920, aged 23 and having survived diphtheria and injury, he and Helen were married and Elizabeth's older sister Mary had been born. He wanted to finish his law course and find a house somewhere just out of Adelaide with some land where they could keep animals. They fell in love with a magical property they christened Maryland, after

---

6 Paul Teesdale Smith, 'A Soldier's Letters 1914–1920', private papers.

their first child. It was a huge allotment at 506 Marion Road, South Plympton. There was a long, tree-lined driveway, an extensive two-storey house with various additions and a self-contained flat, a grass tennis court surrounded by a cypress hedge and sufficient acreage to sustain a working farm. It was the homestead of the Teesdale Smith clan for the next 40 years and it was where, in an atmosphere of industry, laughter, and discussion, Mary (1919), Elizabeth (1920), her younger sister Cecil (1922) and brother Malcolm (1926) were brought up.

While Paul Teesdale Smith founded the firm of Cleland, Teesdale Smith and Harris, his wife ran the suburban farm. They kept cows for milking and churned their own butter, made cheese and ice cream, grew vegetables, tended an orchard of fruit trees, and kept chickens, turkeys, ducks, a large aviary, horses, hound puppies and, for a time, a pack of about 50 beagles. The hunt was their focus and Teesdale Smith won a series of races on his favourite mount, Capture. Helen was one of the Adelaide Hunt Club's most accomplished riders and in 1932 she was the first female winner of the Drag Cup. Mary, Elizabeth and Cecil hunted and rode steeplechase and were praised for their horsemanship in the Adelaide Hunt Club's official history. Aged 15, Mary rode and won a point-to-point steeplechase in 1935 and again in 1936, 1939 and 1940. In 1939 she won the ladies point-to-point on her horse Ali Baba. (The club did not hunt foxes but chased after hounds who trailed the scent of aniseed wiped on the hoof of a horse that had gone ahead and marked the route). The Teesdale Smith girls were mentioned in the list of young horsewomen who in the 1930s could be said to be 'as good as men'.[7]

Elliott met his future father-in-law before he knew Elizabeth. One Saturday morning at Povey Waterhouse, he was asked to deliver legal documents to the office of Mr Teesdale Smith. Elliott presented himself at the front desk and asked permission to hand over a writ. He was astounded when confronted by a tall man who emerged from his office resplendent in a red coat and full hunt regalia. Elliott recovered himself sufficiently to pass on Mr Povey's compliments and deliver the writ. Elliott later came to love and

7 Daly, p. 85.

admire the thoughtful and disciplined man who brought up his girls as intellectual equals, encouraging them to become independent thinkers. The children's partners and friends were welcomed without question into the inner family circle.

In 1939 Elizabeth arrived at the University of Adelaide already covered with glory. In her final year at school she was head prefect of Woodlands and vice-captain of its Clive House. She was a gifted student and sat on the committees of the debating society, the school magazine and the sports and senior science club. At the school speech night in 1939, only Elizabeth Teesdale Smith was singled out. 'I am not going to embarrass her by talking about her in public, so I will simply say this,' the headmistress Miss Monica Millington said, 'that as hockey captain, tennis captain and head prefect she has given of her best and those who know her will realise that Elizabeth's best is a splendid thing'.[8] She was already starting to spread her wings intellectually. One of her teachers at Woodlands, a young female Communist, encouraged her to think deeply about the issues of the day. She was Margot Trafford, later Margot Milner, a French mistress in Elizabeth's senior years. She had joined the Communist Party of Australia in the late 1930s; she was also a talented pianist who had studied music at the Elder Conservatorium at the University of Adelaide. In 1939 she quietly left the school, probably because of her Communism. She and Elizabeth were friends for life and stayed at each other's homes in England and Australia.

When Elliott and Elizabeth met, she was a first-year law student following in the steps of her father. Her beliefs evolved in parallel with Elliott's, but she was happier in the background. She was a key member of the thwarted Radical Club, the Left-wing forum banned by the University during the war, and as its secretary wrote to the University Union in April 1940 to request that the club be represented on the Debating Club sub-committee. In 1939 when Elizabeth was in her first year of law, Elliott was in third year and had been working for two years as an articled clerk with Povey Waterhouse. At the start of 1940, she began doing articles at her father's firm and in 1941, as the war closed in, they began discussing marriage.

---

8 Elizabeth Teesdale Smith, Woodlands Archives, Adelaide.

It was a tumultuous year and at its end, Elizabeth and Elliott were both Communists and Elliott was in military service. Elizabeth, her law degree incomplete, then amazed everyone by being elected secretary of the South Australian branch of the Federated Clerks Union. She nominated for the position after Harry Krantz was called away to war. This was Elizabeth's personal commitment to the war effort and it showed how serious she was about ensuring that the conditions of workers and the interests of the union were protected. She took the job almost on instinct, even though she was mid-way through her degree. 'I thought the experience of working in a union would be very valuable. I tried to do one subject of the law course a year but that was very hard to do', she said.[9] She was the first female secretary of a trade union in South Australia and the first woman delegate and executive member of the South Australian Trades and Labor Council. Holding this role cemented her position as one of the most loved and revered women in South Australia's labour movement.

Elliott had known Harry Krantz from their work on the South Australian Clerks Award, but Elizabeth's decision to replace him was her own. Like her great friend Mary Miller, an organiser for the Munitions Workers (later Ironworkers) Union who sewed cordite into bags for 23-pounder shells at the Munitions Small Arms factory at Hendon, Elizabeth stepped into a man's job. She was the union's only paid employee and did everything, including enrolling new workers under the award rates. It was a struggle; even gaining entry to offices to speak to the clerks was a battle because of employer resentment towards the unionisation of white-collar workers who were in positions of trust the employers believed could be abused. 'It was very, very hard – long hours and very hard work,' Elizabeth said, 'but the fundamental job was to go out and get members, organising, getting out to various offices, getting permission to speak and explaining what the union did'.[10]

The union covered not only members in South Australia but

---

9 Elizabeth Johnston interviewed by Eleanor Ramsay (in *To Unite More Closely. A history of the United Trades and Labor Council of South Australia*, ed. Chris Vevers, United Trades and Labor Council of South Australia, Adelaide, 1984, p. 50).

10 ibid.

also the new Northern Territory branch, which included employees of the Civil Constructional Corps, a civilian force of volunteers and conscripts who built Australia's wartime infrastructure, including the road between Darwin and Alice Springs, airstrips, hospitals, wharves and defensive posts. There were fifty thousand members nationally and most were concentrated in the north of Australia, in Elizabeth's patch. Many of the letters between Elizabeth and her members concerned details of their work conditions. 'I don't recall having dealt with any matter which has been more confused and disorganised, and what will eventually happen is beyond guessing', she wrote of the conditions in which male and female construction workers were to be housed during an infrastructure project in Darwin.

Elizabeth visited workers in the Northern Territory, which at that time was administratively controlled and required a permit to enter. Travelling alone, she caught the train from Adelaide to Alice Springs and contacted members in Alice Springs and Darwin. Harry Krantz thought her very courageous and believed she was the only woman doing such work. Her common sense and directness was noted. 'Monday night's meeting was a revelation to most union members when the general secretary from Adelaide explained award variations, determinations etc, in everyday language', the Federated Clerks Union newsletter *Smoke Signal* noted in August 1945.

At the end of the war, when Harry Krantz had returned home, Elizabeth relinquished the position. She was then elected treasurer of the Trades and Labor Council and became a life member of the Federated Clerks Union. Safeguarding conditions for women during the war proved to be crucial. The entry of more than ninety thousand women into the paid workforce between 1940 and 1945, many of them into the heavy industries, was a milestone in labour relations, opening doors that never fully closed. Women did not revert to their pre-war selves. Their demonstrated capacity for equal work led indirectly to the 1969 ACTU case for equal pay that stripped industrial classifications of gender. The seeds of the liberation of women had been sown and Elizabeth took up a position defending those wartime gains. 'At the end of the war, there was a concern among the unions that the rates established under the

Women's Employment Board (which set rates of pay in jobs previously done by men) should be protected. There was an awareness in the trade union movement that some effort had to be made to try to help, protect, and advance the gains won through the Women's Employment Board', she said.[11]

Elizabeth began married life with Elliott on Christmas Eve, 1945, on his return from New Guinea. They borrowed a friend's flat, then lived with Elliott's family, and later for a time at Maryland until a house became available almost exactly opposite at 513 Marion Road. Maryland remained the heart of their family life and the days of work and laughter were followed by nights of music, cards and parlour games. On special occasions they rolled back the carpet in the sitting room and everyone danced, men and women and women with women. It was sophisticated, free-spirited and exceptional.

The family accepted Elliott and Elizabeth's marriage and politics. Even after Stewart was born and Elliott had travelled a year later to the Peace Congress in Warsaw, visited Russia on the way home and returned virtually penniless to become a full-time Communist organiser, leaving four years later for 18 months in China, no one asked him how he intended to take care of one of the Teesdale Smith girls.

The family was generous to a fault. Sally Smith, a young mother married to a Communist and a friend of Elizabeth's, asked Paul Teesdale Smith in the 1950s if he could make some land available for a Mothers and Babies Health Centre. She and Elizabeth ran an informal child-minding centre at the RSL Hall at Marion, where on Fridays mothers could leave their children while they did the weekly shopping. Sally Smith nervously approached Elizabeth's father, who answered with a kindly, 'Yes, dear, you can have it'. He marked out a corner block of Maryland near an olive grove, made another block available to the Boy Scouts, and leased both to the Marion Council for a peppercorn rent. At the opening of the Mothers and Babies Health Association Centre, which for a time bore the Teesdale Smith name, Paul Teesdale Smith spoke movingly about how he loved to hear the music and sounds of children playing from a corner of his property. It was all done without a fuss.

11 ibid.

When the Teesdale Smith name was erased from the centre years later, Smith rang and wrote to complain (to no avail).

Elliott never considered it odd that a woman from Elizabeth's privileged background should be a Communist, or that she had paid a price. All kinds of people signed up to the Communist Party and the peace movement in response to the horrors of the Depression and the spectre of European Fascism. No one suggested that Elizabeth, wealthy and talented, should aspire to being more than a Communist, let alone marrying one.

She could have chosen not to work at all and to fill her life with art, tennis, horses, literature, travel and music. Lindy Powell found Elizabeth and her family like an Adelaide version of the literary Bloomsbury set. 'Here they all were talking about politics. They had the most interesting dinners. There were Christmas parties where the most fascinating and intelligent women would dance with each other. I was transported', Powell said.

Elliott's father-in-law never spoke to him about being a Communist. 'It simply was not an issue for him that he thought to discuss with me', Elliott said. Paul Teesdale Smith may have had private reservations, and Margot Milner's role in converting Elizabeth to Communism at Woodlands was a subject for discussion in the family. Elizabeth's ASIO file claims that she realised she was 'a great disappointment' to her father, at least until her career took off.[12] But the affection between them did not falter.

Paul Teesdale Smith was a man of such strong principle that he stood up for his son-in-law's rights when, after the war, the RSL tried to block Communists as members. The national policy was accepted by all but the Marion branch, where Paul Teesdale Smith and another man had led opposition to it. A national representative of the RSL went to Adelaide to bring the rebels into line, but failed. Elliott, who had not joined the RSL because he was too busy, could not speak highly enough of his father-in-law. 'He was not a Communist, I don't think he was a Socialist but he believed in the right to hold an opinion. He was a great man', Elliott said.

After leaving the union, Elizabeth put her energy into the

---

12 ASIO, Elliott Frank Johnston, National Archives of Australia, Canberra, 5 June 1957.

Communist Party and helped establish the Left-wing Co-operative Printing Press, which published a South Australian version of the Communist weekly, *Tribune*. She kept their accounts and worked at their print office until late in 1949, when she gave birth to Stewart. It was a difficult, life-threatening birth, and Stewart, born Ian Stewart Johnston and known as Ian until his teens, was their only child. In her 60s, Elizabeth was diagnosed with a clotting disorder, Anti Thrombin 3, a genetic condition that Stewart inherited.

The Marion area was beginning to change from what essentially had been farmland to residential subdivision and in 1950 the Communist Party opened a branch. Elizabeth and Elliott were founding members, along with their good friends, Graham Smith and Dr David Caust. Elizabeth became branch secretary and each week distributed a dozen or more copies of *Tribune*. Elliott had begun his dogged three-decade career as an aspiring Communist candidate by standing for the Marion Council. The Johnston house became a hub of campaign activity, filled with books, people and politics. In 1951 their house was the headquarters for opposition to the Menzies referendum on Communism and strangers would knock on the door seeking information and pamphlets.

Much was expected of the Communist wives, including a willingness to shoulder financial hardship. Sally Smith had a more difficult time with this than Elizabeth. Graham Smith was a militant Communist who lost two jobs and was barred from becoming a teacher. When Elliott was invited to the Sheffield Peace Congress, he also had wanted to go, but Sally, who had a young child and was pregnant with another, opposed it. She says her husband, who later married teacher Leonie Ebert, never forgave her. Elizabeth had her own difficult moments as a Communist wife. She had been left by herself when Elliott went to Sheffield, Warsaw and Russia, and during his trip to China – from 1955 until 1957 – she was out of touch with him for almost 18 months. When he finally returned, he was four months late. Smith remembered that at times Elizabeth found Elliott's absence difficult. But she weathered the storms for the sake of Communism. Even ASIO, as they spied on her, recognised her integrity. 'Elizabeth Johnston is intellectually superior to all the other women in the CPA in this state. It is considered that in all probability her interest in Communism in the first place was due to generous instincts – hatred of injustice, pity for the less fortunate, and impatience with the slowness of social reform … She is one of those people whose sympathy for the "down and outs" overwhelms their judgment and sense of proportion.'[13]

In the late 1950s when Elliott returned to the law, Stewart was a schoolboy and Elizabeth was free to return to the University of Adelaide to complete her law degree. She repeated her articles and completed third-year subjects including Latin. In 1958 she was awarded the Bachelor of Laws degree and went to work part-time with the fledgling Johnston & Johnston, where she handled estates and legal claims, managed the trust account and did the books until the late 1960s, when Jack Lewis and Robyn Layton arrived and the firm moved to Carrington Street.

Elizabeth was too busy to be part of the nightly drinks or Friday lunches at Neddy's restaurant, and she had no office of her own. She worked in a timber-lined room at the back of the building on a makeshift desk made from a door that lay across a bath. In the early 1970s, when Elliott was a Queen's Counsel and the firm became Johnston & Partners, the work flowed in. Elizabeth could have used her strong union ties to build her own client base. However, she left to take up what she considered to be significant work in the Crown Law office with the reformist Dunstan Government.

By the mid-1970s she was part of a circle of influential Adelaide feminists who were implementing Dunstan's agenda. The group consisted of the Women's Adviser to the Premier Deborah McCulloch, the Equal Opportunity Commissioner Mary Beasley, media adviser Carol Treloar and Robyn Layton, who chaired the Classification of Publications Board (known in the Public Service as the 'porn board'). Elizabeth was the least famous of the five women, who in a 1976 profile in *The Australian* were archly referred to as the 'mafiosi', or godmothers, of Dunstan's reformist policy. 'The truth is that there are five women in South Australia who are fundamentally affecting State Government policy and administration and moving both areas more rapidly toward functionally effective sexual equality than Elizabeth Reid [appointed Women's Adviser in Canberra in 1973] would have believed possible for the Whitlam

13 ibid.

Government, and more spectacularly than certainly the Dunstan Government expected', journalist Peter Ward wrote.[14]

Appointed a temporary solicitor in 1971 and made permanent the following year, Elizabeth became a senior solicitor in June 1973. She worked on conveyancing, handled leases registered under the Aboriginal Lands Trust and managed agreements on the conduct of children's homes. She drafted new Regulations under the *National Parks and Wildlife Act 1972* and gave opinions on aspects of the *Workmen's Compensation Act 1971* in the Industrial Court. She represented the Attorney-General on the Legal Aid Committee of the Law Society and chaired a working party to report on the establishment of a Legal Aid Commission in South Australia. She provided legal opinions in a range of areas, including copyright, the development of West Lakes and the ill-fated indenture for a proposed petrochemical plant at Redcliff, a major infrastructure project that did not proceed.

In August 1976, she became the first female assistant Crown Solicitor in South Australia, and in the same year was appointed to her most prominent public role, that of the first chair of the South Australian Sex Discrimination Board. Deborah McCulloch and university lecturer Father Peter Travers were her board members. The *Sex Discrimination Act 1975*, proclaimed in 1976, was the forerunner to the *Equal Opportunity Act* and preceded it by almost a decade. It was more narrowly aimed at outlawing discrimination provoked by sex or marital status in employment, education, the provision of goods and services, and accommodation. It was the work of the Dunstan Government, although it began life as a Private Member's Bill introduced by the Liberal member for Bragg and later Premier of South Australia, David Tonkin, who saw his widowed mother struggle to work in a society that did not grant her equal status. Under the new law, it was illegal to victimise a person who complained about discrimination and it was no longer legitimate to advertise jobs by gender.

The board was entitled to hear complaints and to authorise exemptions if the grounds warranted it. There were some innovative attempts to escape the new law. Noel Teasdale, the manager of

14 Peter Ward, 'Where women have a say', *Australian*, 23 December 1976.

a rundown Hindley Street hotel called the Mediterranean, appealed for the right to keep his front bar a men-only zone. Teasdale claimed that the hotel was overrun by drug users and prostitutes who would service a queue of men lined up outside the toilets. His solution was to ban women from the front bar altogether. He claimed the tactic was working but he needed another four to six weeks to be sure the women moved on. Jill Matthews, a feminist and academic who went into the front bar of the Mediterranean two days before the board met and was refused a drink, argued against it. She was given leave to appear as 'an intervener' and argued that barring women implied they caused the anti-social behaviour, while the men were let off the hook. Elizabeth supported her. 'Whilst the board appreciates that the presence of prostitutes may well lead to prostitution on the premises, it is not convinced that the presence of drug users, criminals and other undesirable persons is accountable to the presence of women', she found.[15] Noel Teasdale was told to rely on the police and the licensing laws.

A more significant finding involved a young nurse who was dismissed by a North Adelaide nursing home because she was pregnant. She wanted to work until her seventh month, but 14 weeks into the pregnancy she was fired. She was told she represented a higher insurance risk and that the owner could not afford to continue to employ her. When she attempted to complain, she was shown the door. Pregnancy was not grounds for protection under the Act and the gender argument was problematic because another woman could replace her. But Elizabeth found a way around it by accepting that pregnancy fell within the meaning of 'a presumed characteristic' exclusive to the female of the species. She was able to bring a finding that the nurse's removal was therefore discriminatory; the nurse was compensated and got her job back.

Cases like these were glamour issues for Elizabeth's board and they were important victories for the women's movement. But she also quietly worked in the background to pressure banks to stop charging women housing interest rates up to four per cent more

15 Sex Discrimination Board, *In the matter of an application by Dawainne Pty. Ltd. for exemption for certain provisions of the* Sex Discrimination Act, 1975, Adelaide, 10 November 1976.

than men and also terminated the time-honoured practice used by companies like Broken Hill Associated Smelters in Port Pirie to demand that working women resign when they married. Elizabeth also pioneered work behind the scenes to bring newspapers in line with the new rules on gender-free advertising. Although the Sex Discrimination Board was a quasi-judicial body, she knew she would achieve more through education and support than punishment. Elizabeth sat down with the managers of Adelaide's largest newspaper, *The Advertiser*, to work through the transition from overtly sexist advertising for women secretaries and typists, to gender-neutral advertisements pitched at the merits of both. Most men were genuinely stumped as to how this could be done and she devoted the best part of a year to showing them what could change. Deborah McCulloch was impressed with Elizabeth's practical approach and the difference that the legislation made. '[There was] a whole range of assumptions about what was women's work and what was men's work. I mean you looked around at jobs like journalism and they were all men. Now there are women everywhere but it all started from the legislation', she said.

Elizabeth let others make colourful public statements about women's rights; her political agenda went further than overdue gains in the gender wars. Her feminism was part of a broader Communist platform demanding deep social realignment. It was the position of many female Communists, with French philosopher Simone de Beauvoir stating it most famously in her 1949 feminist treatise, *The Second Sex.* She defined 'the problem' of being a woman and showed how it curtailed freedom and rights. Elizabeth, who had a collection of books by Simone de Beauvoir in her library, considered that socialism was the solution and believed that problems of access and inequity, like childcare and healthcare, would be ameliorated in a socialist economy. McCulloch disagreed, telling Elizabeth to look at the lives of Russian women who had free childcare, but every morning handed over their babies in order to work long hours in a factory. Elizabeth listened but did not change her mind.

Elizabeth had the courage to face her critics. Not long after the tabloid exposé that 'unmasked' Elliott, Elizabeth went to an education conference at which the former ASIO spy, Anne Neill, was speaking. The conference heard a report from the RSL about the infiltration of Communists into South Australian schools. Elizabeth got to her feet. 'I am not a member of this association but as one of those terrible Communists Mrs Neill has spoken about, I would like to express another opinion', she said. She attempted to continue speaking, but a slow handclap from the delegates showed their disapproval of the Communist in their midst. 'Mrs Neill will say Mrs Johnston is a Communist. I will admit this publicly. However I think it only fair to say the Minister of Education has looked into this alleged Communist activity among South Australian school teachers and that he is apparently quite satisfied that the teachers are doing an adequate job.'[16] She was expelled from the meeting after a motion from the floor prevented her from speaking. 'Slow Clap Halts Communist' was the headline above a newspaper report of their confrontation.

Elizabeth's response to the 1976 strike by the ACTU over the Fraser Government's attempts to water down Medibank illustrated her commitment to principles she held dear. Like Elliott she believed in the universal health care model introduced by the Whitlam Government and although the strike did not involve the South Australian Public Service Association of which she was a member, she went on strike for the day. The government tried to pay her anyway and she had to argue that her salary should be docked. It was a one-woman strike that nobody noticed and she had to fight not to be paid.

She had a peripheral role in the other landmark shift in policy under Dunstan, Aboriginal land rights. She had championed the rights of Aboriginal people and with Elliott attended the 1971 meeting when the Aboriginal Legal Rights Movement was established. She believed that Aboriginal people had been alienated from their land and that white Australia should begin a process by which it could be reclaimed. In the late 1970s a working party was set up under lawyer Christopher Cocks to draft land rights legislation that would hand back to the northern Pitjantjatjara people an area of 102,000 square kilometres, bound on the north by the breathtaking Musgrave Ranges. Cocks travelled to the Pitjantjatjara lands and

16 'Slow clap halts Communist', *Advertiser*, 31 July 1963.

came back with a model for land rights that went beyond communal control and returned ownership to the Indigenous people. Elizabeth was seconded from Crown Law to advise Cocks and his working party on the practical details of the legislation. A Bill introduced into the South Australian Parliament in 1978 picked up almost all of the working party's recommendations, but languished when Dunstan resigned because of ill health. The Liberal Government adopted it after minor changes over mineral rights and in 1981 Dr David Tonkin, then Premier of South Australia, ceremonially handed the land back.

Elizabeth worked in Crown Law for just over 10 years and her employment was a catalogue of the changing times. At age 56, she represented the Attorney-General for three years on the Legal Aid Committee of the South Australian Law Society and chaired a committee reporting on the establishment of the first quasi-independent Legal Aid Commission. Greg Crafter, who was the executive officer, credits her with being the chief driver of the Legal Aid Commission, set up in 1979 and still operating today.

All the while, her bohemian political and home life continued. Crafter remembers strolling with Elizabeth through the Brookman Building in Grenfell Street in the city on the site where later the AMP Centre housed for a time the Federal Court and the Family Court. It was then a lovely old building with a linoleum floor and clusters of legal offices, accountants and coin and stamp collectors. Crafter remarked to Elizabeth that it was a pity it was being pulled down. Yes, she said thoughtfully but without any fuss, the building had been in her family for years and it was a shame to see it go.

As assistant Crown Solicitor she rode around town on an old bicycle, smoked heavily, socialised closely with a circle of women friends and delivered copies of *Tribune* at night and on weekends. She would field domestic calls from Elliott at her office at Crown Law; he once rang to ask how much soap went into the washing machine. A long conversation ensued about exactly how he should do the washing and how much soap powder to use. It would have been easier to tell him to leave it to her, but her principles would not allow it.

Stewart, an only child, was being raised in an unusually informed and politicised environment. The family would sit together at dinner and not begin eating until Stewart correctly named the neighbours of a country nominated by Elliott or Elizabeth, an effective daily lesson in geography. In 1962, aged 12, he came to the notice of ASIO for collecting signatures on a petition to make the southern hemisphere nuclear free. ASIO reported someone saying to Elliott, 'You've got your son on the ball with these peace petitions', and Elliott nodding approvingly.[17]

The Johnstons mixed with a tight group of friends and spent weekends away at a house near Victor Harbor. Later they purchased a house in Moonta, a coastal town with a Cornish mining heritage on Yorke Peninsula, 165 kilometres from Adelaide. It was shabby and rundown but there were plenty of rooms. They held working bees to patch up walls or repair floors, followed by a game of bridge, *vin ordinaire* and a roast leg of mutton prepared by Elliott. At Christmas, the group, which included Mary Miller, Ruth Fletcher and Sally Smith, would arrive after Christmas dinner and stay for a couple of weeks.

Mary Miller had met Elizabeth when they were young Communists and they remained friends for life. She was politically committed, a union activist and an organiser with the Peace Council. She and Marjorie Johnston founded the New Theatre in Adelaide, a drama troupe that performed plays with Left-wing content. Elizabeth joined and one of their biggest productions was the musical *Reedy River*, about the 1892 shearers' strike. The cast, which was comprised mainly of waterside workers, sang revivals of Australian folk songs, including 'Click go the shears'. The troupe tried but failed to persuade Aboriginal players to join and had to make do with white actors in blackface.

Elizabeth remained a close friend of Margot Milner, the radical young French teacher from Woodlands whose extraordinary connections and achievements were recognised in 1995 in an obituary in London's *The Independent*. Milner was troubled throughout her life by unresolved allegations that her husband was an Australian link to the notorious group of Oxford-educated Communist spies who had given secrets to the Russians. In 1940 in Adelaide, Milner had married fellow Communist and diplomat Ian Milner; the couple

17 ASIO, 'Ian Stewart Johnston', National Archives of Australia, Canberra, 13 June 1962.

moved to Melbourne and then to New York, where he took up a position in the Security Council of the United Nations. In 1954, in the fallout from the Petrov affair, Milner, a former Rhodes Scholar at New College, Oxford, was accused of espionage by the Australian Government. The United Kingdom and the United States had jointly deciphered the Soviet Union's Project Venona diplomatic codes and closed in on a ring of Western spies, among them Donald Maclean, Kim Philby and Guy Burgess. Australian Communists were suspected of being involved and Milner was one of two people named. A few weeks later he resigned from his position at the United Nations and went with Margot behind the Iron Curtain. From Prague, he denied being a spy. They divorced and Margot Milner later went to England and worked at the BBC, where she became an expert in early music. She always denied that her ex-husband was part of the Philby-Burgess-Maclean circle of spies, although Elizabeth thought privately he probably was.[18] She and Margot would catch up infrequently in either England or Australia. They were intellectual equals and warm friends.

Paul Teesdale Smith died suddenly of a heart attack on 8 March 1962, and in 1964, the family seat of Maryland was sold. The large holding was divided and demolished and only a few landmark trees remained. Helen Teesdale Smith had been in poor health for some time. In the 1930s, still a young woman, she had fallen from a horse in a crippling accident that broke her back. It left her so badly stooped that her head almost rested on her chest. Nevertheless, she cut an industrious figure striding across the yard in a fine wool poncho woven by her sister Joyce. Although more than a decade older than Paul, she outlived him by ten years, and after the sale of Maryland she moved to Summit Road at Crafers to live at The Glen with Cecil, Elizabeth, Elliott and Stewart. Living almost next door were Elizabeth's other sister, Mary,[19] and her friend, Barbara Wall, a highly regarded senior mistress in English at Woodlands. In 1971 Helen moved to The Gap, also in Crafers, where she lived until her death. Cecil and her partner Ellen Christensen, the headmistress of Presbyterian Girls College (later Seymour College), where Cecil was

18 Interview with Stewart Johnston, 28 September 2006.

19 Mary Teesdale Smith died in 2006.

also much loved as a senior English mistress, built a house nearby at Vantage Way at Crafers and lived there until Cecil's early death from lung disease and the thrombosis related to the family problems with blood clotting. Elliott's parents had died two decades earlier. Elsie Johnston fell ill with stomach cancer when she was relatively young and Elliott and Elizabeth moved into Elliott's old home and cared for her until her death in 1949, aged 59. William Johnston died suddenly of a heart attack four years later, aged 64.

After Helen's death in 1972, Elizabeth, Elliott and Stewart returned to the city. Elizabeth found a solid, stone terrace house in need of renovation at the eastern end of Gilles Street. With beautiful leadlight front windows and high, ornate ceilings, the house was close to the parklands in an enclave that later included the first female Governor in South Australia, Dame Roma Mitchell, and Robyn Layton. They bought Gilles Street for $15,826 and spent as much again doing up the bathroom, adding a laundry and installing a new roof. They filled the lovely old terrace with art and books. Elizabeth's antique furniture and fine bone china were from the Waterhouse and Teesdale Smith connections. They lived modestly and Elizabeth, despite her family wealth, clung to strong ideas about how a Communist should live. She denied herself comforts, believing they were indulgences, and never accumulated personal luxuries, or even conveniences. She owned magnificent furniture and inherited art objects, but she would cook using a hand whisk and refused to buy an electric beater. This self denial was in keeping with the spirit of the Party, although ASIO did report a tiff between her and Elliott when Elizabeth complained about being always short of money.[20] They struggled on for years with an old, broken pressure cooker that was held down by placing a weight on top. Every few months, it would blow its top and coat the kitchen walls with soup.

In her fifties Elizabeth began to travel, visiting China in 1977 with a group that included ALP Legislative Councillor Anne Levy and Stewart, who came at the last minute after someone had dropped out. It was a semi-official visit, organised with the help of the Dunstan Government; their group was among the first tourists

20 ASIO, 'Elliott Frank Johnson', National Archives of Australia, Canberra, 12 January, 1965.

allowed in after the death in 1976 of the Communist leader Mao Tse-tung. In 1974 she joined Elliott on his trip to England to appear before the Privy Council on the appeal by Frits Van Beelen against his conviction for the Taperoo Beach murder. They stopped off in Greece for several days and were pictured climbing the steps of the ancient Parthenon, a couple of middle-age western tourists talked into buying photographs taken by a local who had latched on to them. About a year later Elizabeth visited Indonesia on a study tour, and, in 1979, she fell in love with Europe, particularly Italy and Florence. Some of her long-held inhibitions about enjoying at least some of life's privileges began to abate. She became a great appreciator of Italian art, particularly the dramatic tableaus of Michelangelo and Caravaggio.

Elizabeth went without Elliott on her first trip to Italy, staying first with Margot Milner in England. Elliott had remained in Adelaide to work on a Medicare fraud case. She then met with Mary Miller and Ruth Fletcher in Vienna, and Elliott joined them in Venice. The group went across to Yugoslavia, travelled by boat to Ankara in Turkey, and returned to Bari, where they began a driving tour of Italy. It was winter and there were few tourists. Elliott decided they should visit Plati in Italy's south, the former home of some of his immigrant clients. They caused a stir when Elliott tried to call on the mayor, who was in Naples for a wedding, to pay his respects. Word spread around town about the well-to-do tourists in their Audi hire car and they were welcomed into a stranger's home for bread and olives.

As the party drove up through a remote stretch of the Aspromonte Mountains in Calabria, they came to a section of the road which was blocked by large rocks. They were forced to stop. Ruth Fletcher was driving, with Elizabeth next to her in the front, while Elliott and Mary Miller were in the back. When Elizabeth and Elliott got out of the car to move the rocks, four masked men with rifles emerged from behind an outcrop alongside the road. 'We're Australians! Australians', shouted Elliott (hoping the bandits preferred Americans). He was frisked and the gunmen took his wallet containing 100,000 lire ($110 dollars) but missed a money belt stuffed with notes withdrawn from a bank earlier that day. Ruth Fletcher remembers a rifle trained on them, as the bandits, a local

Mafia gang, attempted to force them from the car. Suddenly, the man on watch shouted a warning and the bandits vanished as a car came down the road. Their bags were stolen and they lost passports, travel documents and reading glasses but no one was harmed. They reported the theft and were told to return along the more populated east coast. 'QC in Armed Holdup' was on the street posters advertising Adelaide's tabloid daily, *The News*, which carried the headline splash, 'Mafia Ambush Adelaide QC: Terror hold-up in Italy'.[21] Stewart read about his parents' ordeal in the paper.

Even on trips away and with close friends whose company they enjoyed, Elizabeth and Elliott, after almost 40 years of marriage, were closer to each other than to anyone else. They would examine paintings or plaques and discuss their history and context. Ruth Fletcher says they were a pair and you didn't intrude. 'No one resented it. It was interesting', she said. An ASIO report of Elliott and Elizabeth noted their close bond and described them as dancing together and whispering, more like lovers than a married couple.

As Elizabeth aged, her appetite for travel became keener and she became more intrepid. While she was a regular visitor to Italy, France and Spain, Stewart had spent long periods travelling through Asia and in the early 1990s Elliott and Elizabeth, both in their 70s, backpacked with Stewart and his wife, Janet, through India, staying in cheap hotels and sleeping rough on the Bangalore Express.

After Elizabeth retired from Crown Law in 1982, aged 62, she studied the history of art at Flinders University but continued to help Aboriginal people and promote the cause of women. She was a member and later secretary of the Aboriginal Education Foundation, founded by Don Dunstan's first wife, Gretel, to encourage Aboriginal children to attend school. Indigenous women in South Australia always had a strong voice and the Aboriginal Women's Council headed by Point Pearce elder Gladys Elphick laid the groundwork locally for the Aboriginal Legal Rights Movement. Shirley Peisley, a field officer in the early days of the ALRM, credited Elizabeth with helping to develop the first Aboriginal preschool centre in South Australia. In her continuing support of

21 Mike Safe, 'Mafia Ambush Adelaide QC: Terror hold-up in Italy', *News*, 18 October 1979.

women's rights, Elizabeth became a mentor to the women's movement, again, away from the limelight. In 1979, the South Australian Working Women's Centre became a practical feminist resource on matters such as workers' compensation, sexual harassment and discrimination at work. It also advised and supported migrant and Aboriginal women. Stephanie Key, then a Flinders University student activist who took over as director of the centre in 1981 aged 26, looked up to Elizabeth as a role model for trade union activism. She found her to be a source of wise counsel, short-tempered at times, but never seeking to lecture or dispense advice from above. Elizabeth's standing in the union movement gave her great sway and Key said that she smoothed the way with Harry Krantz for a women's committee to be established in the Federated Clerks Union. Krantz, whose union was under siege in the 1950s, was suspicious of everyone, including women, but Elizabeth brought him around.

In 1984 Elizabeth joined the Board of the South Australian Housing Trust when a major shift from public to welfare housing was gaining momentum. There was resistance to acknowledging that a fundamental change was taking place in the services the Housing Trust had to provide. The trust had been established as an instrument of economic growth during the Playford years when it built housing for the blue-collar workers needed for the state's manufacturing sector, like General Motors-Holden's at Elizabeth. At the time Elizabeth joined, its services were overshadowed by the crisis demands of welfare housing. The most disadvantaged often needed housing at short notice and other welfare agencies had to be called in. Elizabeth and Stephanie Key, who came onto the board at the same time, wanted a separate emergency housing office set up within the Housing Trust which would deliver a range of social and mental health services. How all this was to be managed became a drawn-out debate that was still going on when Elizabeth left four years later. Elizabeth had an instinct for what mattered; she would grill the rest of the board on details they had not considered, on whether proposed housing was close to schools and public transport and whether there were childcare services nearby. Key, who became a state Labor minister, said some of the board members considered this to be warm and fuzzy thinking; it is now accepted as social impact.

Elizabeth stayed true to Communism, even as it failed in Russia and China, and as the Party crumbled at home. ASIO had predicted in the 1950s that she would be a Communist for the long haul: 'Whilst Elizabeth is not considered to be quite so fanatical as Elliott, it is still felt that her loyalty to the CPA will not change, not for some years anyway'.[22] They were right and she became more brittle and hard-line as time went on. Like Elliott, her causes widened in the late 1990s to include issues that were linked to the Left. She was troubled by the deteriorating state of the River Murray, the lack of progress with Aboriginal reconciliation, and the detention of asylum seekers and their children.

The CPA limped on through the 1980s fighting a rising tide of triumphant materialism and the anti-socialist concept of 'user pays', and Elizabeth's five decades of membership ended with its demise. With the massacre in 1989 of an unknown number of students, intellectuals and activists in Tiananmen Square, where Elliott in the mid-1950s had proudly stood and watched Chairman Mao, the Party entered its death throes. Who could call themselves a Communist at the end of the twentieth century and expect that anyone would support them? The ideals of Communism had been irreparably besmirched by the failings of the Communist regimes.

As numbers dwindled, the Party lived off its assets. Elizabeth spent the latter part of the 1980s managing The People's Bookshop at 25 Angas Street, where die-hard activists would drop in to chat. The Party had moved to the building, known for a time as the theatre, The Red Shed, after it had left its rented Hindley Street shopfront and sold its property at 27 Wright Court.

The end was especially unpleasant for Elizabeth. In March 1991, the CPA held its last congress. After 70 years, the organisation was shattered and demoralised, with all purpose gone. The People's Bookshop and theatre were to be sold and leased. As Elizabeth began clearing books, a shelf fell upon her. Her ankle was broken so badly that surgery at the Wakefield Hospital was required. It was a time of great anguish and the end of a dream.

Just over a decade later, in 2002, Elizabeth died of cancer aged

22 ASIO, Elliott Frank Johnston, National Archives of Australia, Canberra, 5 June 1957.

81, a month from turning 82. She had been ill for a short time and was cared for in the Mary Potter Hospice; she sat propped up with pillows as she bid her friends farewell. Her death was commemorated at the Tandanya Aboriginal Cultural Institute in Grenfell Street. Her friends Sally Smith and Ruth Fletcher were there. Mary Miller, who died the following year, spoke of Elizabeth's fight to preserve women's rights during the war. Other speakers were the former head of ATSIC, Lowitja O'Donoghue, the President of the Law Society of South Australia, Christopher Kourakis QC, and Stephanie Key. Kevin Fisher, an old friend, sang one of the songs from *Reedy River*. Stewart had grown up with Maryland as his own private Arcadia and at the funeral he brought to life something of Elizabeth's extraordinary background. He had found a letter written by his great-grandmother about the charm of the home Helen and Paul Teesdale Smith created after the First World War. 'The family bought the house because they couldn't see anything else they liked so well. They have lived there ever since, such a happy bohemian life, with children who were in sympathy with their tastes', Laura Waterhouse wrote.

Elizabeth's fierce principles denied her the life of privilege she could have led, but provided her fulfilment in another way. Her spirit very much defined her. Stewart at her funeral told a marvellous story from his childhood when, in response to some crisis now forgotten, he ran away from home. He fled from his bath and ran down Marion Road. Elizabeth caught up with him. Instead of being angry, she reassured Stewart there was no need to feel ashamed about walking home naked through the traffic. They returned together, hand in hand, their heads high. 'I cannot fully explain how empowered that made me feel. If it's okay to walk naked with your Mum down Marion Road, it was going to be okay to try a few other things', Stewart said. He followed this with another family story that demonstrated Elizabeth's genuine compassion for others. Only a few years before she died, a burglar broke into Gilles Street while she and Elliott lay sleeping. Elizabeth heard a sound in the kitchen and went down the passage to find a burglar raiding the fridge. No one knew what was said but Elizabeth made him a cup of tea and sat him down for a midnight chat. He left by the front door and Elizabeth went back to bed. Minutes later she answered a knock on the door. The burglar was back to thank her and to return the items he had stolen. Elliott slept through it all.

On her death Elizabeth donated her body to science. Elliott's annual remembrance of Elizabeth is to attend a ceremony of thanks at the University of Adelaide's Elder Hall for the relatives of donors.

Chapter 11

The true believer

Elliott, at 92, is still a Communist. He has slowed down physically and old age has brought increasingly severe bouts of pneumonia, forgetfulness and cataracts that for a time clouded his working eye. But he has never given up his beliefs. Have you ever regretted becoming a member of the Communist Party, he was once asked.

> No, I haven't actually. By that I don't mean to say that one's views on certain subjects don't change, both individually and as a Party. Nor, of course, am I silly enough to suggest that our Party has always been right in the past, or will always be right on political issues in the future. But broadly speaking, and in the broad general developments and our policy, I'm a very ... well I'm very proud to have been a member of the Communist Party.[1]

He belonged, always, to the Left. In his 90s, he was on the management and editorial committees of *Options*, a South Australian-based magazine he co-founded in 1995 as a vehicle for post-Communist discussion. It has struggled to find an audience for its embittered anti-capitalism. 'The ideologues of the global corporations think they are home and hosed. There seems to be no opposition. Socialism, they think, is dead. Long live the dollar. These people should learn that ordinary people are strong. They don't often win but they are never beaten.'[2] The magazine is published four times a year and the management committee meets in Gilles Street, where Elliott lives alone. In his 90s, Elliott was on

1 Talkback interview on Radio 5DN, Adelaide, 10 April 1975.

2 Elliott Johnston, 'Working Nation proposals', *Options,* Adelaide, June, 1995.

the management committee, with Don Jarrett, a second-generation Communist whom Elliott met in Port Augusta, and the editorial sub-committee. Its subscription base in 2008 was less than 1000 and it was trying to find new ways to engender Left-wing discussion.

The Party's sad end had left Elliott in as much despair as it had Elizabeth. By the time the Royal Commission into Aboriginal Deaths in Custody had ended, the CPA no longer existed. Elliott and Elizabeth attended meetings of the New Left party but this organisation also petered out. In the mid-1990s the Soviet-aligned splinter group known as the Socialist Party took the name of the Communist Party of Australia, but neither Elliott nor Elizabeth wanted anything to do with it.

The Party had collapsed in disillusion. It was heavily factionalised, members squabbled about their allegiances to different brands of Communism, and its original vision, he believed, had been lost. 'I thought there was a tremendous amount of dispute about questions that were not important for us, disputes about attitudes towards the Soviet Union which, in my opinion, were irrelevant to us', he said. Like many Communists, he blamed the Party's failure in Australia on the favourable post-war conditions that had allowed workers to flourish. It robbed the working classes of their rage. By and large, Elliott said, Australia did not have as many problems as other countries had.

In Australia, Communism had achieved very little. It was always politically marginal and limited to working-class electorates. Communists did influence some debates and protests, notably those concerning the Vietnam War, and some Communists held office in a small number of unions. Overall though, spirits had flagged and efforts were frustrated. ASIO reported an incident at a branch meeting as early as 1963 where Elliott was discouraged from standing again for council election by his sister, Marjorie, and by David Caust, who turned on him saying, 'You are not the party member you were 20 years ago. You have mixed up your party work and your private work.' But Elliott never gave up. His father had in the 1940s challenged his son over his choice of Communism, telling him the stigma of membership would hold him back. Elliott defended his choice then, and 70 years later he still considered it had been the honourable thing to do. 'I certainly never classed myself as an ex- Communist, I should make that very clear', he said. Along with his family, the law and his unmitigated passion for the Sturt Football Club, Communism had shaped and inspired him. Even ASIO accepted that he was genuine. 'Johnston is one of the few of the leadership of the CPA in South Australia who is sincere and is being a fool to himself. He is an intellectual and one of the few in this category who is accepted by the CPA leadership as a genuine revolutionary.'[3]

Even as the Party began to disintegrate, Elliott's belief in the rights and decency of ordinary people was sacrosanct. He believed Communism was a more evolved way of living and he was far from alone in this. Some Communists felt abandoned after the Party folded because their identities were so enmeshed in the internal politics. But others like Eric Aarons had an independent vision that withstood the Party's collapse. Aarons likened himself to Walter in Frank Hardy's novel about the individual and the state, *But the Dead are Many*. There were values at the core of any cause or movement and they were not lost when the party structure failed.[4]

Elliott recognised that no Communist state had succeeded. He had been in China in the mid-1950s and thought it a workers' paradise, but admiration had later turned to horror and disappointment. He had been inspired by the Russian Revolution and subsequent events, but renounced Soviet practice for something democratic, and Australian. Yet all Australian Communists were to some extent in thrall to the Soviet Union. It was part of the trappings of being a Communist and Elliott was as susceptible as anyone else. He had Communist paraphernalia around the house and he campaigned for the seat of Port Adelaide in 1980 under a poster with a clenched fist. After the 1950s, and particularly after the 1968 Soviet invasion of Czechoslovakia, he was an Australian Communist, along the lines of the emerging Euro-Communist model that matched Marxist theory to a country and its conditions. Without renouncing Russia or China, he had become critical of what each country did.

---

3 ASIO, 'Elliott Frank Johnston', National Archives of Australia, Canberra, 3 October 1955.

4 Eric Aarons, *What's Left?* Penguin Books, Melbourne, 1993, p. 233.

'We were not anti-Soviet but we were "anti" the Soviet invasion of Czechoslovakia and we were "anti" the behaviour of Stalin that had been stated at the 1956 Congress. We were not anti-China but we had been against the attitude Mao Tse-tung adopted in about 1959 when he attacked India, applied control in China and no longer applied the doctrine, "let 100 flowers bloom". We took the point of view that in Australian society we must support democracy', he said.

He took a lead in the Party's internal debates, including in the 1960s, adopting the Soviet line in his criticism of renegade Ted Hill over the Maoist split. The Party had moved back to Russia but in doing so alienated prominent Victorians, including Hill. There was a great deal of internal sniping over who made the better Communists. 'The Little Red Book, *Quotations from Chairman Mao,* is of immense service to all revolutionary workers. It ought to be our constant companion', Ted Hill wrote.[5] Elliott's attack on Hill was in the form of a paper to the state conference that was later published in *Communist Review.* His tone was didactic but he criticised the group whose infatuation with China had provoked the first serious schism in the Australian party. Hill's aggressive pro-China tactics would lead to 'the utter isolation from all the mainstreams of the working class and progressive movements', warned Elliott. He defended Russia, up to a point. 'We do not say that everything that has been said or done by the CPSU [Communist Party of the Soviet Union] is correct. We do not take our understanding of what is to be done from the CPSU; we take that understanding from the fundamental principles of Communism.'[6]

It is difficult to appreciate how deep and bitter the divisions in the 1960s went. A new leadership headed by Laurie Aarons, one of Elliott's companions from China, had emerged, and the Party's base had broadened to include students and young intellectuals. But when the Russian leader Leonid Brezhnev sent Warsaw Pact tanks into Czechoslovakia in 1968 to crush Dubcek's Prague Spring, the Party split again between those, like Elizabeth and Elliott, who

5 Ted Hill, *Looking Backward, Looking Forward: Revolutionary socialist politics against trade union and parliamentary politics,* Melbourne, 1968, p. xi

6 Elliott Johnston, 'The Position of the Hill Group', *Communist Review*, 270, 1964.

were appalled by what Russia had done, and those who clung to the Soviet dream no matter what the cost. The invasion had rocked Elliott and Elizabeth to the core. 'I find it hard to tell you how tremendous the dispute was', Elliott said. 'We had been very interested in various things that were being done in Czechoslovakia before the Soviet Union invaded. They were doing some very democratic things, and winning a lot of support. The Soviet Union just came in and said that had to stop and chucked out the leader. We both [Elizabeth and I] thought it was highly improper.'

In the fallout from the Czechoslovakia invasion, members were asked to declare their support for or against the Soviet Union's actions. Elliott, who attended a meeting held at the Poultry Breeders' Hall in Adelaide's Pulteney Street, wanted to stop the divisive motion even being put, arguing that it encouraged hatred between members. He thought it should be sorted out in a friendly manner before everyone got on with the real Party work. At a follow-up meeting at the Sydney Town Hall, the CPA denounced the Soviet invasion, which pleased Elizabeth and Elliott but triggered another exodus, this time into the Socialist Party of Australia. The atmosphere was bitter, and those who left included Jim Mitchell, a former Port Adelaide wharfie, who was one of Elliott's friends. 'It was tragic that Jim left the Party because he was a great bloke. Virtually the whole of the Port Adelaide branch left, they were mainly people from the maritime industry, and a lot from the Norwood branch', Elliott said. He maintained friendly relations with Mitchell yet he had struggled tremendously with his feelings for his own sister, who was a fierce Maoist.

Marjorie Johnston, younger than Elliott by a couple of years, had become a Communist and peace activist around the same time as Elliott. She attended the Warsaw Peace Congress and on her return to Adelaide gave talks on disarmament and peace. Briefly married but single for most of her life, Marjorie was for a long time close to Elizabeth and Elliott both socially and through the Party. She was part of the New Theatre and, when Elliott and Elizabeth bought their house on Marion Road in the early 1950s, Marjorie moved into their vacant flat at Maryland with her then husband, Max Schmidt, and lived with the Teesdale Smiths for some years. In June 1970 when Johnston & Johnston moved from

Victoria Square to Carrington Street, Elliott offered her a job. Like him, she was eccentric, but thought her own brother's obsession with Communism made him 'a bloody fanatic'.[7] Marjorie worked at Johnston & Johnston for almost a decade, but for much of that time, she and Elliott did little more than exchange pleasantries because of the Soviet–Maoist tensions. Everyone in the office knew that they were fighting but it was hard to take them seriously. Marjorie wore a Chairman Mao badge to work to provoke Elliott and held the line in defence of Chinese Communist practice, despite a mountain of evidence that conditions in China left a lot to be desired. Lindy Powell loved her spirit: 'She was this Maoist and because of it there was this great distancing between sister and brother but at the same time they loved each other like stink – she was the other side of Elliott'. Her presence divided opinion; Brian Withers kept his distance, but McCusker, like Powell, thought her magnificent.

The Party in South Australia was worried in case news of the conflict between brother and sister became public. Elliott's ASIO file recorded a meeting in 1961 at which he and Marjorie clashed but submitted to Party discipline. Marjorie had demanded a written analysis of the differences between China and the Soviet Union, but Elliott resisted. 'I don't care what you say. I just plainly want to read and know what the Chinese say and what the Russians say, and what the Chinese want, and what the Russians want, so I can judge the things in my own way', she told Elliott. ASIO found her 'almost too naïve to be true, but obviously genuine' and by nature a shy woman who found it hard to make friends.[8]

Elliott saw in working people a capacity for greatness. His faith in people was stronger than dogma and he was drawn to others who felt the same. In 1985, he spoke at the funeral of Alan Finger, who had brought to medicine the same Communist ethos that Elliott had brought to the law. Elliott told how his friend converted after working as fruit picker when he was a medical student. The pickers were paid by the bucket and at the end of each day the worker with the lightest load was sacked. Capitalism was brutal, and there

---

7 ASIO, 'Elliott Frank Johnston', National Archives of Australia, Canberra, 6 June 1954.

8 ibid., 1 May 1963.

had to be a better way, Finger had thought. Elliott saw the same qualities in Graham Smith, who had died in 1989. At his funeral Elliott said that all Smith had wanted was to live in a community that cared for the sick, protected the environment and filled people's lives with laughter and enjoyment. These were values straight from a Christian pulpit but they were also seen as the promise of Communism. Elliott and many others like him believed that they were answering the single most important call of their age. In an interview in 1999, only weeks before his death, the former Whitlam Government minister, James (Jim) McClelland, explained how the Depression made him a Trotskyite before he joined the Labor Party.

> The Depression was not a short thing, and it was misery such as the ordinary human being in Australia today can hardly imagine. There were actually gaunt, hungry-looking people confronting you every day, sitting in the parks and couldn't get a feed, couldn't feed their families. It was a type of society the present society just cannot imagine. Now that's what gave birth to the Communist movement in Australia. It was very easy to persuade ordinary sensible people that the form of society which had brought this to pass was an evil society that should be overthrown by any means.[9]

Their commitment to the ideal of a liberating, equalising Communism that safeguarded the welfare of ordinary people kept Elliott and Elizabeth above the spreading taint of Communist practice. They reached their own accommodation with what was being done elsewhere. 'You suggest that the Communist Party stands for bloodshed and so on and so forth – that's not, of course, our position. We stand for fundamental changes in society and that may happen in different places in a number of different ways', Elliott said in 1975.[10] Elliott took refuge in the resolutions of the 1951 Congress that laid out a non-revolutionary blueprint for Australia which was essentially socialist.[11] His Communism did not need blood and turmoil; it would be built on the political power of a united working

9 J. Russell, 'Communism', in *Encounter*, ABC Radio National, 14 February 1999.

10 Talkback interview on Radio 5DN.

11 Communist Party of Australia, *Australia's Path to Socialism*, Sixteenth Congress, Sydney, 1951.

class. He explained this to the South Australian state conference in 1970. 'If they use force, we will have to resist but our force will be defensive only', he said. 'The revolution will be brought about by the working class who make up 80 per cent of the population, so the capitalists will be fighting against pretty great odds. For the same reasons there will not need to be a dictatorship of the proletariat, just democracy, because of the greater majority of the workers.'[12] It may have been naïve to preach of Communism by persuasion, but Elliott meant it.

He moved confidently in Adelaide's legal circles because he was not trying by night to overthrow the system he was part of by day. Even when he campaigned, he used reason, not the threat of revolution. He talked about giving a voice to the disenfranchised and erecting government-owned economic structures that would protect people from extreme poverty. He wanted to give hardworking men and women a fighting chance. Running for the seat of Adelaide in the 1972 federal election he explained, 'I think it is important to demonstrate an alternative set of values and aims. Power in the hands of the people is the essence of what we are trying to put forward – in the factories, universities, schools, hospitals, in foreign policy and domestic policy, so that people can and should take control of the issues that determine their lives.'[13]

Some people genuinely feared his politics, and others did not like his style. But up close, Elliott never looked or sounded like much of a threat. This essential truth was recognised by John Mortimer, the writer and lawyer who created Rumpole of the Old Bailey. Mortimer visited Australia in 1983, just before Elliott became a judge, meeting him in Brisbane at a labour lawyers' conference. Mortimer later wrote of a charming, smiling man in his mid-60s with gold-rimmed glasses and almost shoulder-length white hair. His impressions of Elliott, and the significance of his pending appointment, were perceptive. 'Judge Elliott Johnston, from Adelaide, must be about the only judge in the English-speaking world who was, until his appointment compelled him to sever

12 ASIO, 'Elliott Frank Johnston', National Archives of Australia, Canberra, 17 March 1970.

13 Elliott Johnston, Letter to the *Sunday Mail,* 23 November, 1972.

his political affiliations, a paid-up and publicly-declared member of the Communist Party. Certainly Elliott Johnston was a Euro-Communist, and as such, probably about as much of a threat to society as an English Liberal', he wrote.[14] Mortimer concluded that Australia was in some matters more progressive than the United Kingdom:

> Adelaide is one of the most beautiful and most English of the Australian cities, surrounded by valleys full of the best vineyards, with grey-stone colonnaded buildings, an ivy-covered university and a modern Festival Theatre they ran up when Sydney was still arguing about its Opera House. Now they have a Communist judge, which at least argues sufficient maturity in Australia to realise that all Communists are not little red monsters from outer space, or moles in endlessly incomprehensible English spy stories. It also shows a tolerance in political matters which some say Australians haven't achieved in racial questions.[15]

Given what Communism came to stand for, it is hard to comprehend today the importance exerted by pacifism, equal rights and free speech in Elliott's conversion. In the early 1940s when wartime censorship was in place and anything less than full support for the Australian war effort was considered unpatriotic, Party meetings were a safe place to speak out. The South Australian Parliament still held on to elements of privilege – voting for the state's upper house was limited to those who held property. In contrast to this, Communism promised equal opportunity. At Party meetings, which had to be held in secret, Elliott could talk about the ideas that landed him in trouble at university.

Elliott never gave up these founding ideals and he chased a democratic agenda within the Party. In 1968 he wrote a charter of democratic rights that was accepted by the national conference and later published as a Party document. It was his vision of a peaceful transition from capitalism to communism. Social and class revolution of the scale sought by the Communist Party of Australia histori-

---

14 John Mortimer, 'In the Land of Chazza, Chook and Tinnies', *Advertiser*, 13 August 1983.

15 ibid.

cally had required civil war, but Elliott believed that Australia's circumstances were sufficiently different for it to be achieved through democracy. 'In all these cases the overthrown regimes were despotic and oppressive in the extreme, the people were deprived of elementary rights, and the ruling classes were determined to go to the limit of waging civil war to maintain their power and privileges. Many of them called in foreign military aid from similar regimes. In Australia there are possibilities of carrying through the socialist revolution without such agonising birth pains', he wrote.[16]

No blood would be shed. Communism might take power in coalition with other Left parties and businesses would not be seized. He believed that a socialist Australia would be richer and more satisfying than anyone could imagine. 'Australian Communists reject the slander that socialism would reduce humanity to a uniformly grey, dull level of existence. We proclaim as our aim the concept stated in the Communist Manifesto of 1848, the first great programmatic document of modern socialism: a society in which the free development of each is the condition of the free development of all.'[17] His adherence to free speech and democracy was consistent and ASIO, as they spied upon him, confirmed this. In 1970, with the invasion of Czechoslovakia provoking bitter relations within the Party, ASIO described Elliott giving a longwinded address to congress that boiled down to support for 'democracy flowing everywhere'. He wanted pro-Soviet Party members invited to a meeting, despite their different views. 'We [pro-Czechs] must not ignore "them" [pro-Soviets], no matter what their beliefs. We must invite them as well', he told congress.[18]

Yet in the public eye, Elliott's democratic socialism was obscured by the stigma of his Communist Party membership. He was tolerated for other reasons but his ideas were widely misunderstood. Many of those who opposed his taking silk in 1969 had faltered over the murky question of his loyalty to the Queen and country. By then Elliott had clearly defined himself as an Australian Communist who

---

16 Elliott Johnston, 'Charter of Democratic Rights', Communist Party of Australia, Sydney, 1969.

17 ibid.

18 ASIO, 'Elliott Frank Johnston', National Archives of Australia, Canberra, 27 May 1970.

was fiercely patriotic and he had twice sworn the oath of allegiance with integrity. The Queen was the representative of the people and he was loyal to the people, so where was the problem? The historical incongruity between Communism and democracy was tougher to resolve, and it confused even those who knew him: 'I think the view of Elliott as a Bolshevik committed to the violent overthrow of society was a phony argument, but to be fair there wasn't a big debate about it', Chris Sumner said.

As time passed, it ceased to matter. In the 1968 South Australian election Elliott had won eight per cent of the vote in the seat of Adelaide. Two years later he received four per cent. Communism was declining as a threat, just as society was relaxing its views. The Party faded into obscurity and Elliott's membership became part of his bohemianism, like the flowing silver hair, the quaint sense of humour and a taste for pork pie hats.

When Elliott was sworn in as a Supreme Court justice in 1983 the crowd spilled over to the top of the stairway outside the court. It was the largest gathering of its kind for many years and at the end of the ceremony people broke into spontaneous applause. It was a sign of affection and a nod of recognition for what Elliott had achieved, despite the obstacles Communism had placed before him. The Bannon Government had been nervous about the public's reaction to Elliott's becoming a judge and Chris Sumner took the precaution of phoning key people to warn them when the decision had been made. He was astonished to hear lawyers telling him it should have been done years before. Somewhere, a line had been crossed. Dunstan, despite his disregard for convention, was not ready to put Elliott on the Bench and the short-lived Labor Government of Des Corcoran thought it out of the question. Four years later Chris Sumner was being told it should have happened earlier.

He was popular, and even ASIO conceded he had an agreeable nature. 'He is an egotist, secretive, selfish, but is unusually good tempered', it noted.[19] However, Elliott's assimilation was never fully complete. He won over some colleagues because of the generous spirit he showed towards those who, at the 1969 meeting of the Law Society of South Australia, had voted in support of the Hall Government.

---

19 ibid., 6 June 1960.

One of them, a senior legal man whom Elliott treated as a friend, despite Elliott's knowing how he had voted, was mortified three decades later that he had been once so scared of Communism. But Elliott was a curiosity and some of his colleagues were wary. He tried to put people at ease but was irritated by jibes from fellow lawyers about whether he was going to the 'Moscow circus', as if being a Communist meant he wanted to see Russian horses perform. He took a stand on small matters of privilege and he was one of a very few Supreme Court justices who never joined the Adelaide Club, those elegant, old-fashioned clubrooms on North Terrace which counted most of the judiciary as members. In earlier times, the Bench would walk as one from the courts to the Adelaide Club to take lunch, and the workers in Victoria Square would doff their hats in respect. It was not something Elliott wanted to be part of.

He went along with the privileges of his position, but only up to a point. Kevin Duggan was in the Crown Prosecutor's Office in 1971 during the trial of the murder of Taperoo schoolgirl Deborah Leach. He had briefed Elliott to lead the prosecution of the alleged murderer, Frits Van Beelen. On the appeal to the Privy Council, Duggan went to London with Elliott and got to know him well. After their day in court, the South Australian Agent-General told Duggan he would like to take him and Elliott to lunch at the East India Club. Would Elliott think that appropriate? Elliott was delighted and they went to a glorious London dining room with starched linen tablecloths, crystal goblets and curries served in large tureens covered with ornate silver salvers. Elliott accepted the lunch in the spirit with which it was offered and set out to enjoy it. But in the crowded dining room a young waitress tripped and sent a tureen and its contents splashing over the Agent-General. It caused pandemonium. The Agent-General was taken aside and wiped down and three stiff brandies were brought to the table to steady everyone's nerves. Lunch resumed, but Elliott fell silent and the mood was destroyed. He could not contain his distress and blurted out to the Agent-General, 'That poor girl!' The Agent-General's coat had to be dry-cleaned but the waitress probably had lost her job. 'Elliott could see her almost walking up the street counting her last wages. That told me a lot about Elliott', Duggan said.

On other occasions during the London trip he was urbane and

at ease with his surroundings. He was interested in world affairs and he never embarrassed the Australians by pushing the Communist line. On his own, however, he approached newsagents in London to buy the Communist paper, *Daily Worker*, and a certain impish humour helped him make light of privilege. At dinner in the dining room of the Dukes Hotel in St James's Place, he kept peering at the wine list and then asked the waiter if a bottle of Chateau Mouton Rothschild 1951 could be brought up from the cellar. The attitude of the waiter changed as a group of rank colonials suddenly became paying customers. Both Duggan and Elizabeth thought Elliott had taken leave of his senses. Napkins were unfolded, chairs were adjusted and the wine was carried over in a ceremonial basket. The waiter asked how many glasses were needed. 'Oh, we don't want to drink it', Elliott replied, and asked if he could look at it. He took the bottle, cradled it like a newborn baby, then passed it to Elizabeth and suggested she do the same. 'Thank you. I just want to go back to Australia and say I held a bottle of wine that cost $700', he said.

Elliott lacked cynicism and was guileless, and he had a disarming personality. By 1970 Germaine Greer had published *The Female Eunuch* and women were no longer the weaker sex in need of male protection. Elliott believed in women's liberation, and in the Clerks Award in the late 1940s he sought equal pay for women. Women at Johnston & Johnston were made partners along with the men, and maternity leave was granted there before most Adelaide firms. He was married to the woman who headed South Australia's first Sex Discrimination Board and who was a beacon of female independence and achievement. But he had about him a streak of old-fashioned gallantry and a liking for romantic gestures that had to be taken at face value by the women with whom he worked.

He loved the way women looked and he occasionally bought the women in the office gifts. He did so openly and innocently a dress, a pair of shoes, a piece of jewellery. They were young and attractive and he wanted them to look nice. No one was embarrassed and the female lawyers took it as a rather sweet example of Elliott's quaint ways. In the 1970s Elliott was in his 50s and, like many men, he struggled with the daily practice of gender politics even while he believed the theory. He had a flirtatious manner that was largely harmless.

Elliott was similarly on the cusp of generational change in courtroom style and manners. He was slow and old fashioned and took so long to get to the point that some of the judges, including Sam Jacobs, were irritated. He was prone to asking long and convoluted questions that revealed themselves in transcript to be coherent and well constructed. He would consider a matter on his feet in total silence while the clock ticked and people fidgeted. Unfazed by the court's irritability, he would finally ask a detailed question expressed just as he meant it to be.

He drilled through complex and hostile arguments in a voice that was unfailingly courteous. John Scott, who in the 1970s was secretary of the Amalgamated Metal Workers and Shipwrights Union (AMWSU) in South Australia, remembered Elliott during the Gnatenko case. During cross-examination of a defence witness, Elliott thought for a while, twiddled his glasses and waited until the court was completely quiet before observing very calmly, 'Well that's not what you told me before'. It was a lethal attack on the credibility of the company's witness, said Scott: 'The witness almost shit himself, it was just remarkable. He just demolished him. I'll never forget that. It was the day I saw a witness melt away.'

The Supreme Court in South Australia in the 1970s led by John Bray was highly regarded and included Roma Mitchell, Andrew Wells, Charles Bright, David Hogarth, George Walters and Howard Zelling. The tenor of their language was learned and formal and reflected courtroom practice. With his occasional oratorical flights and debating school charm, Elliott was a student of this old school. He was well after the days of legendary figures like Frank Villeneuve Smith KC, who was said to bully hapless victims on the stand through the sheer grandeur of his eloquence, or Edward Erskine Cleland KC, who, when refused the right to address the Full Bench of the Supreme Court, turned to the wall and spoke to it for 20 minutes, bowing courteously at the close.[20] Elliott's barrister's career was a colourful flourish at the tail-end of a remarkable generation of lawyers whose style belonged to an earlier time.

After the Royal Commission into Aboriginal Deaths in Custody had ended, his public life was all but complete. He edited the *South*

---

20 Jack Elliott, *Memoirs of a Barrister*, Wakefield Press, Adelaide, 2000, p. 9.

Australian Law Reports with great enthusiasm and kept up to date with the decisions of the Supreme Court of South Australia. He saw a great deal of his old friends, Andrew Collett, Paul Heywood-Smith, Robyn Layton, Peter McCusker, Lindy Powell, Mick Doyle, Ann McLean and others. He played croquet with Elizabeth, Ruth Fletcher and Sally Smith and regularly attended Sturt Football Club matches with Brian Withers and others.

In 1991 the first Dean of Law at Flinders University, Professor Rebecca Bailey-Harris, invited Elliott to contribute to the development of a new law course. He helped to establish the Flinders Law School and was Associate Professor of Law from 1992 until 1995, teaching Legal Method. In 1996 Flinders University awarded him an honorary Doctorate of Philosophy.

The idea of Elliott as a threat to Australia's interests or its legal order had dissipated and in the end he was honoured for having held so nobly and naively to his youthful beliefs. In 1994 he was made an officer of the Order of Australia, which he accepted without hesitation, and with pride. He also accepted a modest and strictly factual entry in the Australian version of *Who's Who.* In 2006 when Elliott was awarded a PhD *honoris causa* by Adelaide University, the Vice Chancellor, Professor James McWha, praised him as an advocate for the oppressed and the working class. At a time of almost free-rein capitalism after years of deregulation and the outsourcing of community facilities, Elliott's socialist values were prized. It would have been churlish to mention during the ceremony at Adelaide University's Bonython Hall that more than six decades earlier he had been stood down by the Vice Chancellor for wanting to discuss his beliefs.

In old age Elliott is greatly loved. His loyalty to a chosen path, the unwavering belief that turning Left was always right, became an inspiration to others. In 2007, the Adelaide Festival of Ideas was dedicated to Elliott, and the Chief Justice, John Doyle, praised his 'unassuming but powerful example'. At his ninetieth birthday in February 2008, Elliott was celebrated for personal attributes, which included an abiding analytical interest in the Australian political landscape. 'We love you for your uniqueness and for the indelible difference which you have made in each of our lives', Robyn Layton said. It was not just sentiment. He always thought the best of people and did not curry favour. He has been secure in his beliefs, without caring what others thought. When confronted with a large file containing the evidence of decades of ASIO's surveillance, he was genuinely uninterested. 'A lot of crap', he remarked, without even looking at it.

He knew how to conduct himself. Both he and Elizabeth were from backgrounds that made their radicalism an act of choice, not a shot across the bows in the class war. She was from a colourful branch of Adelaide's horse and tennis set, and her father was a lawyer and Deputy Coroner. They were wealthy, and Elizabeth's sister, Mary, never took on paid work. Elliott was from humbler stock but he was also a private school boy. He came to Prince Alfred College on a scholarship but it placed him in the right social milieu. They were Communists but their social backgrounds were middle and upper-middle class. At times there was even uncertainty within the family about whether their lifestyle had strayed too far from their beliefs. In the mid-1960s Elliott's phone was being tapped. ASIO's records show that, after a heated conversation at the Johnston dinner table, Elizabeth's sister, Cecil, rang a friend to complain that Stewart, who was then a teenager, preferred Marjorie to her. They were both Communists but Stewart thought Cecil was 'idle rich' and not sufficiently working class. The situation *was* rather confusing when you thought about it, she said to her friend – with Elizabeth and Elliott both Communists and their son a student at PAC. 'Their position isn't really logical', Cecil said.[21]

The Johnstons' private school connections had attracted sniping criticism from within the Communist Party. In 1966 ASIO quoted Charles McCaffrey, a Maoist rival of Elliott and friend of Marjorie's, as saying the Johnstons' situation was laughable. 'They are living it up in the country, sending their boy to a private school, and he [Elliott] claims to be a defender of the workers', McCaffrey scoffed.[22] Stewart's enrolment at Elliott's old school had baffled ASIO: 'This office was not aware of the possibility that Elliott Frank Johnston's son attends Prince Alfred College, a school which is run under the auspices of the Methodist Church. Action will be taken to confirm

21 ibid., 14 September 1965.

22 ibid., 11 July 1966.

identity and a further report will follow'.[23] Stewart grew up understanding that his family was different. Magazines came into the house from China and Russia showing pictures of happy peasants and hard-working factory hands. He dreamed about Lenin as some kind of benevolent father figure. At school, he was challenged over his background and learnt to stand up for his parents' politics. 'I was certainly prepared to justify my parents' position, which I had to do at Princes', he said. He studied Marxist economics at the University of Adelaide and became a schoolteacher, travelling widely and living in Sydney.

Football, Elliott's other great passion, was the great humanising thread that won people over and helped break down barriers in Stewart's school community. Elliott and Elizabeth were often at the school, supporting Stewart, who was a good footballer. They ran morning and afternoon teas during the football season and showed such an attachment to the game that suspicions about them were at least partially allayed. Elliott was unrelentingly obsessed with the Sturt Football Club, his home team from childhood. He told long and funny stories about football and for years pursued a Friday night joke about having just run into the mother of one of Sturt's players, a Mrs Kutcher, who had given him the inside running on the next day's game. He is still going to Sturt's games in his 90s.

Elliott's name is linked nationally to the modern move towards Aboriginal reconciliation, and in the end his greatest historic legacy was outside the Communist Party. The final recommendation of the Royal Commission into Aboriginal Deaths in Custody highlighted the compelling need for black and white Australia to take a long-overdue first step. The report, with its willingness to confront a nation's difficult history, advocated that white Australia show initiative. In 2006 the Aboriginal and Torres Strait Islander Social Justice Commissioner, Tom Calma, described how pivotal the report had been for Australian race relations. 'The report,' he said, 'smashed the so-called great Australian silence by making explicit the connections between the history of treatment of Indigenous peoples and its ongoing, contemporary impact'.[24]

23 ibid., 18 May 1965.

24 Tom Calma, *From Rhetoric to Reconciliation: Addressing the challenge of*

More than 15 years later the advances Elliott hoped for had not been realised. The crisis in black Australia has only deepened. The federal Howard Government refused to say 'sorry', and turned the clock back to autocratic white rule, earning Elliott's contempt. He still believes that reconciliation has to be worked out *with* Indigenous leaders, not by white people for them. To this end he has remained a patron of Reconciliation South Australia, along with Lowitja O'Donoghue. Despite the fact that the then Prime Minister of Australia, Kevin Rudd, made an apology to Aboriginal Australians on 13 February 2008 for their past treatment, reconciliation has barely begun.

In his eighties, Elliott contributed to the Search Foundation, which was formed to explore alternatives to capitalism after the failure of Communism. It managed the archives and residual business interests of the Communist Party and searched for a new language for the old ideas. Elizabeth left the foundation a considerable sum in her will and Elliott attended meetings, but his thinking was from another era. At a forum in 2006 to discuss a new book by academic David McKnight, *Beyond Right and Left,* Elliott talked about the need for a democratically elected government that would control water, power, transport and health. Australia was being destroyed by the domination of global capital and he wanted the major corporations to be government-owned. No one else in the group seemed to know quite what to say. His ideas were too big and too late. The discussion reverted to the poor polling of the federal ALP leader, Kim Beazley.

The chance for a new world had come and gone. In the 1930s, the hold of old structures and systems on the Australian psyche had been prised loose by war and Depression. For a time, Communism, with its goals of equality and international peace, occupied the high moral ground. Oxford and Cambridge graduates with a social conscience joined the Communist Party because they believed that this was the decent thing to do. Seventy years later there was nothing worthwhile left to pay allegiance to. Elliott finally came to believe that the CPA had failed the Australian public by not differentiating

---

equality for Aboriginal and Torres Strait Islander People in criminal justice processes, Elliott Johnston Tribute Lecture, Flinders University, Adelaide, 2006.

itself strongly enough from Soviet Communism. The distinction between Australian and Russian Communism was clear to him, but not to others. Encouraged from the late 1940s to fear Communism and bolstered by the cruelties of life in Russia, Eastern Europe and China, ordinary people understandably confused cruel dictatorships with Communist politics.

In hindsight, Elliott believed that a change of name and a clearer statement of the Australianness of what was proposed would have helped. 'Whilst we did not make it absolutely clear, now looking back, that we were saying we were against armed uprising, we made it clear we were advocating a parliamentary proposal and were seeking support for that. But we didn't come out and make it clear we were not advocating exactly what they had in the Soviet Union', he said. He was not the only old Communist to believe that the Australian Party had stayed too long in the shadow of the Soviet Union. Eric Aarons wrote in his memoir that, in the lead up to the 1974 Congress, there had been pressure from the Soviet Union's Communist Party in Moscow to reclaim Russia as the model for Australia. In response to this pressure, Aarons wrote a long critique of Soviet society which rejected it as something to which Australian Communists should aspire. The fault then was in not going far enough:

> The umbilical cord tying us to the Soviet Union, which we had nurtured for the first forty-five years of the CPA's existence, we found to be too strong to sever in our final twenty-five. We were still judged by most Australians on their view of Communism as practised in the Soviet Union, rather than by what we actually stood for.[25]

Elliott believed that the logic of the socialist model was undeniable and that common sense had to triumph, that reason alone would persuade people to choose a society that put their welfare ahead of one that worshipped money. He stood up to younger critics who argued for a moral memory of Communism that linked Marxist theory with 'murderous Communist practice'. He argued that Communism as practised in the Soviet Union was not the same as Marxism, and it was wrong to suppose that Communist parties everywhere were the same.

---

25 Aarons, p. 202.

Historian Amirah Inglis, who was for a time married to a Communist, held strong views on the practical good that some Australian Communists achieved through trade unions, in running mothers' clubs for Aboriginal people, in encouraging tolerance towards migrants, and in helping the marginalised. She mentioned a friend, a Communist who had fought in the Spanish Civil War and who had left the Party over Stalinism. He delivered Meals on Wheels until he died. Her argument was that people who joined the Communist Party because they were dedicated to doing good works kept on doing good works when they were no longer Communists. She might have been talking about Elliott, who did more practical good outside the Party than in it.

In the twenty-first century, Elliott became part of a Left coalition that supported action on global warming and climate change; he opposed the United States invasion of Iraq and Afghanistan and fought against the Howard Government's harsh industrial relations agenda. He was saddened at the way the rights of workers were undermined, while in Sydney the rich jockeyed for the best Harbour views. In 2004 he agreed to become the patron of the newly formed Australian Friends of Palestine Association and put his name to a number of high-profile, public criticisms of Israeli Government policy. He hated the exorbitant salaries of the executive class, and the sale of the Commonwealth Bank by a Labor Government, which caused its shares to skyrocket and its profits to soar. He despaired over the move to privatisation and the sale of the Electricity Trust of South Australia, which had been established 50 years earlier by another Liberal Premier, Tom Playford, then sold by the South Australian Liberal Government of John Olsen. These events pained him deeply. He read the platform of the Rudd Government and was dismayed to find no mention of socialism.

By 2008 most of his contemporaries had gone. Elizabeth had died in six years earlier and he had attended countless funerals of family and friends, including in 2005 that of his communist colleague Laurie Aarons, and in 2006 of Harry Krantz and Elizabeth's oldest sister, Mary. He still goes to the football, plays weekend croquet and enjoys his circle of friends. He is amusing and interested company and within the limits of his health he is active and involved. In 2005 he was appointed as a delegate to a reconciliation workshop in Canberra and he attends protest meetings to preserve the Adelaide parklands.

In 2007 Elliott wrote an article on the future of the Left, in it identifying the domination of capital as Australia's chief problem. Capitalism made enemies of others, while socialism joined them as friends. His thinking had not changed much in 70 years, even though little of what he had fought for had been achieved. It was unrealistic in today's globalised world to believe that Australia's largest companies would ever be nationalised, but he still believed they should be. Towards the end of a happy life, he is still agitating for change and he has never resigned himself to accepting Australia as it is.

Elliott Johnston's footprint can be found more on the law than on politics, but his desire to improve the world defines him. He has given more than most to the fight for democracy, fairness and equality. A battle that began in the late 1930s has continued for seven decades, and there is no end in sight. 'It may well be quite a way off but if we do not keep up the argument, it will be even further away', he said. 'Our duty is clear.'

Index

I

J

K

L

M

Q

R

S

T

Roma the First

A biography of Dame Roma Mitchell

Susan Magarey and Kerrie Round

Here is Roma Flinders Mitchell, 1913–2000, her life spanning a century scarred by war and depression, illuminated by a vision of new freedoms and opportunities for women, a vision in which she became a central inspiration. She was Australia's first female Queen's Counsel, the first woman in Australia appointed to a superior court, the first woman invited to present the Boyer Lectures, the first woman elected Chancellor of an Australian university, the first woman to be appointed Governor of an Australian state. She was necessarily formed by her times, but she also contributed importantly to those times, pioneering a new kind of womanhood.

Roma Mitchell's life is a story about contradictions. A life-long and devout Catholic, she achieved prominence in a society known justly as a 'paradise of dissent'. Her religion aligned her with Irish working-class Outsiders, yet she gained the top position at the heart of a Protestant Establishment, and prized the honours awarded her as a loyal member of the British Commonwealth of Nations. She was deeply committed to the Common Law, but sought to change it. A reformer, she was also a traditionalist. An internationalist, she was also a loyal local. A woman, she gained authority in a world dominated by men. As generous as she was ambitious, she shines and shines like a good deed in a naughty world.

ISBN 978 1 86254 780 3

For more information visit www.wakefieldpress.com.au

Supreme Federalist

The political life of Sir John Downer

J.C. Bannon

Sir John Downer (1843–1915), first in line of a political dynasty, was born in humble circumstances in Adelaide, yet he became an outstanding scholar, brilliant barrister, premier of his colony and a founding father of the Australian federation. He was one of the committee of three men who drafted the Commonwealth Constitution, and in 1901 was elected to the first Senate.

As a political leader, Downer was an enigma. He was a democratic nationalist and Australian patriot, but his vision of a great Australian nation was always in the context of the British Empire and his English origins. A conservative with liberal values, he championed legal reform, introduced legislation for the advancement of the rights of women and children, and opposed the White Australia policy.

In *Supreme Federalist* John Bannon, an historian well-versed in the intricacies of public life, tells the story of John Downer's intriguing career, providing us with a fresh perspective on Australia's political transformation from a group of colonies to the modern federal nation.

ISBN 978 1 86254 835 0

For more information visit www.wakefieldpress.com.au

Wakefield Press is an independent publishing and
distribution company based in Adelaide, South Australia.
We love good stories and publish beautiful books.
To see our full range of titles, please visit our website at
www.wakefieldpress.com.au.